SHAKESPEARE FILMS
IN THE CLASSROOM

SHAKESPEARE FILMS
in the
CLASSROOM

A Descriptive Guide

by Jo McMurtry

Archon Books
1994

29311806

First published 1994 as an Archon Book,

an imprint of

The Shoe String Press, Inc.,

Hamden, Connecticut 06514.

Library of Congress Cataloging-in-Publication Data

McMurtry, Jo, 1937–

    Shakespeare films in the classroom : a descriptive guide / by Jo

McMurtry.

      p. cm.

    Includes bibliographical references and index.

    ISBN 0-208-02369-0 (alk. paper)

    1. Shakespeare, William, 1564–1616—Study and teaching—Audio-

visual aids—Catalogs.   2. Shakespeare, William, 1564–1616—Film

and video adaptations—Catalogs.   3. English drama—Film and video

adaptations—Catalogs.   I. Title.

PR2987.M36   1994

016.79143′75—dc20   93-39431

                                          CIP

The paper used in this publication meets the minimum requirements of

American National Standard for Information Sciences—

Permanence of Paper for Printed Library Materials, ANSI Z39.48-1984. ⊗

Book design by Abigail Johnston

Printed in the United States of America

⁊ This book is dedicated to my grandson,

CURTIS EDWARD MCMURTRY,

who at the age of three is not quite ready

for Shakespeare but already likes a good story.

ᐁ Contents

🝆 Acknowledgments

My greatest debt is to my students, responsive and outspoken as always, who served as guinea pigs for this enterprise. I hope their encounters with Shakespeare on film as well as the printed page have enhanced their education and fostered a lifelong Shakespeare habit.

At the University of Richmond, the staff of the Media Resource Center has indefatigably sought out films for me. Paul Porterfield, Dywana Saunders, and Tom Campagnoli went far beyond the call of duty. Lois Morley and Cely Coleman, of the university's computer center, have generously shared their expertise.

I am grateful to the University of Richmond's faculty and administration for maintaining an environment in which research is seen as a component of teaching rather than a distraction from it. David Leary, Dean of Arts and Sciences, along with Barbara Griffin and Ray Hilliard, successively chairs of the English department, have greatly assisted this project by arranging my teaching schedule and other responsibilities so that I could find blocks of time to work on it. Wendy Thompson, English department secretary, has helped me keep my commitments in balance during an often frenzied year and a half.

In the wider world of Shakespearean scholarship, my experiments in using films in the classroom have been encouraged by Bernice Kliman and Kenneth Rothwell, editors of the *Shakespeare on Film Newsletter* (1976–92), during seminars sponsored by the Shakespeare Association of America as well as less structured conversations.

Jim and Diantha Thorpe of The Shoe String Press have been supportive as always, combining practical suggestions with a far-sighted view of this book's usefulness to the audience for which it is intended.

The manuscript has benefited from copyeditor Carolyn Marsh's quick eye. She has caught numerous errors and inconsistencies. I take responsibility for any which may have escaped her vigilance.

❧ SHAKESPEARE FILMS IN THE CLASSROOM ⸻⸻

❧ Introduction ⎯⎯⎯⎯⎯⎯⎯⎯⎯⎯⎯⎯⎯⎯⎯⎯⎯⎯⎯

What This Book Is For

This book is meant for teachers who like to show films of Shakespeare plays to their classes, and also for librarians forming collections of these films or advising teachers in their purchase and rental choices.

So many Shakespeare films are now available, especially in easy-to-use forms like videotape and videodisk, that we face an embarrassment of riches. It is hard to find time to see so many films. And sometimes, having seen them, it is hard to keep them all straight. I hope this book will simplify decisions, encourage experiment, and jog the memory.

A further limitation obtains. The classes and the students here envisioned are concerned primarily with literature, not with the history or technology of film as such. Detailed information on the cinematic aspects of most of the films in this list can successfully be sought elsewhere. (For some pointers, see the bibliography in the back of this book and its introductory note.)

This book includes at least one film of each play in the Shakespeare canon. Many plays are represented by several films; *Macbeth*, for example, has nine as of this writing. The total is just over a hundred. All are full-length renditions, allowing for a certain amount of cutting and thinning, almost inevitable in any performance. All are on videotape and/or videodisk. (I am using the word *film* as a blanket term for all formats.) All, or almost all, are easily available from distributors. A few elusive titles are listed anyhow, in the hope that circumstances will improve.

What to Expect in the Entries

In the description of each film, I have emphasized the kind of thing most students notice and can discuss, so to speak, from a standing start. These include primarily what is on the screen—the actors and actresses, the costumes, the sets.

The degree of familiarity students have with the text at the time they watch the film will depend, of course, on the way the class is conducted. Some instructors prefer to use film as an introduction to the study of the text, while others do it the other way round. Either way, notice of cuts and rearrangements is useful, and I go into some detail on this point.

Information about film techniques and history—camera angles, for example, or the careers and quirks of film directors—is slighted here, as noted above. Most students consider these matters tangential to a course in literature. Similarly, I have not given music the attention it deserves, crucial as a background score can be in influencing the audience's emotions and creating atmosphere.

Individual films are numbered by a system which I hope will simplify cross-references. Each film has two numerical elements. The first category is by play. These are arranged alphabetically and numbered, so that all films of *A Midsummer Night's Dream*, for example, will have a "21" as their first element. Within that category, the films themselves are arranged chronologically. Thus Max Reinhardt's *Midsummer Night's Dream*, released in 1935 and the first in this queue, is numbered 21.1. The 1982 version by the British Broadcasting Company happens to be fourth and is numbered 21.4.

Films which are not full-length versions of a Shakespeare play but are in some way related to one or more Shakespeare plays can be found in Appendix A, "Analogues and Variations." The numbering system is the same except that individual films are given letters as their second elements. *West Side Story* is categorized under *Romeo and Juliet*, number 27 in both the main listing and Appendix A. As *West Side Story* (1961) is chronologically the earliest *Romeo and Juliet* derivative to be recorded here, its number is 27.A. At the end of this particular category, the most recent *Romeo and Juliet* entry is a 30-minute cartoon version released in 1992 (27.E). For a more detailed explanation of the contents of Appendix A, see the introductory note (p. 235).

Alert readers may note a numbering discrepancy. The standard Shakespeare canon contains 37 plays; I seem to deal with only 35. The explanation is that I have lumped together all three parts of *Henry VI*. The three parts are always performed as a unit, and to separate them would create unnecessary repetition.

Most entries in the main listing include a brief bibliography headed "Reviews and Studies." Items here are focused essentially on that one film, as though it existed alone on an island. This policy saves both space and frustration. It is annoying, I think, to look up a reference and find that the film one is teaching is mentioned only in passing, the rest of the essay being devoted to the body of a director's work or to a comparison of that film with five or six others. Of course, it is possible that one's students are equally concerned with the five or six others, but for most syllabi the odds are against it. More all-encompassing works about films of Shakespeare's plays may be found in the general bibliography.

Entries under "Reviews and Studies" are not complete, again for reasons of space. Subtitles are generally omitted, and the only publishing information given is the date. For a more complete listing, see, once again, the general bibliography.

Under "Purchase/Rental Inquiries," I have listed distributors who were handling a certain film at the time of this writing. The situation here is in constant change. Distributors are generally receptive to inquiries; if they no longer sell or rent the film in which one is interested, they will often suggest someone who might do so. Distributors' addresses can be found in Appendix B.

My references to Shakespeare's texts follow the act, scene, and line numbering of the Riverside edition of Shakespeare's works (Boston: Houghton Mifflin, 1974). I have also followed the Riverside edition's Americanized spellings.

The Films Herein: Silents, Talkies and Blockbusters

Silent films are more useful for a Shakespeare class than one might at first think, despite several drawbacks. The poetry, in its aural dimension, is obviously missing. And the extravagant acting style of the early twentieth century can reduce students to roars of laughter quite unintended by the actors. But the faces and gestures still convey emotions. In a comparative scene analysis, for example, a few minutes of a silent film can elicit some provocative ideas.

Unfortunately, the silent-film footage that still survives is for the most part stored in archives, to be viewed by special arrangement, and is not available on videotape or videodisk. This situation may improve. In the meantime, a 1922 silent film of *Othello* is sometimes available from distributors and is listed in Appendix A, "Analogues and Variations" (23.A).

More accessible in terms both of student response and of easy purchase or rental are the big-screen box office hits that began with Laurence Olivier's *Henry V* of 1944 (10.1). Olivier's *Hamlet*, 1948 (7.1), and *Richard III*, 1955 (26.1), were also popular and remain so today. Students may find them a bit quaint, but the adjustment is not difficult.

Even more appealing are the big-budget Shakespeare films of the 1960s, a decade eternally young and eternally welcoming. Today's students seem to feel as much at home there as their parents did. Franco Zeffirelli's *The Taming of the Shrew*, 1966 (28.2), and *Romeo and Juliet*, 1968 (27.3), remain magical. Roman Polanski's *Macbeth*, 1971 (17.4), chronologically past the 1960s but not by much, has kept its compelling attraction.

The phenomenon of big-budget films of Shakespeare's plays has been revived in recent years with Zeffirelli's *Hamlet*, starring Mel Gibson, 1990 (7.8), and Kenneth Branagh's *Henry V*, 1989 (10.3), and *Much Ado about Nothing*, 1993 (22.3).

In the meantime, many of the more budget-conscious films of the past several decades have become available and are well received by students. Several of Orson

Welles's Shakespeare films have been reissued in video formats that attempt to clear up such technical problems as fuzzy soundtracks. (See *Chimes at Midnight*, 8.1; *Macbeth*, 17.1; *Othello*, 23.1.)

Foreign films of Shakespeare's plays are generally less effective in the classroom, but as students become more globally aware this blind spot may clear up. And, of course, an instructor's job is to open eyes and minds. Listed in this book are, among other films with English subtitles, Kozintsev's *Hamlet* (7.3) and *King Lear* (15.2). Several films of the Japanese director Kurosawa, which reflect Shakespeare at a somewhat oblique angle, are listed in Appendix A, "Analogues and Variations." An example is *Throne of Blood* (17.A), related to *Macbeth*.

Television: The British Broadcasting Company

On turning to the small screen, we find ourselves in a posture of transatlantic indebtedness. Shakespeare classrooms would be considerably poorer were it not for "The Shakespeare Plays," the British Broadcasting Company's massive series of the entire canon. Thanks to the BBC, there is now at least one film version of everything.

The project ran from 1978 until 1985. During this time the 37 plays were telecast in Great Britain and the United States, over public broadcasting stations in the latter case.

Considerable funding came from the United States. Major donors included Time-Life, Inc.; Exxon Corporation; Metropolitan Life Insurance Company; and Morgan Guaranty Trust Company of New York. WNET, a PBS station in New York City, was energetically involved in the fund-raising.

Three producers were sequentially involved in the project—Cedric Messina (1978–80), Jonathan Winters (1980–82), and Shaun Sutton (1982–85). Directors of individual films included, among many others, Elijah Moshinsky, Stuart Burge, James Cellan-Jones, Don Taylor, Kevin Billington, and Jane Howell. Jonathan Winters served as both producer and director of a number of films.

Several plays from this series were re-run in the United States as "The Shakespeare Hour," introduced by Walter Matthau, in the spring of 1985.

In the classroom, the BBC films are useful because they show great respect for the text and seldom make major cuts. (There are a few exceptions.) The acting is of a high standard. Often one finds an actor or actress performing a role which he or she has done on stage, perhaps many times in various productions, so that each word and phrase has been carefully thought through.

Costumes typically are not only sumptuous but credible. They look like clothes people would actually wear, given a sufficiently grand context, and they add authority to the characterization.

There are a few disadvantages. Films can be very long, three hours' running time in some cases. Budgets, while adequate, were far from lavish, especially with regard to studio sets. The results can seem uninteresting to viewers accustomed to special effects and frequent changes of scene.

Other Televised Shakespeares

Besides the BBC, numerous films made for television have become available for classroom use.

Laurence Olivier's last Shakespearean role was performed for Granada Television, which filmed *King Lear* in 1983 (15.6). It did not suffer from budget restrictions, being the most expensive production in British television history at that time, and it surrounded Olivier with other well-known Shakespearean actors. Telecasts in England and America drew large audiences. The film's popularity in videotape remains high.

Thames Television has also filmed several Shakespeare plays which can be obtained on video. Among these are *Romeo and Juliet* (27.6) and *King Lear* (15.8).

In the United States, a group of Shakespeare films have been made by Bard Productions in association with what appears to be a varied confederation of sponsors. This group, based in California, films its plays in an Elizabethan-style theater with a thrust stage and minimal scenery. The result is not exactly a filmed stage production, since there is no live audience, but the effect is similar. American actors are used, many of them familiar faces from non-Shakespearean movies and television. Among the sponsors listed in the various films' credits are the Shakespeare Video Society; Santa Barbara Gazebo Theatre One, Inc.; KCET, public television for Southern California, Los Angeles; and Bard Productions, Ltd.

Bard films include *Antony and Cleopatra* (2.4), *King Lear* (15.7), *Macbeth* (17.6), *The Merry Wives of Windsor* (20.1), *Othello* (23.6), *Richard II* (25.2), *Romeo and Juliet* (27.5), *The Taming of the Shrew* (28.4), and *The Tempest* (29.3).

These films vary in quality, but they add to the variety of classroom resources. The Elizabethan staging is instructive in itself.

Filmed Stage Performances

A very useful kind of Shakespeare film, especially since students are more likely to have had personal experience in staging plays than in making full-scale movies, is the videotaped stage performance. These are often of surprisingly high technical quality, in view of the difficulties—low auditorium lighting, limited camera angles, and so on. The acting is often delightfully fresh and convincing. Pehaps the reason is that the scenes are performed in their natural sequence, rather than at the behest of a studio shooting schedule, and actors create their own pace and momentum.

Examples listed here include an *As You Like It* performed by the Stratford Shakespeare Festival of Ontario, Canada (3.3); a *Midsummer Night's Dream* performed in New York's Central Park (21.5); and a *Macbeth* performed at the Lincoln Center for the Performing Arts (17.7).

A particularly noteworthy series of films in this category was made by the English Shakespeare Company, headed by Michael Bogdanov and Michael Pennington. In the late 1980s this group put together and toured with a twenty-hour stage production of Shakespeare's history plays called *The Wars of the Roses*. The cycle was filmed before a live audience in Swansea, Wales. For more information, see under *Richard II* (25.3), the first of the series.

The videotaped stage performance might be seen as bringing Shakespeare films full circle, since some of the earliest attempts to record Shakespeare on this strange new medium were influenced by stage productions and/or performed by stage actors. Robert Hamilton Ball has described many of these efforts in his book on Shakespearean silent film. (See the general bibliography, p. 248.) A few minutes were filmed from Herbert Beerbohm Tree's stage *Tempest*, for example, in 1908. And Sarah Bernhardt, whose interpretation of Hamlet is among her most famous roles, performed the duel scene before a movie camera in 1900.

But if the effect is circular, the circle is certainly not a closed one. The filming of Shakespeare's plays, and the making of these films available for classroom use, goes on apace. Consequently, I compile this list in the certain knowledge that, by the time my reader picks it up, it will be incomplete. This problem is on balance a happy one, however, and in the meantime I hope these pages prove to be useful.

1 ❧ ALL'S WELL
THAT ENDS WELL_____

❧ 1.1. *All's Well that Ends Well.* 1980. British Broadcasting Company/Time-Life Television: The Shakespeare Plays. Color, 160 minutes. Producer: Jonathan Miller. Director: Elijah Moshinsky.

HELENA	Angela Down
BERTRAM	Ian Charleson
COUNTESS OF ROSSILLION	Celia Johnson
LAFEU	Michael Hordern
KING OF FRANCE	Donald Sinden
PAROLLES	Peter Jeffrey
DIANA	Pippa Guard
WIDOW	Rosemary Leach
LAVATCH	Paul Brooke
FRENCH LORD	Robert Lindsay

Pluses   A carefully thought-through film, realizing the potential of many of the minor roles.

Minuses   Pace is sometimes slow.

Textual Cuts and Rearrangements   The third scene of act three, in which the duke of Florence appoints Bertram "general of our horse," is omitted, giving us that much less evidence that Bertram has some military talent and isn't entirely a selfish brat. The epilogue, spoken by the king of France, is omitted.

Some passages are thinned of presumably redundant lines. The first scene of act three, the French volunteers' arrival in Florence, is also omitted.

Settings   Interior scenes are inspired by seventeenth-century Dutch painters—Vermeer, Pieter de Hooch, Jan Stern. Typically, we see a sequence of connecting rooms, their doorways receding into perspective, while clear daylight pours through side windows.

At night, the lighting shifts to baroque effects. Candles flicker; flames leap in fireplaces.

In the house of the countess of Rossillion, a dignified and orderly way of life is suggested by the polished tile floors, the tapestries, and the harpsichord at which Helena muses on the hopelessness of her love for Bertram.

Costumes   Dress matches the early-seventeenth-century setting. Characters wear gathered breeches, doublets with slashed sleeves and starched ruffs, plumed hats. The braggart Parolles (Peter Jeffrey), of course, outdoes his companions in sartorial flourish.

Helena wears a pilgrim's gown, something like a friar's costume, for her journey to Florence. The rest of the time she prefers simple gowns with touches of white.

Interpretation of Roles   Angela Downs presents Helena as a thoughtful, determined young woman. Her fair coloring and high cheekbones make her look at once vulnerable and strong. Her unconventional wooing strategy—she cures the king of France of a wasting disease, then asks the hand of Bertram as her reward— is only her first challenge; she must then win the love of her indignant husband.

As the king of France, Donald Sinden gives his role a sexual twist that can create misunderstanding in student audiences. Helena begins her treatment (II.i) by walking her fingers over his forehead and gazing deeply into his eyes, after which she and the king melt into a passionate kiss and the screen blacks out. Students can hardly be blamed for assuming that the cure consists of a roll in the hay and that Helena's pregnancy, announced in the final scene, might as easily be the king's doing as Bertram's. An instructor may wish to exonerate Shakespeare from this train of events.

The often thankless role of Bertram is ably undertaken by Ian Charleson. As an adolescent tired of being controlled by others and longing to make a name for himself, this Bertram's reactions become understandable. He is summoned to the king's court, then forbidden to leave with the other adventure-seekers (II.i.27). In this production Bertram serves as a sickroom nurse and even appears in one scene carrying a vial containing, we assume, the king's urine. When he is abruptly married off to a woman he considers his social inferior, the audience is hardly surprised when he first runs away to the wars and then tries to seduce a woman he has at least chosen for himself.

Diana, the object of Bertram's affections, is played by Pippa Guard with a quiet, self-confident sensuality. As Bertram woos her before a cozy fire (IV.ii), she persuades him to give her his ring by delicately nibbling the end of his finger. Bertram concedes at once. The ring, of course, is the one Bertram has vowed Helena must show him if he ever acknowledges her as his wife.

Bertram's mother, the countess of Rossillion, is played with dignity and authority by Celia Johnson. Like her courtier friend Lafeu (Michael Hordern), the countess represents a benevolent older generation, pleased to work out happy endings for the young people and puzzled when the young people insist on finding obstacles.

Production History   *All's Well* was shown on English television in January and on American television in May of 1981. It was the fifteenth of the British Broadcasting Company's series of the entire Shakespeare canon (1978–85).

Reviews and Studies   Bulman, J. C., and Coursen, H. R., eds. *Shakespeare on Television.* 1988. Extracts from reviews of the BBC *All's Well*, pp. 273–74.

Hunter, G. K. "The BBC's *All's Well that Ends Well.*" In J. C. Bulman and H. R. Coursen, cited above. Pp. 185–87.

Rothwell, Kenneth S., and Melzer, Annabelle H. *Shakespeare on Screen.* 1990. Item 3, p. 22.

Willis, Susan. *The BBC Shakespeare Plays.* 1991. Pp. 149–52.

Purchase/Rental Inquiries   Ambrose Video; Filmic Archives; Insight Media; The Writing Company. See Appendix A for addresses.

2 🍃 ANTONY AND CLEOPATRA* _____

🍃 2.1. *Antony and Cleopatra.* 1972. Folio Films, London. Color, 160 min. Producer: Peter Snell. Director: Charlton Heston.

ANTONY	Charlton Heston
CLEOPATRA	Hildegarde Neil
CHARMIAN	Jane Lapotaire
OCTAVIUS	John Castle
ENOBARBUS	Eric Porter
LEPIDUS	Fernando Rey
MENOCRATES	Fernando Bilbao
MENAS	Peter Arne
EROS	Garrick Hagan
SOOTHSAYER	Roger Delgado
PROCULEIUS	Julian Glover
IRAS	Monica Peterson
OCTAVIA	Carmen Sevilla
MARDIAN	Emiliano Redondo
ALEXAS	Juan Luis Caliardo
POMPEY	Freddie Jones
AGRIPPA	Doug Wilmer
VENTIDIUS	Aldo Sambrel

Pluses   Students like this film's action and verve, the battle scenes in particular.

Minuses   Textual changes (see below) can make the plot hard to follow.

Textual Cuts and Rearrangements   The film begins in a rush of action. Instead of a dialogue between two of the Roman soldiers who attend Antony in Alexandria, we have the arrival of Caesar's messenger, a quite non-Shakespearean entity, galloping from the ship to Cleopatra's palace.

---

* Note: For films related to Shakespeare's *Antony and Cleopatra*, see Appendix A, "Analogues and Variations."

The gods' abandonment of Antony (IV.iii), a curious scene involving oboes under the stage, is omitted.

A large proportion of the textual changes make the main characters more sympathetic and also less ambiguous. For example, we hear Enobarbus' description of Cleopatra ("Age cannot wither her, nor custom stale/Her infinite variety," II.ii.234) after Antony has married Octavia and is living with her in Athens (III.iv). Antony is wandering about the house after Octavia bars him from her bedroom—a rejection not mentioned in Shakespeare's text and here functioning to justify Antony's return to Egypt.

Ventidius' practical advice on how to succeed in a hierarchy by flattering one's superiors (III.i) is omitted, presumably because the superior in this case is Antony.

All references to Cleopatra's children disappear. The moral ambiguity of her suicide is thus lessened, since she is not seen to be abandoning anyone to the conquering Octavius Caesar.

In the final scene, the role of Caesar's officer Proculeius (who in Shakespeare's text betrays Cleopatra by first winning her trust and then capturing her for Caesar) is merged with that of Dolabella, the officer who tells Cleopatra of Caesar's intent to lead her in triumphant procession. Antony's dying advice to Cleopatra ("None about Caesar trust but Proculeius," IV.xv.48) thus turns out to be sound. In the original text we find that Antony has been mistaken in his evaluation of Proculeius as in so many other things.

Settings   Settings are large scale. Interiors in Alexandria, Rome, and Athens have marble staircases, columns, statuary, high ceilings, and wide, polished floors. Cleopatra's palace is also seen from the outside, where a swimming pool gives additional scope for revelry. Her monument, where she shuts herself up with her attendants at the end, is a pyramid in the lonely desert.

Land battles are fought in open country, with plenty of room for horses and extras. The viewer is definitely in the middle of things. Sea battles appear to use model ships interspersed with close-up action, including shots of the galley slaves below deck.

Costumes   Costumes are ornamentally Roman. Soldiers wear elaborate breastplates and helmets with plumes. Cleopatra wears such a helmet herself when she briefly goes in for the military life (III.vii). Women's gowns have simple lines, with pleats and low necks. For her death scene, Cleopatra wears a huge golden collar and a headdress complete with coiled golden snake.

Interpretation of Roles   Hildegard Neil's harsh and mechanical Cleopatra disappoints many viewers. Cleopatra's self-centered vanity comes across, but not her grandeur. Nevertheless, she has her moments. When she questions a messenger about her rival Octavia (III.iii), doing her makeup the while with an array of creams and powders, she achieves a bouncy charm. Her attendant Alexas can be seen cueing the messenger with the correct answers.

Heston has more success interpreting Antony as a bluff soldier, more at home with action than with politics. Even his suicide becomes an exercise in physical endurance. After failing to stab himself effectively (IV.xiv), he refuses help, walks under his own power to Cleopatra's monument, and climbs to an upper window.

As Octavius Caesar, John Castle exudes a smooth, youthful confidence that contrasts with Heston's craggier, sweatier efforts.

Fernando Rey brings out the ineffectual good nature of the hapless third triumvir, Lepidus. While important negotiations take place, Lepidus is out feeding the swans; when Antony and Octavia leave for Athens, he runs in with his farewells at the last minute, having apparently just been told of the departure.

The soothsayer, a minor character in Shakespeare's text, is here given greater importance. He replaces an anonymous messenger in V.i, bringing Antony word that Cleopatra is alive after all, and it is he who brings the asps to Cleopatra's monument and wishes her "joy of the worm" (V.ii).

Cleopatra's attendants include Jane Lapotaire (later to play Cleopatra in the BBC film) as a sprightly Charmian.

Production History   This film did not do well at the box office and was not widely distributed.

Reviews and Studies   Rothwell, Kenneth S., and Melzer, Annabelle H. *Shakespeare on Screen*. 1990. Item 20, p. 28.

Purchase/Rental Inquiries   Embassy Home Entertainment. See Appendix B for address.

❧ 2.2. *Antony and Cleopatra*. 1974. Royal Shakespeare Company. Color, 162 min. Producer: Lorna Mason. Director: Trevor Nunn.

ANTONY	Richard Johnson
CLEOPATRA	Janet Suzman
ENOBARBUS	Patrick Stewart
OCTAVIUS CAESAR	Corin Redgrave
THIDIAS	Ben Kingsley
PROCULEIUS	Tim Pigott-Smith

MAECENAS	Patrick Godfrey
DOLABELLA	Martin Milman
CHARMIAN	Rosemary McHale
IRAS	Mavis Taylor Blake
OCTAVIA	Mary Rutherford
LEPIDUS	Raymond Westwell
EROS	Joe Marcell
VENTIDIUS	Constantin De Goguel
SOOTHSAYER	John Bott
ALEXAS	Darien Angadi
MARDIAN	Sidney Livingstone
AGRIPPA	Philip Locke

Pluses   Excellent acting, roles convincingly cast. The story flows energetically. A favorite with student audiences.

Minuses   Viewers are divided about the film's close-up camera work. Some find the result monotonous; others are drawn to the actors' subtle changes of expression.

Textual Cuts and Rearrangements   Cuts serve to keep the film's emphasis on the relationship between Antony and Cleopatra. Protruding bits of plot, such as military expeditions, are snipped off, along with subtle bits of characterization and miscellaneous comments on human experience.

The episode of Pompey and the pirates, a substantial part of the second act, is omitted, though the existence of these threats to Roman rule is mentioned. The party aboard Pompey's galley is changed to a Roman celebration. Here Lepidus is manipulated into drinking too much, and Antony's soldiers demonstrate an Egyptian dance.

The text's alternation between Alexandria and Rome, in the first half of the play, is changed to allow longer sojourns in each setting. Ventidius' account of his adventures in Parthia (III.i) is lost in this shuffle.

Scenes frequently lose their beginning and ending lines, and passages are thinned. Part of the gods' abandonment of Antony remains, however (IV.iii), a rarity in film versions, and Proculeius' betrayal of Cleopatra is essentially unchanged (V.ii). Cleopatra's and Caesar's brief references to Cleopatra's children remain. The episode with Cleopatra's treasurer, Seleucus, is cut.

Passages of descriptive dialogue are often illustrated with pantomimic renditions of whatever is being talked about. We hear Caesar's voice-over explanation of Antony's return to Cleopatra (III.vi), while we see, in a shimmer of god-like habiliments, Antony, Cleopatra, their several children, and Caesarion, solemn and big-eyed under their golden headdresses. (Caesarion, according to some ancient authorities, was Cleopatra's son by Julius Caesar, predecessor of Octavius Caesar.)

Settings   Settings are more stylized than realistic. Alexandria is indicated by hanging draperies, some of them white and translucent, together with luxurious carpets and cushions. Cleopatra and her attendants occasionally move out to the desert sands for a sunbath. Rome is simply a white floor and backdrop, in a glare of white light, against which the inhabitants find themselves squinting.

In this film, characters are seldom alone. Even the most intimate lines are spoken for effect, as part of the characters' public personae, and are rewarded by laughter and applause from spectators whose heads float in and out of the camera frame, inches away from the faces of the speakers.

Sound effects include rushing winds, clashing swords, distant revelry, barking or neighing animals. When so much of the screen is covered by faces, the sounds are useful in implying a spatial context.

Costumes   Egyptian costumes are elaborate and stylized, colorful, reminiscent of the more expensive items in a museum's gift shop. The golden collars, covering the shoulders and set with gems, are especially dazzling. Romans wear togas. Antony and his soldiers buckle breastplates over basic leather tunics.

Interpretation of Roles   Janet Suzman's Cleopatra is both imperious and earthy. Supremely self-assured, she controls Antony with a shrugging shoulder and a defiant glance. Only when she hears of his marriage to Octavia is she crushed; and, since in this film the passage of time is speeded up, she seems to get him back almost at once. Suzman follows Shakespeare's directions by showing herself "with Phoebus' amorous pinches black," or at least deeply tanned. Her dark, heavy hair hangs to her shoulders in a very Egyptian manner. Appropriately for the play, Suzman is not in her first youth, but her vitality and sexuality are extraordinary.

Richard Johnson's Antony lacks the complexity of the character Shakespeare created. At least in part because of textual cuts, this Antony does not seem deeply torn between Roman self-discipline and Alexandrian self-indulgence. His marriage to Octavia seems a temporary aberration. Physically, however, he is grizzled and handsome, and Cleopatra's passion for him is explicable.

Patrick Stewart, familiar to students today through his television role in *Star Trek: The Next Generation*, plays Enobarbus as a no-nonsense soldier whose common sense tells him to desert Antony and whose loyalty, once he has done so, tells him to die.

As Octavius Caesar, Corin Redgrave is blond and cool, though given to passionate outbursts. Ben Kingsley, later to win acclaim in the title role of the film *Ghandi*, here turns up as Thidias, messenger from Caesar to Cleopatra.

Mary Rutherford makes the small role of Octavia into a gem of characterization. Fragile, hesitant of speech, focused entirely on making others happy and creating harmony around her, she is the opposite of Cleopatra.

Cleopatra's attendants are a strange lot. When viewed through the desert haze, carrying enormous fans and walking in close formation, they look like a surreal mirage. The number of waiting women has been augmented. Besides Charmian and Iras, three or four others hover in the background and even accompany Cleopatra on her final journey to the monument, though they seem to have slipped away when it is time for the asp.

Mardian the eunuch, plump and bald, speaks in falsetto tones. In most of his scenes he is joined by three others in like case, carrying and sometimes playing Egyptian musical instruments.

Production History The Royal Shakespeare Company's stage version opened at Stratford-upon-Avon in 1972. It moved to the Aldwych Theatre, London, the following year. The television version was shown on British television in 1974 and in the United States in 1975.

Reviews and Studies Bulman, J. C., and Coursen, H. R., eds. *Shakespeare on Television*. 1988. Extracts from reviews of this film, pp. 246–47.

Rothwell, Kenneth S., and Melzer, Annabelle H. *Shakespeare on Screen*. 1990. Item 21, pp. 29–30.

Purchase/Rental Inquiries Viewfinders, Inc. See Appendix B for address.

❧ **2.3.** *Antony and Cleopatra*. 1980. British Broadcasting Company/ Time-Life Television: The Shakespeare Plays. Color, 177 min. Producer: Jonathan Miller. Director: Jonathan Miller.

ANTONY	Colin Blakely
CLEOPATRA	Jane Lapotaire
OCTAVIUS CAESAR	Ian Charleson
ENOBARBUS	Emrys James
LEPIDUS	Esmond Knight
EROS	Simon Chandler
CHARMIAN	Janet Key
IRAS	Cassie McFarlane

OCTAVIA	Lynn Farleigh
MENACRATES	Desmond Stokes
MENAS	George Innes
VENTIDIUS	Jonathan Adams
SOOTHSAYER	Howard Goorney
DOLABELLA	Geoffrey Collins
ALEXAS	Darien Angadi
MARDIAN	Mohammed Shamsi

Pluses   Since almost every scene is included, this film is useful for comparative scene analysis. Individual speeches are typically well-thought-out and effectively delivered.

Minuses   Slow pace and lack of spectacular effects can make the experience tedious. Students are often annoyed at Colin Blakely's middle-aged Antony.

Textual Cuts and Rearrangements   Most of the text is retained, in its original sequence. Some passages are thinned out, complex metaphors and classical allusions removed. The first and/or last exchanges in a scene are often cut, so that the audience has to make abrupt shifts in time and place.

Ventidius' advice on flattering one's superiors (III.i) disappears, as does the gods' abandonment of Antony (IV.iii) and Cleopatra's exchange with her treasurer (V.ii.138–83).

Settings   Sets are generally small-scale and simple, becoming even simpler as the play progresses. Early scenes include luxurious props for Cleopatra's court (ceremonial umbrellas, for example), a banquet of fruit for the meeting of Antony and Octavius (II.ii), and, for Pompey's party, the deck of a ship, where Enobarbus leads a dance reminiscent of Zorba the Greek.

Virtually all the battle scenes involving Antony and Cleopatra (beginning with III.vii) take place against a sort of pinkish-red cloth, suggesting a tent or the sail of a ship. As in Shakespeare's text, action is described rather than shown. Caesar's battle headquarters is also a tent interior. Cleopatra's monument consists of dark, simple shapes—a rectangular doorway, a chair or two.

The audience has little sense of geography or of the relationship of one place to another. The fact that violence is not seen and only occasionally heard removes from the last two acts any sense of danger or even pressure. Antony and Cleopatra seem to be killing themselves on a whim.

Costumes   Costumes follow the director's choice of the paintings of Veronese (Paolo Cagliari, 1528–88) as a visual reference. Colors and textures are rich. Cleopatra attends the battle of Actium in ruffled décolletage. Occasional variations imply Roman or Egyptian influence, and there is a touch of the late nineteenth century, as when Caesar and his staff appear in high-necked blue tunics.

Interpretation of Roles   Colin Blakely gets the most reaction from viewers, and it is generally negative. An Antony of short stature, paunchy figure, and thinning hair, afflicted with an apologetic grin, does not find favor with student audiences.

Jane Lapotaire as Cleopatra, though somewhat dried-up looking, gets better notices, perhaps by default. Her mixure of playfulness and self-confidence comes through. Reminiscing about Antony during his absence (I.v), she writhes orgiastically about on a couch. In her last moments she is imperious to the extent of defying gravity, dead but nevertheless sitting bolt upright on her throne.

Emrys James plays Enobarbus as a matter-of-fact army buddy. During the angry exchange between Antony and Octavius and the diplomatic marriage arrangements that follow (II.ii), Enobarbus just goes on eating.

Ian Charleson's Octavius Caesar is young, pale, erect, intellectual, and, as his icy self-control contrasts with Antony's emotional urgency, very convincing.

Cleopatra's attendants convey an appropriate Alexandrian frivolity. Iras (Cassie McFarlane) has raised tattoos on her face and an exotic, Nubian air; at one point (I.ii) she carries a pet monkey. Charmian (Janet Key) is demonstrative, almost gushing, teasing her mistress but, like the more reserved Iras, with her to the death.

Production History   Part of "The Shakespeare Plays," the British Broadcasting Company's series of the entire canon, this film was first shown on British television in 1980, and in the United States in April of 1981.

Reviews and Studies   Bulman, J. C., and Coursen, H. R., eds. *Shakespeare on Television.* 1988. Extracts from reviews of this film, pp. 270–73.

David, Richard. "Shakespeare in Miniature: The BBC *Antony and Cleopatra.*" In *Shakespeare on Television*, ed. Bulman and Coursen, cited above. Pp. 139–44.

Rothwell, Kenneth S., and Melzer, Annabelle H. *Shakespeare on Screen.* 1990. Item 23, pp. 30–31.

Purchase/Rental Inquiries   Ambrose Video; Filmic Archives; Insight Media; The Writing Company. See Appendix B for addresses.

ô 2.4. *Antony and Cleopatra*. 1985. The Bard Series. Color, 183 min. Producer: Ken Campbell. Director: Lawrence Carra.

ANTONY	Timothy Dalton
CLEOPATRA	Lynn Redgrave
OCTAVIUS CAESAR	Anthony Geary
SOOTHSAYER	John Carradine
ENOBARBUS	Barrie Ingham
VENTIDIUS	Michael Billington
CHARMIAN	Nichelle Nichols
IRAS	Kim Miyori
MARDIAN	James Avery
ALEXAS	Anthony Holland
EROS	Brian Kerwin
DOLABELLA	John Devlin
PROCULEIUS	Henry Sutton
LEPIDUS	Earl Boen
OCTAVIA	Sharon Barr
SELEUCUS	Ralph Drischell
POMPEY	Walter Koenig
MENAS	Ted Sorel
MAECENAS	Earl Robinson
AGRIPPA	Tom Rosqui

Pluses   A lively, vivid production.

Minuses   Some of the acting is wooden, with mechanical gestures and stilted speeches.

Textual Cuts and Rearrangements   There are surprisingly few cuts. Some passages are thinned. As seems to be usual in film, no gods abandon Antony (IV.iii), although the opening lines of the scene are kept. But Ventidius gives most of his advice on how to get ahead (III.i). Cleopatra's scene with Seleucus, her treasurer, often cut, is retained and works well. When Seleucus says she has not put anywhere near the total of her possessions into the list she gave the conquering Caesar, Cleopatra pretends to be furious and Caesar roars with laughter, convinced that the queen wants to live and that his plan to lead her in his triumphal procession is safe (V.ii.138–75). Seleucus' role, incidentally, is built up by being combined with that of Diomedes (IV.xiv).

Settings   The single set is designed to suggest Elizabethan staging. Everything is made of dark, polished wood. Two staircases curve toward each other to the main acting area; above, a narrow railed passage provides an upper level. Numerous entrances are possible.

Geographical shifts are indicated with on-screen titles (e.g., "Athens: Antony's House," at the beginning of III.iv).

Costumes   Romans wear elaborate breastplates and helmets; Egyptians, looser garments. Antony often appears in a leather jacket, unlike anyone else, and in the final battle scenes combines a loose striped robe with a Roman breastplate. Women, whether Roman or Egyptian, wear long, form-fitting gowns with pleats, usually in bright colors.

Interpretation of Roles   For students, encountering in Shakespearean roles actors they associate with something quite different can have a curiously positive effect. It is as if Shakespeare has been authenticated by a higher power. This film provides three such cases. Lynn Redgrave, who first made a mark in *Georgy Girl*, recently appeared in *Getting It Right*; Timothy Dalton has reached a wide audience in his James Bond films; and Anthony Geary is a familiar face on daytime television, especially *General Hospital*.

Lynn Redgrave plays Cleopatra with flashing eyes and assured diction. In bidding goodbye to Antony (I.iii), she does not burst into tears, as Cleopatras often do. But when she learns that Antony is married (II.v), queenly dignity abandons her and she kicks the messenger in the crotch. In the final scene she becomes unfortunately laughable; she bugs out her eyes and speaks her dying words in slow motion.

Dalton's Antony wears a grizzled beard and an intent expression. In dialogue with Caesar he is quietly arrogant, leaning back in his chair while Caesar stands above him and rages. With Cleopatra, Dalton alternates between states of love and fury.

As Caesar, Geary is more hot than cool—an interesting contrast to the BBC film's Ian Charleson. He enjoys physical demonstrations of his higher status; as everybody laughs at the drunken Lepidus (II.vii), Caesar condescendingly pats Lepidus' cheeks, part pat and part slap. (This gesture is repeated a few minutes later when Pompey, rejecting Menas' suggestion of a triple assassination, pats Menas on the cheeks.)

Cleopatra's attendants work well together, creating an intimate, luxurious atmosphere. Iras (Kim Miyori) makes her character's silence plausible with her demure Oriental grace. Nichelle Nichols, as Charmian, responds with instant and natural warmth to whatever happens around her. She is black, as is James Avery's cheerful and muscular Mardian.

Production History   Bard Productions, based in California, have made numerous films of Shakespeare's plays. For others in the series, see the general introduction (p.5).

Reviews and Studies   Rothwell, Kenneth S., and Melzer, Annabelle H. *Shakespeare on Screen*. 1990. Item 27, p. 32.

Purchase/Rental Inquiries   Crest Video; Filmic Archives; The Writing Company. See Appendix B for addresses.

3 ❧ AS YOU LIKE IT*_____

❧ 3.1. *As You Like It.* 1936. Twentieth Century British Fox. Black and white, 97 min. Producer: Joseph Schenck. Director: Paul Czinner.

ORLANDO	Laurence Olivier
ROSALIND	Elizabeth Bergner
DUKE FREDERICK	Felix Aylmer
JAQUES	Leon Quartermaine
TOUCHSTONE	MacKenzie Ward
CELIA	Sophie Stewart
PHEBE	Joan White
AUDREY	Durice Jordred
ADAM	J. Fisher White
CORIN	Aubrey Mather
DUKE SENIOR	Henry Ainley
OLIVER	John Laurie
CHARLES	Lionel Branham
WILLIAM	Peter Bull
AMIENS	Stuart Robinson

Pluses   Considerable charm, provided one does not expect too much.

Minuses   Tends to over-cuteness.

Textual Cuts and Rearrangements   Both cuts and rearrangements are frequent. Apparently it was thought necessary to reduce the playing time. Propriety seems the motive in some cases; cynical Jaques and ribald Touchstone lose many lines. Touchstone does retain some of his bawdy verses, however (III.ii). Rosalind in Shakespeare's text tells Celia, who has asked if her sorrow is caused by her banished father, that it is in fact "for my child's father"—Orlando, with whom she has just fallen in love (I.iii.11). In this film she claims to feel "for my father's child"—herself. This chaste variation, without textual authority, was a favorite in Victorian times, to judge from surviving promptbooks.

Some songs are added, including "Hey, Nonny Nonny" from *Much Ado about Nothing* and "Tell Me Where Is Fancy Bred" from *The Merchant of Venice.*

---

* Note: For films related to Shakespeare's *As You Like It,* see Appendix A, "Analogues and Variations."

Settings   Oliver's estate, Duke Ferdinand's palace, and the forest of Arden have a solid spatial presence and are filled with people and animals. Orlando eats with his brother's farmhands at a sort of picnic table while horses and chickens look on (I.i). On Duke Frederick's manicured grounds, swans drift about an ornamental lake. In Arden, Rosalind and Celia live in a thatched cottage beside a picturesquely arched bridge. From time to time flocks of sheep rush past the camera.

Costumes   Ladies at Duke Frederick's court wear conical caps and wimples. Only their faces show, and as a result the audience finds it fairly believable that they can change their identities along with their clothes. Attire in the forest is more casual. Celia wears a full-skirted shepherdess outfit. Rosalind's disguise includes a pair of trousers sufficiently loose to hide the shape of her legs, although she looks thoroughly feminine nevertheless.

Interpretation of Roles   Laurence Olivier makes Orlando a faithful friend to his aged servant, Adam, and a bedazzled lover of Rosalind. The role is not a particularly challenging one, and Olivier seems at loose ends, as if wondering why he were there.

Elizabeth Bergner, by contrast, does a great deal with her role as Rosalind, but some viewers may feel she does the wrong things. She is kittenish and coy, with a high, twittery voice and an accent that can seem affected. (Bergner was born in Vienna, to do her justice. Her casting as Rosalind would seem to have been non-negotiable, as she was married to director Paul Czinner.)

The rest of the cast go about their jobs in an amiable manner. Duke Ferdinand (Felix Aylmer) is heavily villainous in the opening scene, to the extent that his sudden conversion by "an old religious man" (V.iv.160) would seem preposterous were it not for the fantasy ambiance of Arden. Celia (Sophie Stewart) is sprightly, and the exiled duke, Rosalind's father (Henry Ainley), sonorous and dignified.

Production History   The film was moderately well received but does not seem to be cited among the personal triumphs of any of the people involved.

Reviews and Studies   Rothwell, Kenneth S., and Melzer, Annabelle H. *Shakespeare on Film*. 1990. Item 34, pp. 34–35.

Purchase/Rental Inquiries   Filmic Archives. See Appendix B for address.

❧ 3.2. *As You Like It*. 1978. British Broadcasting Company/ Time-Life Television: The Shakespeare Plays. Color, 150 min. Producer: Cedric Messina. Director: Basil Coleman.

ROSALIND	Helen Mirren
ORLANDO	Brian Stirner
JAQUES	Richard Pasco
DUKE SENIOR	Tony Church
TOUCHSTONE	James Bolam
DUKE FREDERICK	Richard Easton
ADAM	Arthur Hewlett
CHARLES	Dave Prowse
CELIA	Angharad Rees
PHEBE	Victoria Plucknett
AUDREY	Marilyn Le Conte
LE BEAU	John Quentin
AMIENS	Tom McDonnell
CORIN	David Meredith
WILLIAM	Jeffrey Holland
SILVIUS	Maynard Williams
SIR OLIVER MARTEXT	Timothy Bateson
HYMAN	John Moulder Brown
JAQUES DE BOYS	Paul Bentall

Pluses   A conscientious production with many good moments.

Minuses   Overall, curiously somber.

Textual Cuts and Rearrangements   The text is generally followed with care. A few passages are thinned, and some scenes lose their opening and/or closing lines.

Setting   The film was shot on location at Glamis Castle, Scotland, in what appears to have been pleasant summer weather.
   The setting does not make a distinction between Oliver's and Duke Frederick's estates. Both seem composed of terraces and topiary. The forest offers more variety; trees are of different sizes, some spots have bracken and some do not, and there are a few open glades.

Costumes   Dress at Duke Frederick's is pompous, requiring elaborate headdresses for women and a great deal of brocade and velvet for everyone. In the forest things are simpler. Rosalind's disguise reveals her short, curly hair and makes her look somewhat different, but she is still recognizable, and audiences tend to assume that Orlando knows who she is but is willing to play the game.

Interpretation of Roles   Helen Mirren plays Rosalind quite morosely. Celia's early plea that she cheer up a bit (I.ii.1) is in vain; gloom for a banished father would seem to conquer all. She then falls in love, to such an extent that Rosalind admits she has no time to think of her father even though she and Celia had originally set out to seek him in Arden; but love makes her even sadder. Eventually, however, when she has Orlando at her beck and call, she does begin to smile.

Celia (Angharad Rees) is petite and perky, a welcome contrast. When she and Oliver meet (IV.iii), they are obviously smitten with each other before they have a chance to speak.

Brian Stirner's Orlando puzzles many viewers as it is difficult to understand what Rosalind sees in him, beyond the fact that both have had a hard time in life. He has long, stringy hair and a half-hearted little moustache, a weak chin, and a generally hangdog air. Student audiences tend to label him a wimp. His defeat of Charles the wrestler is ludicrous (I.ii). This mystery does not clear up.

As the misanthrope Jaques, Richard Pasco gives a consistent performance as an alienated looker-on. He makes most of his speeches from the edge of the group, wine cup in hand. During his "seven ages of man" speech (II.vii. 139ff.), his fellow exiles, far from admiring his insights, go on eating and pay little attention. (On this occasion, however, Jaques endears himself to the audience by taking an instant dislike to Orlando.)

Touchstone (James Bolam), on the cheerful side of this film's emotional dichotomy, revels in language and will debate anybody on anything. Duke Senior and his court applaud after he gives his "seventh cause" speech (V.iv). Audrey (Marilyn Le Conte), the country lass Touchstone marries, is not nearly as ugly or awkward as Touchstone keeps saying she is; she has a healthy, natural grace. The audience assumes Touchstone is spreading negative propaganda for fear of being cuckolded.

Production History   As You Like It was offered during the first season of the British Broadcasting Company's series "The Shakespeare Plays," which eventually filmed the entire Shakespeare canon. It was shown on British television in December of 1978 and in the United States in February of 1979.

Reviews and Studies   Bulman, J. C. "As You Like it and the Perils of Pastoral." In Shakespeare on Television, ed. J. C. Bulman and H. R. Coursen. 1988. Pp. 174–79.

Shakespeare on Television, cited above. Extracts from reviews of this film, pp. 251–52.

Rothwell, Kenneth S., and Melzer, Annabelle H. *Shakespeare on Screen*. 1990. Item 42, pp. 37–38.

Purchase/Rental Inquiries Ambrose Video; Filmic Archives; Insight Media; The Writing Company. See Appendix B for addresses.

❧ **3.3. *As You Like It*.** 1985. Stratford Shakespeare Festival, Canada. Color, 158 min. Producer: Sam Levene. Directors: John Hirsch, Herb Roland.

ROSALIND	Roberta Maxwell
JAQUES	Nicholas Pennell
ORLANDO	Andrew Gillies
CELIA	Rosemary Dunsmore
DUKE FREDERICK	Graeme Campbell
ADAM	Mervyn Blake
TOUCHSTONE	Lewis Gordon
PHEBE	Mary Haney
SILVIUS	John Jarvis
OLIVER	Stephen Russell
DUKE SENIOR	William Needles
CORIN	Deryck Hazel
AUDREY	Elizabeth Leigh-Milne
DENNIS	Nicolas Colicos
CHARLES	Jefferson Mappin
LE BEAU	Keith Dinicol
AMIENS	John Novak
SIR OLIVER MARTEXT	Maurice E. Evans
WILLIAM	Hardee T. Lineham
PAGE	Graham Abbey
PAGE	Christopher Cook
JAQUES DE BOYS	Christopher Gibson

Pluses Warm, lively, and intelligent, with the all-of-a-piece momentum often found in a filmed stage production.

Minuses This film is hard to fault.

Textual Cuts and Rearrangements   Changes in the text are usually made for clear reasons. Rosalind, for example, is not noticeably taller than Celia, and references to this physical discrepancy are cut. In Touchstone's speech about honor, "meat pies" replaces "pancakes" (I.ii.79), presumably because the former are more compatible with mustard in present-day gastronomy.

Setting   The play takes place before a live audience on the open thrust stage of the Stratford, Ontario, Shakespeare Festival. This stage manages to be simultaneously large and small. Two or three people can converse on it without looking lonely, and fifteen or twenty can romp about without looking crowded. It has numerous acting areas—platforms, stairs, upper levels—and camera angles can give additional variety.

Props are occasionally used to establish place. The forest of Arden has a tree, for example, a leafy trunk.

Costumes   Costumes are basically nineteenth century, though within this period the mix is eclectic. The opening scene implies a cold night in a London market, with people rushing about in mufflers and shawls. The effect is of a Dickensian Christmas. Oliver de Boys wears a tall hat, a tailcoat, and heavy boots. He carries a whip. Orlando, less expensively clad, has to make do with a sweater and muffler.

At Duke Frederick's court, the color scheme is black and silver. The duke's female companion, a silent addition to the text, wears a curious headdress with a crescent moon, along with a supercilious expression. Touchstone is dressed as a circus clown, red nose and all, and carries a hand puppet.

In the forest, the exiled duke and his men also wear coats and mufflers, but as the weather gradually warms up they appear in knee breeches and vests. Touchstone exchanges his clown outfit for a gaudy version of civilian dress—blue cutaway coat, yellow vest, red bow tie.

Women in Arden wear, typically, a full skirt with a laced bodice and a blouse with large sleeves. Rosalind's disguise gives her a Huckleberry Finn appearance, trousers and jacket with a straw hat.

Interpretation of Roles   Roberta Maxwell's Rosalind is a mixture of common sense and playfulness. When she confronts Orlando in the forest and suggests that she pretend to be Rosalind (III.ii), she is nervously improvising; when he goes along with the game (without giving any indication of recognizing her), she is just as clearly delighted.

Orlando (Andrew Gillies) is here a decent, dependable person, quite relieved to find that one does not have to be a desperado to survive in Arden (II.vii).

Rosemary Dunsmore's cheerful and adaptable Celia seems capable not only of falling in love with Oliver at a moment's notice but of remaining true to him.

This production offers an unusual Jaques (Nicholas Pennell), more sensitive than vituperative. At the end of his "seven ages of man" speech, he is quite affected by the picture he has conjured up, as if he had thought of the dire effects of age for the first time (II.vii). He holds out his trembling hands, perhaps wishing he could stop the process.

Another unusual touch is presented by Orlando's servant and companion, Adam, played by Mervyn Blake. Adam has no lines after the second act, and in some productions he disappears from the action. Here, however, he remains among the duke's merry men, growing increasingly stronger, and on Oliver's arrival in the forest he is overjoyed at the brothers' reconciliation (V.ii).

Production History   The play was given in 1983 at the Stratford Shakespeare Festival in Stratford, Ontario. A 30-minute version of this film is available in the "Page to Stage" video series (see Appendix A, 3.A).

Reviews and Studies   Rothwell, Kenneth S., and Melzer, Annabelle H. *Shakespeare on Screen*. 1990. Item 45.1, p. 39.

Purchase/Rental Inquiries   Insight Media. See Appendix B for address.

4 ❧ THE COMEDY OF
ERRORS_____

❧ 4.1. *The Comedy of Errors.* 1984. British Broadcasting Company/ Time-Life Television: The Shakespeare Plays. Color, 110 min. Producer: Shaun Sutton. Director: James Cellan-Jones.

AEGEON	Cyril Cusack
SOLINUS	Charles Gray
AEMELIA	Wendy Hiller
ADRIANNA	Suzanne Bertish
THE TWO DROMIOS	Roger Daltrey
THE TWO ANTIPHOLUSES	Michael Kitchen
LUCIANA	Joanne Pearce
THE COURTESAN	Ingrid Pitt
BALTHAZAR	David Kelly
ANGELO	Sam Dastor
PINCH	Geoffrey Rose

Pluses Colorful, fast-paced.

Minuses Viewers expressing discontent with this film generally turn out not to have been in the mood for farce.

Textual Cuts and Rearrangements Cuts are extensive, serving not only to speed the action but to rescue the audience from jokes which may have been funny to the Elizabethans but which have not stood the test of time. The Syracusans' catechism of jokes about hair (II.ii) is an example of repartee whose absence is not missed.

Setting A studio set of considerable ingenuity. Both functional and nonrealistic, its colorful jauntiness adds to the sense of comedy. The three houses—the Porpentine, home of the Courtesan; the Phoenix, home of Antipholus of Ephesus and his wife Adrianna; and the Abbey, where a long-lost wife and mother is discovered—surround a central acting area the floor of which is painted with a map of the eastern Mediterranean. An overhead shot at the beginning lets the viewer get his bearings.

Costumes   Since the plot involves two pairs of long-lost identical twins who also happen to wear identical clothing, costumes can come under severe scrutiny. Colorful, cartoon-like designs predominate, with some subtle variations among the twins; Antipholus of Syracuse wears his collar up, Antipholus of Ephesus wear his collar down. As the play continues, of course, they can be further distinguished according to who is and who is not wearing a gold chain.

The duke of Ephesus wears an elaborately plumed helmet and ornamental breastplate. He is accompanied, as an echo of the twin motif, by a tiny page wearing a version of the same gear.

Women's costumes emphasize their stations in life. Adriana displays the rich fabrics of a merchant's wife, her sister Luciana prefers virginal simplicity, and the Courtesan's clothes are occupationally revealing. The Abbess wears a traditional religious habit, as do the various nuns glimpsed from time to time walking calmly through the frenetic street life of Ephesus.

Interpretation of Roles   When the same actor plays two roles in a film, one assumes that both roles will not appear in the same shot, and throughout most of *The Comedy of Errors* this stipulation is easily met by the plot. At the end, when the twins meet, this film uses split-screen techniques that produce a satisfactory result and greatly interest student audiences.

As the two Dromios, rock musician Roger Daltrey is outstanding. He differentiates between his two parts, making the Ephesian Dromio a bit more baffled by events and the Syracusan Dromio a bit more in control.

Michael Kitchens similarly brings out the difference between the hot-tempered Antipholus of Ephesus and his more sophisticated and generally pleasanter brother of Syracuse.

Suzanne Bertish makes Adrianna more a sympathetic figure than a nagging wife.

Aegeon, the old man in search of his family, as acted by Cyril Cusack, becomes a human being and not just a catalyst for the plot. His long exposition in the opening scene is enlivened by a mime troupe acting out his words. Throughout the rest of the action we see him wandering about, often just missing an encounter with one or the other of his sons.

Charles Gray plays the duke with authority, and Wendy Hiller as a bubbly Abbess makes her surprise appearance to wind up the plot.

Production History   *The Comedy of Errors* was shown on British television in December of 1983 and in the United States in February of 1984. It was the thirtieth of the British Broadcasting Company's 37-play series of Shakespeare's entire canon.

Reviews and Studies   Bulman, J. C., and Coursen, H. R., eds. *Shakespeare on Television*. 1988. Extracts from reviews of this film, pp. 303–04.

Roberts, Jeanne Addison. "The Shakespeare Plays on TV: *The Comedy of Errors*." *Shakespeare on Film Newsletter* 9.1 (1984): 4.

Rothwell, Kenneth S., and Melzer, Annabelle H. *Shakespeare on Screen*. 1990. Item 55, p. 44.

Willis, Susan. *The BBC Shakespeare Plays*. 1991. Pp. 260–91, 341.

Wood, Robert E. "Cooling the Comedy: Television as a Medium for Shakespeare's *Comedy of Errors*." *Literature/Film Quarterly* 14 (1986): 195–202. Also reprinted in Bulman and Coursen, cited above.

Purchase/Rental Inquiries   Ambrose Video; Filmic Archives; Insight Media; The Writing Company. See Appendix B for addresses.

5 ❧ CORIOLANUS*

❧ 5.1. *Coriolanus.* British Broadcasting Company/Time-Life Television: The Shakespeare Plays. Color, 145 min. Producer: Shaun Sutton. Director: Elijah Moshinsky.

CORIOLANUS	Alan Howard
VOLUMNIA	Irene Worth
TITUS LARTIUS	Peter Sands
COMINIUS	Patrick Godfrey
AUFIDIUS	Mike Gwilym
MENENIUS AGRIPPA	Joss Ackland
YOUNG MARCIUS	Damien Franklin
BRUTUS	Anthony Pedley
SICINIUS	John Burgess
VIRGINIA	Joanna McCallum
VALERIA	Heather Canning
GENTLEWOMAN	Patsy Smart

Pluses   An interesting psychological study, well acted.

Minuses   Stylized battle scenes can become tedious.

Textual Cuts and Rearrangements   The text has been cut a great deal, omitting much of the political dimension in order to focus on Coriolanus' personal relationships. Many transitional passages, such as the opening lines of scenes, are cut. Crowd scenes are often shortened. The sequence of scenes is occasionally changed.

The intense and ambivolent releationship between Coriolanus and Aufidius — they are enemies, then allies, then enemies again — is emphasized when, on Coriolanus' visiting Aufidius (IV.v), the opening as well as the closing dialogues between the household servants are cut. The servants are not even present. Nobody else is listening as Coriolanus offers to lead Aufidius' troops against his own city, Rome, which has just thrown him out. Soon Aufidius is standing behind Coriolanus and massaging his neck, then embracing him as Coriolanus rhetorically offers his throat for cutting (IV.v.95). Although in Shakespeare's text these lines have a high degree of intimacy ("Let me twine/ Mine arms about that body,

---

* Note: For films related to Shakespeare's *Coriolanus*, see Appendix A, "Analogues and Variations."

where against/ My grained ash an hundred times hath broke," says Aufidius), the servants' presence would ordinarily give the scene some emotional insulation.

Settings   The play's historical period—or legendary period, rather—is approximately the fifth century B.C., but the sets for this production are meant to suggest the early seventeenth century, the time of Shakespeare's original audience. Interiors have ornate Renaissance tables and vistas of receding doorways. Exteriors seem less spacious than interiors, rather oddly. Roman streets are narrow; even the marketplace is miniature. A result, presumably intended, is that a small number of extras can more convincingly impersonate a crowd.

Costumes   Military characters when not in the field wear bits of armor incorporated with their dark, seventeenth-century civilian clothes; a metal breastplate may be topped with a ruffled collar, for example. For battles, however, the costumes shift not to Renaissance combat gear but to stylized tunics and helmets reminiscent of ancient Greece.

Coriolanus wears a loose and rough-woven robe in order to stand in the marketplace, show his battle scars, and solicit the plebians' votes (II.iii). He puts on this garment (a "gown of humility," according to the First Folio's stage direction) with as much reluctance as he fulfills the rest of this political assignment.

Interpretation of Roles   Alan Howard was, at the time the film was made, in his thirties. While he might seem too old for the impetuous Coriolanus, so desperate for his mother's approval and so inflexible in his concept of honor, the viewer gets used to this chronological misalignment. He plays the part with vigor and makes us sympathize with his longing, so familiar to us all, for the rules of life to be simple.

Irene Worth brings an effortless authority to the role of Volumnia, Coriolanus' mother. When she boasts of her son's battle wounds (I.iv), she does so in a quiet conversational tone, without rhetorical rant. And it is she who persuades Coriolanus to spare Rome after all (V.iii), thus, as it turns out, dooming him to death at the hands of Aufidius.

Coriolanus's wife, Virginia, is played by Joanna McCallum as a quiet and thoroughly nonviolent person, a contrast to Volumnia.

A problem with this production, for many viewers, is that so many of the actors look alike. Menenius (Joss Ackland), Sicinius (John Burgess), and several of the anonymous senators have silver hair and beards, and it can be hard to keep up with what is happening.

Production History   *Coriolanus* was among the last of the British Broadcasting Company's 37-film series of Shakespeare's plays. It was shown on British and American television in the spring of 1985.

Reviews and Studies   Bulman, J. C., and Coursen, H. R. *Shakespeare on Television*. 1988. Extracts from reviews of this film, pp. 304–6.
Rothwell, Kenneth S., and Melzer, Annabelle H. *Shakespeare on Screen*. 1990. Item 97, p. 49.
Willis, Susan. *The BBC Shakespeare Plays*. 1991. Pp. 156–60.

Purchase/Rental Inquiries   Ambrose Video; Filmic Archives; Insight Media; The Writing Company. See Appendix B for addresses.

6 ❧ CYMBELINE

❧ **6.1. Cymbeline.** 1982. British Broadcasting Company/Time-Life Television: The Shakespeare Plays. Color, 175 min. Producer: Shaun Sutton. Director: Elijah Moshinsky.

CYMBELINE'S QUEEN	Claire Bloom
IMOGENE	Helen Mirren
CYMBELINE	Richard Johnson
POSTHUMUS	Michael Pennington
IACHIMO	Robert Lindsay
BELARIUS	Michael Gough
CORNELIUS	Hugh Thomas
PISANIO	John Kane
HELEN	Patsy Smart
ARVIRAGUS	David Creedon
GUIDERIUS	Geoffrey Burridge
CLOTEN	Paul Jesson
JUPITER	Michael Hordern

Pluses A thorough treatment of a play which interests students because of its mixture of genres—a parody of *Snow White*, as they sometimes conclude.

Minuses Slow pace.

Textual Cuts and Rearrangements The text is occasionally cut, but the results do not make the story any stranger than it already is. Iachimo, attempting to win a bet by seducing Imogene, loses several of his ironic asides (I.vi). Cymbeline's defiance of the Roman general (III.i) is shortened. Imogene's and Pisanio's dialogue as they walk through Wales, when Pisanio reveals his order to kill Imogene and is persuaded not to follow it, is thinned somewhat (III.iv).

A few scenes, or parts of scenes, are transposed. When Cloten dresses himself in Posthumus' garments (III.v), a source of great confusion after Cloten is beheaded, he speaks lines from the first scene of act four.

Posthumus' vision, incorporating various deceased members of his family and the god Jupiter (V.iv), takes place on a reduced scale, with some cutting of lines and no eagle for Jupiter to ride.

Settings Almost all the action takes place indoors. Prehistoric Britain and ancient Rome are envisioned similarly, as if painted by Vermeer or Rembrandt.

Roman rooms are a touch more elegant than their British counterparts; people play chess beneath sparkling chandeliers.

Imogene's bedchamber is furnished with the tapestry and ornaments which Iachimo notes when he crawls out of the trunk, and which he describes to Posthumus as proof that he has won his bet (II.iv).

Guiderius and Auviragus, the stolen princes brought up as children of nature, live not in a cave but in a comfortable log cabin. The bodies of Cloten (headless) and of Imogene (not really dead) are laid out on the cabin floor, rather than left outdoors and strewn with flowers (IV.ii).

Costumes   Court gentlemen dress in black doublets and breeches, with small white ruffs at the collar. Cloten, when wearing his own clothes, goes in for brighter hues. Cymbeline wears a fur collar, which seems to associate him with a concept of primitive force. Iachimo and the queen, both villains in their respective segments of the plot, wear black—satin for the queen, leather for Iachimo.

Interpretation of Roles   Helen Mirren's Imogene is virtuous, loyal, and ingenious, living in fact a more interesting life in disguise than she does as the devoted wife of Posthumus.

Michael Pennington has the unrewarding role of Posthumus, so unsympathetic to present-day audiences, but he goes through with it. On being reunited with Imogene in one of her disguises as a page, he strikes her energetically, as required by the text (V.v.224), knocking her to the floor. During the interminable explanations of the final scene, he is properly apologetic.

Claire Bloom as Cymbeline's queen and Imogene's stepmother cooks up wicked potions; Robert Lindsay as Iachimo schemes and slithers.

A minor role, that of Cornelius the physician, played by Hugh Thomas, is augmented with the lines of several of the "Gentlemen" who open scenes by discussing the latest turn of the plot. He is thus a familiar figure by the time he adds his bit to the final scene's explanations, to the effect that he had concocted for the queen not a deadly poison but a sleeping draught (V.v.2249).

Production History   *Cymbeline* was telecast in England and the United States in 1982, part of the British Broadcasting Company's project (1978–86) of filming all of Shakespeare's plays.

Reviews and Studies   Bulman, J. C., and Coursen, H. R., eds. *Shakespeare on Television*. 1988. Extracts from reviews of this film, pp. 289–90.

Rothwell, Kenneth S., and Melzer, Annabelle H. *Shakespeare on Screen*. 1990. Item 73, p. 53.

Willis, Susan. *The BBC Shakespeare Plays*. 1991. Pp. 155–57.

Purchase/Rental Inquiries   Ambrose Video; Filmic Archives; Insight Video; The Writing Company. See Appendix B for addresses.

7 ❧ HAMLET*

❧ **7.1.** *Hamlet.* 1948. J. Arthur Rank Enterprises. Black-and-white, 152 min. Producer: Laurence Olivier. Director: Laurence Olivier.

HAMLET	Laurence Olivier
OPHELIA	Jean Simmons
MARCELLUS	Anthony Quayle
POLONIUS	Felix Aylmer
CLAUDIUS	Basil Sydney
GERTRUDE	Eileen Herlie
HORATION	Norman Wooland
LAERTES	Terence Morgan
OSRIC	Peter Cushing
GRAVEDIGGER	Stanley Holloway
BARNARDO	Esmond Knight
FRANCISCO	John Laurie

Pluses   A classic, authoritative film with excellent performances and beautiful photography.

Minuses   Omission of several characters and simplification of the play generally.

Textual Cuts and Rearrangements   Fortinbras of Norway is omitted entirely, taking with him much of the play's political dimension and depopulating the final scene. Horatio's "Good night, sweet prince" becomes by default the concluding speech (V.ii.359).

The loss of Rosencrantz and Guildenstern is perhaps more noticeable to present-day viewers, familiar with Tom Stoppard's 1960s play *Rosencrantz and Guildenstern Are Dead* (later a film; see Appendix A, 7.G), than it was to audiences of 1948. The absence of these two characters diminishes the theme of false friends and hypocrisy. It also relieves Hamlet of the guilt of sending them to their deaths.

The play within a play, which enables Hamlet to observe Claudius' reactions and thus to detect his guilt, consists of the preliminary pantomimic dumb show only. The text itself is omitted (III.ii.155ff.)

---

* Note: For films related to Shakespeare's *Hamlet*, see Appendix A, "Analogues and Variations."

Among the long speeches that disappear is Hamlet's "O what a rogue and peasant slave am I" (II.ii.550ff.), a puzzling omission. Here Hamlet berates himself for inaction; and this film, in its opening titles, announces itself as "a play about a man who could not make up his mind." Audiences may wonder if this oversimplified label actually describes Olivier's interpretation. This Hamlet may proceed slowly, but he proceeds.

The sequence of scenes are occasionally changed. Hamlet's "To be or not to be" soliloquy takes place after rather than immediately before Ophelia's conversation with Hamlet while Polonius and Claudius eavesdrop (III.i). Since Ophelia lies to Hamlet during this exchange, claiming her father is at home when in fact he is behind the arras, it is possible that Hamlet's disillusionment spurs him immediately to thoughts of suicide. On the other hand, he could hardly be surprised by Ophelia's rather minor deceit, since in this film he is shown overhearing Claudius' and Polonius' plan in the first place (II.ii.162 ff).

A few scenes, or brief vignettes rather, are added to the text. When the ghost tells Hamlet about Claudius' pouring poison in his ear, we see it happen (I.v.59ff.). And when Gertrude describes Ophelia's drowning, we see that too, complete with garlands of flowers adrift on the water (IV.vii.166ff.).

Settings The camera in this film has a life of its own. It wanders unaccompanied about the castle, up and down stairs, through corridors, peering into empty rooms and pausing before pieces of furniture—Gertrude's bed, Hamlet's chair.

The castle thus explored has considerable depth and texture, with its round arches, colonnades, carved pillars, and frequent splashes of sunlight. External scenes are shown in their relationship to the castle. The flowery hillsides where Ophelia wanders can be glimpsed through the arches. The churchyard with its gravestones is adjacent to one of the courtyards.

Costumes While the set suggests the eleventh century, the period of the legendary figures more or less analogous to Shakespeare's characters, costumes are of a later period. Hamlet, following theatrical tradition as well as the text, wears a "customary suit of solemn black" (I.ii.78), here interpreted as tights and doublet. Gertrude wears low-cut dresses; Ophelia, virginal white. Occasional bits of embroidery on both men's and women's garments give a Scandinavian touch.

Interpretation of Roles Olivier's Hamlet naturally dominates the film. Pensive, withdrawn, not given to snarling or raging in the manner of some Hamlets, this self-contained prince may not at first appeal to student audiences, but longer acquaintance usually improves the relationship. The final scene is explosive. Hamlet comes very much to life, fights Laertes with nimble skill, then hurls himself from a height to attack the king (V.iii). His attitude toward Ophelia is gentle; he does berate her while pretending to be mad, but this exhibit is for the benefit of Claudius and Polonius (III.i). (Following another stage tradition, on the conclusion of this scene Olivier tiptoes back to stroke Ophelia's hair. Ironically, her weeping face is turned away and she does not see him.)

When planning the film, Olivier was influenced by Ernest Jones's theory that Hamlet is the victim of an unresolved Oedipus complex—that he cannot kill Claudius because he unconsciously identifies with him, Claudius having acted out Hamlet's buried fantasy of killing his (Hamlet's) father and marrying his (Hamlet's) mother. (Jones later explained his ideas more fully in his *Hamlet and Oedipus*, 1949.)

The extent to which this Freudian underpinning comes through to an audience is open to question. Gertrude (Eileen Herlie) is played as a handsome woman in early middle age. She hovers over Hamlet, insisting he remain at court and kissing him on the mouth (I.ii), while he looks uncomfortable. Her "closet" (in Shakespeare's language merely a private room, not necessarily a sleeping chamber) contains an enormous bed. While the audience might see these as Freudian clues, they could hardly be blamed for seeing only an ordinarily dutiful young man and a woman with sumptuous tastes in home decoration.

As Ophelia, Jean Simmons displays a consistently innocent beauty. There is no hint that she knows what she is singing about in her bawdy songs, many of which have been severely cut anyhow (IV.v). With her brother she is playful, teasing him while Polonius gives his lecture on proper behavior (I.iii); with her father she is dutiful, handing over Hamlet's letters (II.i). When Hamlet rejects her she is devastated. Her madness apparently stems from this moment. Her lines beginning "O what a noble mind is here o'erthrown" (III.i.150) have been cut, and Polonius makes no move to comfort her, so that she is left sobbing on the floor, speechless and alone.

Basil Sydney plays Claudius as a conniving and rather small-scale villain, suspicious of being found out, cutting his eyes sideways and obviously wondering what might be coming up behind him.

Claudius's late brother, the ghost, is more formidable. He walks the ramparts in clouds of mist, wearing armor, accompanied by the sounds of a giant heartbeat (I.i, iv). Hamlet's reaction to the sight of him is to grovel. In Gertrude's closet, the ghost appears in a doorway (III.iv) as a faint glimmer of armor.

Production History   This film was greeted with fanfare and in the late 1940s played at movie theaters all over Britain and America, often to coachloads of schoolchildren. It won Academy Awards both for best picture and for best actor, as well as awards from the Venice Film Festival and the British Film Academy. In later decades it has become a staple of school media centers.

Reviews and Studies   Davies, Anthony. *Filming Shakespeare's Plays*. 1988. Pp.
60–64; 190–91.

Davison, Peter. *Text in Performance: Hamlet*. 1983. Pp. 47–54.

Donaldson, Peter. "Olivier, Hamlet, and Freud." *Cinema Journal* 26.4 (1987):
22–48.

Jorgens, Jack J. *Shakespeare on Film*. 1977. Pp. 207–17; 296–300, 327–28.

Kliman, Bernice W. *Hamlet: Film, Television, and Audio Performances*. 1988.
Pp. 23–36.

Manville, Roger. *Shakespeare and the Film*. 1971. Pp. 40–47.

McCarthy, Mary. "A Prince of Shreds and Patches." In Charles Eckert, ed.,
Focus on Shakespearean Films. Pp. 64–67.

Rothwell, Kenneth S., and Melzer, Annabelle H. *Shakespeare on Screen*. 1990.
Item 98, pp. 61–62.

Purchase/Rental Inquiries   Filmic Archives; The Writing Company. See Appendix B for addresses.

ᏋᎯ **7.2. *Hamlet*.** 1964. Classic Cinemas. Black-and-white, 199 minutes.

Directed by John Gielgud and starring Richard Burton, this is a film of a stage
performance at the Lunt-Fontanne Theatre in New York. Burton created a powerful, "angry" Hamlet. The play was done in modern dress, turtleneck sweaters
and other "rehearsal clothes."

The film is currently available only in archives.

ᏋᎯ **7.3. *Hamlet*.** 1964. Lenfilm. Black-and-white, 148 minutes. In Russian with
English subtitles.

Directed by Grigori Kozintsev, this film has received a great deal of notice among
film scholars. It is currently unavailable.

---

๕ **7.4. Hamlet.** 1969. Woodfall Productions/ Columbia Pictures. Color, 117 minutes. Producer: Leslie Linder. Director: Tony Richardson.

HAMLET	Nicol Williamson
CLAUDIUS	Anthony Hopkins
OPHELIA	Marianne Faithfull
LAERTES	Michael Pennington
COURT LADY	Anjelica Huston
GERTRUDE	Judy Parfitt
POLONIUS	Mark Dignam
HORATIO	Gordon Jackson
OSRIC	Peter Gale (Osric)
ROSENCRANTZ	Ben Aris
GUILDENSTERN	Clive Graham

Pluses   Unusual ideas, memorable scenes.

Minuses   Student audiences react negatively to Hamlet's being played by Nicol Williamson, who they see as geriatric and fuddy-duddy.

Textual Cuts and Rearrangements   Cuts are so frequent that one sometimes wonders if the actors are simply speaking every other line. However, the pace is brisk.

Some scenes are rearranged. Polonius' suggestion of spying on Hamlet (II.ii) is immediately acted upon, with a jump to the "lawful espials" scene (III.i). Claudius' attempt to pray (III.iii) here occurs after Hamlet has killed Polonius rather than before.

Fortinbras is cut, though Rosencrantz and Guildenstern remain.

Settings   The film was made in a former locomotive shop, now converted to a theater. Little of this interesting space shows in the film because so many shots are done in close-up. A rough brick wall appears behind the characters' heads, sometimes varied with tapestry. Ocasionally we see tunnels or a brick-lined corridor. There are a great many torches and candles.

Costumes   The court dresses lavishly in a somewhat eclectic but not modern-day style. Men wear dark suits with frilled collars. Women wear bare-shouldered gowns. Ophelia's dress is so high-waisted that student audiences are convinced she is pregnant. Since Marianne Faithfull's Ophelia has a knowing air, this diagnosis might seem to be possible.

Interpretation of Roles   According to Shakespeare, Hamlet is thirty years old (V.i.146, 161), unless we assume some lapse in the transmission of the text or, within the play, of the gravedigger's memory. Hamlet is usually played as considerably younger, however. Nicol Williamson's receding hairline and permanently furrowed brow thus comes as a shock to tradition. Williamson looks, in fact, a good deal older than thirty. Hamlet's fellow student, Horatio, played by Gordon Jackson, is similarly ravaged by time.

Those who can accustom themselves to Williamson's definitely postgraduate appearance find him a vigorous actor, throwing himself physically into the role.

Judy Parfitt plays Gertrude as a sensual and shallow woman, in her early forties at most, eager to get back into bed with Claudius and impatient with other details of daily life. At one point, in fact, she and Claudius have not bothered to get out of bed; they welcome Rosencrantz and Guildenstern from the comfort of that piece of furniture, where they are also eating and playing with a collection of dogs (II.ii). Later, in Ophelia's mad scene (IV.v), Gertrude treats her with little sympathy. Presumably she feels guilty because Hamlet killed Ophelia's father. She does seem genuinely sorry upon Ophelia's death.

Gertrude's own death is unusually long and agonized (V.iii). The audience has an opportunity to see the action from Gertrude's perspective; she suddenly knows who has poisoned her and who the killer intended to kill instead. Her pain is partly the shock of broken illusions.

As Claudius, Anthony Hopkins (recently seen in *The Silence of the Lambs* and *The Remains of the Day*) is quick and alert, promoting what one might call a public sense of humor. His first court scene (I.ii) resembles a cocktail party, the guests chuckling at, for example, Laertes' request to return to France. When all is lost and Hamlet is about to kill him, Claudius still seems to assume his court will come to his rescue, and is surprised when his "Defend me, friends" (V.iii.323) brings no reaction.

Marianne Faithfull's Ophelia has succumbed to the corruption of the court. If she is not in fact promiscuous (or even, as the passion with which she kisses Laertes might hint, incestuous), she does not have an aura of innocence either. She accosts Hamlet not by walking about with a prayer book but by lying indolently in a hammock and kissing him lingeringly at "I was the more deceived" (III.i.119). Historically minded viewers may remember Marianne Faithfull as part of the 1960s "swinging London" scene, romantically linked with rock star Mick Jagger.

The ghost in this production exists only as a blaze of light, and we do not see him directly. Instead, we see (close up) the faces of those who do see him.

Production History   As a stage play (in London's Roundhouse Theatre, where the film was shot), this *Hamlet* was a definite success. It also went on tour, playing in New York among other places. The film has attracted considerable notice among Shakespeareans and film scholars.

Reviews and Studies   Kliman, Bernice W. *Hamlet: Film, Television, and Audio Performances.* 1988. Pp. 167–79.

Manvell, Roger. *Shakespeare and the Film.* 1971. Pp. 127–30.

Mullin, Michael. "Tony Richardson's *Hamlet*: Script and Screen." *Literature/ Film Quarterly* 4 (1976): 123–33.

Rothwell, Kenneth S., and Melzer, Annabelle H. *Shakespeare on Screen.* 1990. Item 123, pp. 72–73.

Purchase/Rental Inquiries   Filmic Archives. See Appendix B for address.

≥ 7.5. *Hamlet.* Hallmark Hall of Fame. Color, 115 min.

Directed by Peter Wood. With Richard Chamberlain (Hamlet), John Gielgud (Ghost), Michael Redgrave (Claudius), Margaret Leighton (Gertrude), Clara Madden (Ophelia). Nineteenth-century costumes; Hamlet in ruffles, handsome and well-behaved.

This film was shown on NBC Television in November of 1970. It is currently not available.

≥ 7.6. *Hamlet.* 1980. British Broadcasting Company/ Time-Life Television: The Shakespeare Plays. Color, 210 min. Producer: Cedric Messina. Director: Rodney Bennett.

HAMLET	Derek Jacobi
GERTRUDE	Claire Bloom
CLAUDIUS	Patrick Stewart
OPHELIA	Lalla Ward
PLAYER KING	Emrys James
HORATIO	Robert Swann
LAERTES	David Robb
ROSENCRANTZ	Jonathan Hyde
GUILDENSTERN	Geoffrey Bateman
FORTINBRAS	Ian Charleson
GHOST	Patrick Allen
MARCELLUS	Paul Humpoletz
BARNARDO	Niall Padden

FRANCISCO	Christopher Baines
REYNALDO	Raymond Mason
FIRST GRAVEDIGGER	Tim Wylton
SECOND GRAVEDIGGER	Peter Benson
OSRIC	Peter Gale

Pluses   Some excellent performances. Attention paid to parts of the play that are often omitted or scanted.

Minuses   Jacobi's unusual Hamlet, whose pretended madness occasionally sends him over the brink into the real thing, alienates some viewers.

Textual Cuts and Rearrangements   Despite the film's length of three and a half hours, there are some cuts. Bernice Kliman gives a detailed account of these in *Hamlet: Film, Television, and Audio Performance* (see "Reviews and Studies," below), pp. 62–86. Ophelia suffers considerably, both in the loss of her own lines and of the lines of people talking to her; Laertes' warning about Hamlet's intentions is shortened, for example (I.iii).

Gertrude does not mention the bribe offered to Rosencrantz and Guildenstern — "such thanks/ As fits a king's remembrance" (II.ii.25). The First Player's sample speech about Pyrrhus at the fall of Troy is cut by twenty lines, so that Polonius' complaint, "This is too long" (II.ii.498), seems a more trivial piece of carping than it would in the original.

The film nevertheless retains a great deal, including many scenes that seldom survive in production. We have both the clowns (gravediggers), though a few lines have disappeared; many productions cut the first part of the scene and begin with the entrance of Hamlet and Horatio (V.i). Earlier, we see Hamlet teasing Rosencrantz and Guildenstern when they try to find Polonius' body; this whole scene is often omitted. And we have Fortinbras, certainly an infrequent visitor.

Settings   Sets suggest a bare-bones stage presentation. Exterior scenes do not attempt realism but content themselves with the wooden studio floor and a cycloramic curtain. Occasionally there is a painted backdrop. Interior spaces are slightly more elaborate, and the great hall has plenty of room. The play within a play — *The Mousetrap,* as Hamlet calls it — does have a picture-frame stage with painted perspective, and in this way it is differentiated from the space of *Hamlet.*

Costumes   Unlike the sets, the costumes are realistically lush, reflecting the status of the wearer. Hamlet himself is usually in disarray.

Interpretation of Roles   Jacobi's Hamlet spends much of the play in a state of hysteria. His encounter with the ghost leaves him laughing (I.v). When Ophelia tries to return the remembrances he once gave her, he whimpers at her in mock pity, then throws her furiously about the stage and ends up embracing her and weeping. "It *hath* made me mad," he whispers, suddenly recognizing his condition (III.i.146).

When the court comes to watch *The Mousetrap*, Hamlet is all over the place, holding a skull mask before his face and leaping onto the stage while the players are trying to get on with their job (III.ii). His antic disposition costs him the information he is trying to get. Claudius does not react to the play but calls for lights to look closely at Hamlet, who hides his face and giggles. Why Hamlet and Horatio then feel convinced of the king's guilt is mystifying.

In the final scene, however, Jacobi's Hamlet achieves an ironic self-control that brings the play into focus. The text is carefully thought through, and the action is photographed from a sufficient distance for the audience to tell what is happening. The "brother's wager," the discovery of treachery, the death of the queen, and Hamlet's attack on the king all build convincingly. Hamlet forgives Laertes with apparent sincerity, clasping his hand, and is passionate in his plea to Horatio to stay alive and tell the story. Hamlet's bestowal of his "dying voice" on Fortinbras as his successor seems to come from a perfectly sane wish to put the kingdom into some sort of order before he departs from it.

Patrick Stewart plays Claudius with the authority which student audiences expect from Stewart's extraterrestial "Star Trek" adventures. He is not a weak Claudius, nor a drunk one. He instantly grasps the fact that Fortinbras, far from offering peace, is in fact threatening an invasion, and his promise to "read, answer, and think upon this business" (II.ii.82) is made in awareness of the implications. His remorse for his crime is genuine, as is his honesty in admitting that he does not want to give up the things he has gained by the crime. All in all, Stewart gives Claudius the complexity the role deserves.

Claire Bloom makes Gertrude a dignified, affectionate woman, distressed at Hamlet's madness and eager to find a cure for it. There is no hint that she suspects Claudius of evildoing or credits Hamlet's accusation. At the end, of course, she finds out otherwise.

Ophelia (Lalla Ward) has a fragile, desperate air even before her troubles begin. In her mad scenes she embraces Claudius and kisses Laertes while singing her songs in a suggestive manner, but this apparent sexual abandon may disguise a more childlike wish to be taken care of.

The ghost is essentially a glimmer of armor, whether seen by the soldiers or by Hamlet.

Production History   *Hamlet* was shown on British and American television in 1980. It was the twelfth of the 37-play series filmed by the British Broadcasting Company between 1978 and 1985.

Reviews and Studies   Bulman, J. C., and Coursen, H. R., eds. *Shakespeare on Television*. 1988. Extracts from reviews of this film, pp. 263–65.

Kliman, Bernice W. *Hamlet: Film, Television, and Audio Performance*. 1988. Pp. 62–86, 195–201.

Maher, Mary Z. "Hamlet's BBC Soliloquies." *Shakespeare Quarterly* 36 (1985): 417–26.

Rothwell, Kenneth S., and Melzer, Annabelle H. *Shakespeare on Screen*. 1990. Item 140, pp. 78–79.

Willis, Susan. *The BBC Shakespeare Plays*. 1991. Pp. 213–14.

Purchase/Rental Inquiries   Ambrose Video; Filmic Archives; Insight Media; The Writing Company. See Appendix B for addresses.

&. **7.7. *Den Tragiska Historien om Hamlet, Priz av Danmark*** [Hamlet, Prince of Denmark]. 1984. Swedish Television. Color, 140 min. In Swedish, with English subtitles.

This film, directed by Ragnar Lyth and with Stellan Skarsgaard as Hamlet, was shown on American television in February of 1987. It is currently unavailable.

&. **7.8. *Hamlet*.** 1990. Warner Brothers. Color, 135 min. Producer: Dyson Lovell. Director: Franco Zeffirelli.

HAMLET	Mel Gibson
GERTRUDE	Glenn Close
CLAUDIUS	Alan Bates
GHOST	Paul Scofield
POLONIUS	Ian Holm
OPHELIA	Helena Bonham-Carter
HORATIO	Stephen Dillane
LAERTES	Nathaniel Parker
ROSENCRANTZ	Michael Maloney
GUILDENSTERN	Sean Murray
OSRIC	John McEnery
GRAVEDIGGER	Trevor Peacock
BARNARDO	Richard Warwick

MARCELLUS   Christian Anholt
FRANCISCO   Dave Duffy
REYNALDO   Vernon Dobtcheff

Pluses   A vivid, fast-paced film, immensely appealing to student audiences.

Minuses   Story and characters are simplified.

Textual Cuts and Rearrangements   Textual changes seem to have been made for the purpose of speeding up the action and clarifying the story. The first scene is omitted, and the film opens not with soldiers on the battlements but with the funeral of the late King Hamlet. This scene does not exist in Shakespeare's text, but it efficiently gets the plot under way and emphasizes Gertrude's passionate if temporary grief.

Fortinbras is omitted, along with the political dimension of the play. This absence makes the play's last few lines rather stark, since nobody can talk about what will become of the kingdom. Hamlet fills part of the gap with a non-Shakespearean "I die, Horatio," repeated several times; and Horatio's "Good night, sweet prince," as usual under these circumstances, closes the play (V.ii.359).

Ophelia loses many lines, including the passage beginning "O what a noble mind is here o'erthrown" (III.i.150ff.). She drifts wordlessly away after Hamlet has rejected her, and Polonius moves the focus back to Hamlet with a non-Shakespearean line, "We must watch him, and that most carefully."

In *The Mousetrap*, the dumb show is cut, along with much of the players' dialogue (III.ii). There is only one clown (gravedigger) (V.i).

Numerous passages have been shifted about. Hamlet's "To be or not to be" here follows the conversation with Ophelia (the so-called nunnery scene referred to above, III.i) and is itself followed by Hamlet's meeting with Rosencrantz and Guildenstern, moved from II.ii.

A few shots have been added to the play. We see the ship sailing for England with Hamlet, Rosencrantz, and Guildenstern; we then see Hamlet "fingering their packets" while his voice explains his actions to Horatio (V.ii). Next we see the execution of Rosencrantz and Guildenstern. (The means of Hamlet's return to England remain unspecified, with no mention of pirates.) We also see Ophelia's drowning, briefly, followed by Gertrude's report of this event to Claudius and Laertes (IV.vii).

Settings   A realistic medieval castle. The audience becomes familiar with various parts of it—the courtyard, crowded with servants going about their business; the library, where Hamlet tries to be alone with his thoughts; the family crypt, the scene not only of the late king's funeral but of Hamlet's "To be or not to be"; the great hall; a high-windowed weaving room where Ophelia and other women do embroidery; the surrounding walls and ramparts. Unlike the empty, echoing castle in Olivier's film, this one bustles with inhabitants. People live in one another's pockets, and eavesdropping seems inevitable.

Costumes   Dress is simple but effective. Soldiers wear chain-mail doublets, as do Hamlet and Laertes as they begin their sword fight (V.ii). Women's dresses have a medieval flow. Gertrude is partial to blue, Ophelia to white.

Interpretation of Roles   Mel Gibson's Hamlet is frustrated but not neurotic. His madness is clearly an act, although he throws himself into it with energy and also with ingenuity. When Polonius asks what he is reading, Gibson does not reply "Words, words, words," in scornful haste. Instead he looks carefully into the book, sees that it contains words, then flips the pages and is surprised to find even more of them (II.ii.192).

With his mother, Gibson's Hamlet is for the most part subdued and respectful, despite his disapproval of her remarriage. The closet scene (III.iv), in which he tries first to find out if she is an accessory to her first husband's murder and then to persuade her that Claudius is guilty of the crime, is an exception. Here Hamlet throws Gertrude onto the bed and continues his argument with body language that is close to coital. This is the most extreme and, except perhaps for Gertrude's snuggly kisses as she begs her son to remain in Denmark (I.ii), the only evidence of an overheated passion between the two. Whether this scene is meant as a key to their relationship is hard to tell.

Helena Bonham-Carter makes the role of Ophelia a powerful one despite the cuts in her dialogue. Her youth—she looks scarcely fifteen—adds to the intensity of her emotions. Before her meeting with Laertes in act one, she runs into the weaving room singing "Tomorrow is Saint Valentine's Day," apparently a favorite song, yet despite the bawdiness of the lyrics her air of innocence remains. (Gibson, in the article by Michael Jensen cited in "Reviews and Studies" below, remarks that when Ophelia hugs Laertes she "does something with her eye" that "tells the viewer she is experiencing her first sexual moment.")

In the first episode of her mad scene (IV.ii), Bonham-Carter is seen harassing a soldier on guard, embracing and singing to him while he shifts uncomfortably from one foot to the other, before she is brought before the king and queen. She is belligerent rather than sentimentally sweet, though there is pathos in her repeating a mannerism of her late father—a quick "hnnh?" at the end of a question or statement. She collapses in sobs, and Horatio carries her bodily away, accompanied by three nuns who have materialized from among the castle retainers. Her second mad episode begins as Laertes hears her weeping, then finds her in the great hall, sitting on Gertrude's throne and playing with the chicken bones and bits of straw that will serve as the flowers she distributes to the court (IV.ii.175ff.).

As Gertrude, Glenn Close is sincere and warmhearted, longing for harmony in her family. We see her at the funeral of her first husband prostrated with grief. On her next appearance she is lighthearted and gay, smiling up at Claudius, then running to mount her horse and canter away with him on a hunting expedition. So swift a consolation may serve as evidence of shallowness in her character; certainly it dismays Hamlet. Nevertheless she retains the audience's sympathy as a person who lives for the moment and wants not only her own happiness but everyone else's.

In the final scene Gertrude is overjoyed that Hamlet is behaving so normally, taking part in a "brother's wager" with Laertes and speaking politely to the king. But once again she is able to adapt to change. On drinking the poison, she instantly realizes the truth and puts all her remaining strength into warning Hamlet.

Alan Bates's Claudius is a curiously jolly regicide, plump, constantly reaching for his wine cup, not terribly bright. The audience wonders how he managed the murder in the first place. After the queen takes her fatal drink, he plops down on his throne to figure out what spin to put on this one. He has reached no conclusion by the time Laertes accuses him—"the king's to blame" (V.iii.320)—so he weakly tries to laugh it off.

Claudius' predecessor, King Hamlet, is memorably played by Paul Scofield. Far from the terrifying, distant and armor-clad apparition to which audiences are accustomed, Scofield turns his ghostly utterance into a cozy chat with his son. The encounter makes it clear that Hamlet undertakes his revenge as much from love as from duty.

Production History   Moviegoers were startled that Mel Gibson, popular in action-filled television and movie roles, would attempt *Hamlet*. Nevertheless the film was a success both with the public and with most critics. It holds a place with director Zeffirelli's earlier Shakespeare films, *The Taming of the Shrew* (28.2) and *Romeo and Juliet* (27.3).

Reviews and Studies   Grant, Edmund. "Hamlet." *Films in Review* 42.3/4 (March/ April 1991): 108–9.

Impastato, David. "Zeffirelli's *Hamlet*: Sunlight Makes Meaning." *Shakespeare on Film Newsletter* 16.1 (1991): 1–2.

———. "Zeffirelli's *Hamlet* and the Baroque." *Shakespeare on Film Newsletter* 16.2 (1992): 1–2.

Jensen, Michael P. "Mel Gibson on Hamlet." *Shakespeare on Film Newsletter* 15.2 (1991): 1,2,6.

Quinn, Edward. "Zeffirelli's *Hamlet.*" *Shakespeare on Film Newsletter* 15.2 (1991): 1,2,6.

Purchase/Rental Inquiries   Filmic Archives; The Video Catalog; The Writing Company. See Appendix B for addresses.

 7.9. *Hamlet.* 1990. PBS Television. Color, 150 min.

Directed by Kevin Kline and Kirk Browning, with Kevin Kline as Hamlet. A modern-dress production on a nearly bare stage. Shown on PBS as part of "The Great Performances" series, in November of 1990.

The film is unavailable at present.

8 ✍ HENRY THE FOURTH, PART ONE*

✍ **8.1.** *Chimes at Midnight/ Falstaff/ Campanadas a media noche.* 1966. Internacional Films Espanola. Black-and-white, 119 min. Producers: Emiliano Piedra, Angel Escolano. Director: Orson Welles.

SIR JOHN FALSTAFF	Orson Welles
KING HENRY IV	John Gielgud
NARRATOR	Ralph Richardson
PRINCE HAL	Keith Baxter
HENRY PERCY, NICKNAMED HOTSPUR	Norman Rodway
EARL OF WORCESTER	Fernando Rey
JUSTICE SHALLOW	Alan Webb
SILENCE	Walter Chiari
PISTOL	Michael Aldridge
POINS	Tony Beckley
HOSTESS QUICKLY	Margaret Rutherford
DOLL TEARSHEET	Jeanne Moreau

Pluses   A film much studied in the context of Orson Welles's work. Inventive, with some excellent performances.

Minuses   Bewildering to an audience primarily concerned with Shakespeare's text. Bad sound and murky picture, especially in videotape.

Textual Cuts and Rearrangements   Welles took to pieces the two parts of *Henry IV* and reassembled them, along with occasional slices of *Henry V* and *The Merry Wives of Windsor*, into a pattern of his own devising.

Falstaff becomes the centerpiece of the play. The Battle of Shrewsbury (*Part One*, IV.iii—V.v) is the film's only military conflict, with the episode of Gaultree Forest, in *Part Two* (IV.i), omitted. Hal's public rejection of Falstaff (*Part Two*, V.v) is followed by Hostess Quickly's description of Falstaff's death (*Henry V*, II.iii). An enormous coffin is then put on a cart and rolled away.

The film opens with Falstaff's visit to Justice Shallow in *Part Two* (III.ii). In

---

* Note: For films related to Shakespeare's *Henry IV* plays, see Appendix A, "Analogues and Variations."

reminiscing about old times, Falstaff speaks the film's title: "We have heard the chimes at midnight, Master Shallow" (III.ii.215).

Students with experience in the tributary plays will enjoy spotting the sources. For other student audiences, this film should perhaps be used with caution.

Settings   The Boar's Head tavern is very large, a sort of barn, and is clearly a house of ill repute, where bevies of loose ladies drape themselves around Prince Hal.

The battle scenes are realistic, with horses, longbows, and clouds of dust.

Court scenes make use of the film's Spanish shooting locale, with romanesque interiors standing in for the more gothic architecture of medieval London.

Costumes   On a small budget, Welles had much resort to gowns and capes. The results are quite satisfactory.

Interpretation of Roles   Welles, with his extraordinary voice and presence, dominates the film. His Falstaff is a complex creation. He is both lovable and detestable, both generous and selfish.

Prince Hal, sensitively played by Keith Baxter, conveys his difficulty in shifting from the world of Falstaff to the world of official duties. After the Battle of Shrewsbury (in which Falstaff has deliberately led his ragamuffin soldiers to their deaths), Hal joins his old friend in toasting victory. As Falstaff launches into his praise of "good sherry sack" (*Part Two*, IV.iii.96), the prince suddenly throws down his cup and walks away.

John Gielgud creates a memorable Henry IV, loving both his son and his hard-won kingdom, and distressed that the first seems to have no interest in the second.

Margaret Rutherford, as a jolly Hostess Quickly, and Jeanne Moreau, as a jaded Doll Tearsheet, ornament the Boar's Head.

Production History   As seems to have been usual in his career, Welles made *Chimes at Midnight* under a financial cloud. Complications included the necessity of pretending he was actually making a film of *Treasure Island*, under which pretext he had obtained some money.

Most of the shooting was done in Spain. Battle scenes, for example, were made in the Casa de Campo, a large park in Madrid.

Chimes at Midnight was shown at the Cannes Film Festival in 1966. When released to theaters it did not do well, but it has attracted critical attention ever since.

Reviews and Studies   Davies, Anthony. *Filming Shakespeare's Plays*. 1988. Pp. 26–37, 189–90.

Jorgens, Jack J. *Shakespeare on Film*. 1977. Pp. 106–21, 268–72, 320.

Lyons, Bridget Gellert, ed. *Chimes at Midnight: Orson Welles, Director*. 1988. Includes script, interviews, commentary.

Rothwell, Kenneth S., and Melzer, Annabelle H. *Shakespeare on Screen*. 1990. Item 161, pp. 88–89.

Purchase/ Rental Inquiries   *Chimes at Midnight* is occasionally available from distributors.

**꒜ 8.2. *Henry the Fourth, Part One*. 1979. British Broadcasting Company/ Time-Life Television: The Shakespeare Plays. Color, 155 min. Producer: Cedric Messina. Director: David Giles.

SIR JOHN FALSTAFF	Anthony Quayle
KING HENRY IV	Jon Finch
PRINCE HAL	David Gwillim
HENRY PERCY, NICKNAMED HOTSPUR	Tim Piggott-Smith
EARL OF NORTHUMBERLAND	Bruce Purchase
EARL OF WORCESTER	Clive Swift
OWEN GLENDOWER	Richard Owens
POINS	Jack Galloway
LADY PERCY	Michele Dotrice
HOSTESS QUICKLY	Brenda Bruce
BARDOLPH	Gordon Gostelow
PRINCE JOHN, DUKE OF LANCASTER	Rob Edwards
PRINCE HUMPHREY, DUKE OF GLOUCESTER	Martin Neil
PRINCE THOMAS, DUKE OF CLARENCE	Roger Davenport
EDMUND MORTIMER, EARL OF MARCH	Robert Morris
LADY MORTIMER	Sharon Morgan
EARL OF DOUGLAS	John Cairney
SCROOP	David Neal
SIR MICHAEL	Norman Rutherford
SIR RICHARD VERNON	Terence Wilton
EARL OF WESTMORELAND	David Buck
SIR WALTER BLUNT	Robert Brown
GOWER	Brian Poyer
PETO	Stephen Beard

Pluses   Well-conceived and well-acted.

Minuses   Flaws are few.

Textual Cuts and Rearrangements   There is little cutting. Prince Hal's rather baffling exchange with the Boar's Head drawer, Francis (II.iv), has disappeared. The dialogue between Glendower and his daughter, Lady Mortimer (III.i), indicated in the text only by such directions as "the lady speaks in Welsh," is here lengthy and emotional. Lady Mortimer's song is a traditional Welsh lullaby, "Suo Gad."

Settings   Many interiors seem cramped. The Boar's Head has a low ceiling and is almost claustrophobic. During the Battle of Shrewsbury, many conversations take place either inside or next to tents, and there is a liberal use of terrain-concealing smoke.

Costumes   Dress is colorful. Henry IV and Prince Hal wear father-son armor, with red and blue surcoats. Court costumes approximate the dress of the early fifteenth century, doublets and breeches.

Interpretation of Roles   Jon Finch as Henry IV continues his characterization from the BBC's *Richard II* (25.1). In the present play he has become older and gloomier. He continually washes his guilty hands—a mannerism which critics have found irksome but which student audiences seem to enjoy discovering.

Anthony Quayle's Falstaff is both jolly and conniving. In the middle of a joke his little pig eyes glance round to make sure the prince is sufficiently amused. He huffs and wheezes, exaggerating his supposed frailty with paradoxical vigor.

As Prince Hal, David Gwillim shows a curious coldness. He seems to find the Boar's Head a tedious milieu and to have forced himself to frequent it only for the public-relations value of a future transformation. In the play-acting scene (II.iv), Hal berates Falstaff with a cruel glint in his eye, promising in ringing tones to banish "kind Jack Falstaff." After the knock on the door stops the play and brings in the sheriff's officers, Hal takes his time before deciding to protect Falstaff from the law. Gwillim's is a logical interpretation of the text, but it threatens to make the prince's ultimate choice seem less wrenching and thus less dramatic.

Hotspur, Hal's opposite number in personality as well as in politics, is played by Tim Piggott-Smith with appealing warmth. He is convincing in his affection for his wife, his impulsiveness, and his impatience with his more prudent elders. Some student audiences cheer for Hotspur rather than Hal when the two meet on Shrewsbury field (V.iv). Hotspur's death, blood gushing from his mouth, becomes a gory illustration of Falstaff's speech on the superficiality of honor a few scenes earlier (V.i.126).

Viewers following the story from the BBC's *Richard II* must adjust to different actors for both Hotspur and his father, the earl of Northumberland.

Production History   This film was shown on British television in 1979 and in America in the spring of 1980. It was the seventh to appear of the British Broadcasting Company's 37-play series.

Reviews and Studies   Bulman, J. C., and Coursen, H. R., eds. *Shakespeare on Television*. 1988. Extracts from reviews of this film, pp. 257–58.

   Clark, Meara T. "The PBS *Henry IV, Part One.*" *CEA Forum* 12 (December 1981): 7–9.

   Rothwell, Kenneth S., and Melzer, Annabelle H. *Shakespeare on Screen*. 1990. Item 166, pp. 90–91.

Purchase/Rental Inquiries   Ambrose Video; Filmic Archives; Insight Media; The Writing Company. See Appendix B for addresses.

8.3. *The Wars of the Roses: Henry the Fourth, Part One*. 1991. The English Shakespeare Company. Color, 145 min. Producers: John Paul Chapple, Andy Ward. Director: Michael Bogdanov.

PRINCE HAL	Michael Pennington
SIR JOHN FALSTAFF	Barry Stanton
HENRY PERCY, NICKNAMED HOTSPUR	Andrew Jarvis
KING HENRY IV	Michael Cronin
HOSTESS QUICKLY	June Watson
LADY PERCY	Ann Penfold
POINS; EARL OF DOUGLAS	Charles Dale
BARDOLPH	Colin Farrell
LADY MORTIMER	Jennifer Konko
EARL OF NORTHUMBERLAND	Ben Bazell
EARL OF WORCESTER	Philip Bowen
DUKE OF EXETER	Ian Burford
SIR RICHARD VERNON	Paul Brennan
PRINCE JOHN, DUKE OF LANCASTER	John Dougall
OWEN GLENDOWER	Sion Probert
SCROOP	John Derrell
FRANCIS	John Tramper
LORD CHIEF JUSTICE	Hugh Sullivan

Pluses   Exciting and imaginative, part of a seven-play series beginning with *Richard II* (25.3) and filmed as a live stage performance.

Minuses   Repertoire players' habit of switching from one role to another can confuse viewers.

Textual Cuts and Rearrangements   Shakespeare's text is not greatly altered, despite the sometimes startling ways it is acted.

The film begins with the rendition of a non-Shakespearean "Ballad of Harry Le Roi," a king who was mighty but wild as a boy, sung by Charles Dale (who plays first Poins and then the earl of Douglas) while the actors gather onstage.

The dialogue of the carriers in the inn at Gad's Hill (II.i) has been cut, and Falstaff's hyperbolic claim to have killed Hotspur is here moved to the end of the play, when King Henry IV and other nobles are present. The king apparently believes Falstaff and looks with distrust at Prince Hal, who has already given his version of the event. Hal's anger at Falstaff adds to the growing gulf between them and explains why, in *Part Two*, his hard-won reconciliation with his father has to be done all over again.

Settings   The bare stage becomes an inn, a palace, or a battleground as props are carried in and out. King Henry IV sits behind a large table rather than on a throne, and his advisors are ranged in a statically symmetrical formation on either side. The Boar's Head has numerous tables crowded with drinkers and card players.

Costumes   An eclectic mix. The king and his court evoke late-Victorian dignity in dark frock coats and military uniforms trimmed with gold braid. At the Boar's Head, the clientele favor punk-rock haircuts and black leather.

Interpretation of Roles   Michael Pennington as Prince Hal does not find universal favor with student audiences because he looks too old—"another middle-aged guy trying to be cool in blue jeans," as one viewer put it. Nevertheless, Pennington's anti-heroic interpretation attracts interest. When on the field at Shrewsbury Hotspur has him pinned at sword's point, Hal grovels and weeps (V.iv.75ff.); when Hotspur then returns his sword to him, Hal gives a roar of humiliation and fury, and promptly skewers Hotspur.

Barry Stanton's Falstaff is debonair, light of foot despite his bulk, an enjoyer of life. On the way to Shrewsbury he rides at his ease in a handcart pulled by the faithful trombone-playing Bardolph (Colin Farrell). His function as jester to Prince Hal is certainly a deliberately chosen role, and he has an eye to the advantage of being a crony of the heir apparent, but one feels he would live the same life whether an ultimate reward beckoned or not.

As Hotspur, Andrew Jarvis becomes an amazing combination of the grotesque and the powerful. His bald head, toothy grin, and lurching gait make him a unique presence. His instant recognizability, in fact, can confuse the audience in the Boar's Head scenes, where he appears as an entirely different character, in a green mohawk haircut, playing a flute.

Ann Penfold is a vigorous and forthright Lady Percy. She wrestles her husband to the ground when he refuses to tell her where he is going; and yet their affection for each other is obvious.

Production History; Reviews and Studies   See the English Shakespeare Company's production of *Richard II* (25.3).

Purchase/Rental Inquiries   Films for the Humanities and Sciences. See Appendix B for address.

9 🕭 HENRY THE FOURTH, PART TWO

🕭 *9.1. Henry the Fourth, Part Two.* 1979. British Broadcasting Company/
Time-Life Television: The Shakespeare Plays. Color, 155 min. Producer: Cedric
Messina. Director: David Giles.

SIR JOHN FALSTAFF	Anthony Quayle
PRINCE HAL	David Gwillim
KING HENRY IV	Jon Finch
POINS	Jack Galloway
HOSTESS QUICKLY	Brenda Bruce
DOLL TEARSHEET	Frances Cuka
BARDOLPH	Gordon Gostelow
PISTOL	Bryan Pringle
SHALLOW	Robert Eddison
SILENCE	Leslie French
DAVY	Raymond Platt
LORD CHIEF JUSTICE	Ralph Michael
EARL OF NORTHUMBERLAND	Bruce Purchase
LADY NORTHUMBERLAND	Jenny Laird
LADY PERCY	Michele Dotrice
PRINCE JOHN, DUKE OF LANCASTER	Rob Edwards
EARL OF WESTMORELAND	David Buck

Pluses   Thoughtfully planned and well-acted.

Minuses   None of moment.

Textual Cuts and Rearrangements   Cuts are frequent but usually not obvious. Justice Shallow's conversation with his servant Davy, for example, does not include reference to one William Visor, a disreputable friend of the latter (V.i), but an audience simply following the action would hardly miss it.

Minor characters' lines are sometimes reshuffled, as in IV.iv., when Harcourt's lines are given to Westmoreland. The allegorical figure Rumor, described in Shakespeare's text as "painted full of tongues," does not appear but introduces the play as a voice-over.

Settings   Most of the play was shot in the studio, including the street scene in which Hostess Quickly has Falstaff arrested by officers Fang and Snare (II.i). Here a minimal number of extras do duty as interested passersby. The episode at Gaultree Forest, on the other hand, takes place in an actual forest.

Costumes   Costumes are plausibly early-fifteenth-century and also denote the wearers' status and personality. Doll Tearsheet, for example, though not young, is got up in red in order to look professionally sexy.

Interpretation of Roles   Jon Finch continues his portrayal of Henry IV, and by this time his inward guilt at usurping the throne of Richard II seems to have eaten him away. His hands are bandaged and his face haggard. (The historical Henry IV is said to have suffered from a skin disease.)

Prince Hal, played by David Gwillim, looks sincerely regretful when his father once again upbraids him for loose living (IV.iv). But Hal's turnaround is not achieved without struggle. Though he rejects Falstaff's attempt to crash his coronation (V.v), banishing him from his person and sending him (temporarily) to prison, he pronounces this doom with sorrow. The viewer who remembers Prince Hal's rather glib plan of cultivating lowlife acquaintances in order to throw them off when the time is right (*Part One*, I.ii. 195 ff.) cannot help wondering if the prince has learned a lesson in humility in spite of himself.

As Falstaff, Anthony Quayle brings out the more mercenary side of the character. He concocts his plan to make use of Shallow as comedy material, fodder for amusing Prince Hal, with a diabolical leer (V.i.77 ff.) When the prince rejects him he is crushed, but the viewer feels he has brought it on himself, and sympathy generally swings to Prince Hal.

Production History   This film was shown on English television in December of 1979 and in North America in the spring of 1980, in each case following *Part One* by a week or so. It was the eighth of the BBC's series of the entire Shakespeare canon.

Reviews and Studies   Bulman, J. C., and Coursen, H. R., eds. *Shakespeare on Television*. 1988. Extracts from reviews of this film, pp. 258–60.

Rothwell, Kenneth S., and Melzer, Annabelle H. *Shakespeare on Screen*. 1990. Item 167, pp. 91–92.

Purchase/ Rental Inquiries   Ambrose Video; Filmic Archives; Insight Media; The Writing Company. See Appendix B for addresses.

№ 9.2. *The Wars of the Roses: Henry the Fourth, Part Two.* 1991. The English Shakespeare Company. Color, 145 min. Producers: John Paul Chapple, Andy Ward. Director: Michael Bogdanov.

PRINCE HAL	Michael Pennington
SIR JOHN FALSTAFF	Barry Stanton
KING HENRY IV	Michael Cronin
POINS; PRINCE HUMPHREY, DUKE OF GLOUCESTER	Charles Dale
HOSTESS QUICKLY	June Watson
DOLL TEARSHEET	Francesca Ryan
BARDOLPH	Colin Farrell
PISTOL	Paul Brennan
SHALLOW	Clyde Pollit
SILENCE	Philip Bowen
LORD CHIEF JUSTICE	Hugh Sullivan
EARL OF NORTHUMBERLAND	Roger Booth
LADY NORTHUMBERLAND	Susanna Best
LADY PERCY	Ann Penfold

Pluses   A lively portion of the seven-play sequence *The Wars of the Roses.*

Minuses   Actors often play several roles in the same play, with potentially confusing results.

Textual Cuts and Rearrangements   There are numerous cuts. The induction spoken by the allegorical figure Rumor is gone, and there is no epilogue. Falstaff's capture of "Coleville of the Dale" at Gaultree Forest has disappeared. Henry IV's soliloquy on the sleep-devouring responsibilties of kingship—"Uneasy lies the head that wears the crown" (III.i.4ff.)—has been cut, and many passages are severely pruned.

Settings   The bare stage is transformed with particular inventiveness for the street scenes. Falstaff accosts the Lord Chief Justice in a sidewalk cafe (I.ii). Fang and Snare are British bobbies, complete with bicycle (II.ii). And for Prince Hal's coronation the stage is draped with Union Jacks, while Falstaff and his gang wave miniature flags (V.v).

Costumes   Modern-dress anachronisms continue, as in the earlier plays in this series. Doll Tearsheet has spiky, multi-colored hair, black lace stockings, and a leopard-patterned miniskirt. Pistol celebrates the coronation in a black leather jacket with "Hal's Angels" inscribed on the back. Falstaff is resplendent in a blue striped suit, an array of medals pinned on his lapel.

By contrast, Henry IV and his court are almost indistinguishable in dark suits of Victorian cut, their personalities submerged, presumably, for the good of the country.

Interpretation of Roles   Michael Pennington continues to act Prince Hal with great furrowing of brow.

Barry Stanton's Falstaff is crushed by Hal's rejection in the last scene and walks away into the darkness. He has many ebullient moments before this point, however. When Hostess Quickly (vividly played by June Watson) attempts to extract from him the money he owes her, he soon has her smiling through her tears, begging for the pleasure of his company at supper, and, of course, making him another loan.

Charles Dale gives the role of Poins a slouching, self-confident authority. When Prince Hal rails at him for being, in essence, of a lower social class and ends the scene with a peremptory "Follow me, Ned" (II.ii.176), this Poins reacts with seething resentment.

Dale's last appearance as Poins occurs when he and the Prince disguise themselves as waiters at the Boar's Head (II.iv), but he reappears shortly thereafter in the role of Humphrey of Gloucester, one of Prince Hal's younger brothers, and marches beside the prince in the coronation procession. Since the brotherly relationship has not been made entirely clear, some confusion is possible. Viewers may get the idea that Poins has been promoted.

Production History; Reviews and Studies   See entry on the English Shakespeare Company's production of *Richard II* (25.3).

Purchase/Rental Inquiries   Films for the Humanities and Sciences. See Appendix B for address.

10 🕮 HENRY THE FIFTH*‎‎

🕮 **10.1.** *Henry the Fifth.* 1944. Twin Cities Films. Color, 137 min. Producer: Laurence Olivier. Director: Laurence Olivier.

KING HENRY V	Laurence Olivier
CHORUS	Leslie Banks
PRINCESS KATHERINE OF FRANCE	Renee Asherson
HOSTESS QUICKLY	Freda Jackson
PISTOL	Robert Newton
BARDOLPH	Roy Emmerton
NYM	Frederick Cooper
BOY TO PISTOL, BARDOLPH, AND NYM	George Cole
ARCHBISHOP OF CANTERBURY	Felix Aylmer
BISHOP OF ELY	Robert Helpmann
KING CHARLES IV OF FRANCE	Harcourt Williams
QUEEN ISABEL OF FRANCE	Janet Burnell
LOUIS, DAUPHIN OF FRANCE	Max Adrian
CONSTABLE OF FRANCE	Leo Genn
ALICE, LADY-IN-WAITING TO PRINCESS KATHERINE	Ivy St. Helier
EARL OF SALISBURY	Griffith Jones
DUKE OF GLOUCESTER	Michael Warre
DUKE OF EXETER	Nicholas Hannon
EARL OF WESTMORELAND	Gerald Case
FLUELLEN	Esmond Knight
GOWER	Michael Shepley
MACMORRIS	Niall MacGinnis
JAMY	John Laurie
MONTJOY	Ralph Truman
SIR JOHN FALSTAFF	George Robey

Pluses   A classic film, still able to stir an audience.

Minuses   From some perspectives, Olivier's vision of good-old-ourside patriotism may seem oversimplified.

* Note: For films related to Shakespeare's *Henry V*, see Appendix A, "Analogues and Variations."

Textual Cuts and Rearrangements   Cuts are numerous. The effect in general is to streamline the action, but many of them also streamline the play's built-in ambiguities. The viewer is not permitted to see this King Henry in a negative light.

The king does not execute the traitors Cambridge, Scroop, and Grey (II.ii); does not threaten the citizens of Harfleur with the horrors of war—"your naked infants spitted upon pikes"—(III.iii.38); does not order his troops to kill their French prisoners (IV.vi.37).

Settings   Sets fall into three categories. We have the charming reproduction of the Globe Theatre, where an Elizabethan audience watches the opening scenes and the epilogue. In a different mode, French cities and palaces are shown as ornamental miniatures, dolls' palaces in a sense, the designs based on illuminated medieval manuscripts. The Battle of Agincourt takes place on a full-sized realistic landscape. (The battle scenes were in fact shot in Ireland.)

The shift from one kind of space to another can be disconcerting, but audiences soon adjust.

The Battle of Agincourt includes several historic touches taken from contemporary chronicles and thus authentic, though not mentioned in Shakespeare's text. We watch as the English soldiers set up a line of sharpened stakes, angled to stop a charging horse. And as the French begin their charge, the volleys of arrows from English longbows literally darken the sky.

Like the rest of the film, the Agincourt scenes portray war as a glorious game. Plumes flutter, flags fly, the sky remains a bright, picture-postcard blue. But there are hints of the darker side. The French cavalry is reflected on the surface of a puddle, advancing to battle as lightly as if the horses were engaged in a dance. After the horses pass, the camera remains focused on the puddle. Then we see foot soldiers standing in the mud, slugging wearily at each other with cudgels.

Costumes   Dress gives something of a medieval-costume-party effect. The English soldiers besieging Harfleur wear clean and tidy uniforms. Macmorris, Jamy, and Fluellen even have their national badges sewn on (shamrock, thistle, and leek).

French costumes are particularly ornamental, often in combinations of blue and silver spotted with fleurs de lis. The Constable of France wears black armor painted with the golden stars mentioned in the text (III.vii.71).

Olivier's haircut, a simple round bowl that bares the back of his neck, sometimes elicits comment from student audiences. The look is historically accurate, based on a portrait of Henry V in the National Portrait Gallery.

Interpretation of Roles   Olivier's King Henry, with his look of eagles and his consistently heroic air, is nevertheless not grim or forced. The manner seems to come naturally.

King Henry's opposite number is the French heir apparent, Louis the Dauphin, played by Max Adrian as spoiled, self-centered, and uninformed.

The French king, Charles VI, was in real life subject to fits of insanity, and historians are divided as to whether he was in or out of his right mind in the autumn of 1415. Directors and actors thus have a choice. Harcourt Williams here plays the king as wispily senile, his voice a thin pipe, his sentences trailing vaguely away.

Princess Katherine, played by Renee Asherson, is kittenish and coy, obviously delighted with her royal suitor. She hangs shyly back in the courtship scene, one suspects, simply in order to prolong the fun.

The courtship sequence ends as Henry and Katherine, seen from behind, walk toward the altar on what has suddenly become their wedding day. When they turn around, we see that we are back in the Globe Theatre. Henry wears his heavy stage makeup, and Katherine is now played by the young boy we saw in our glimpse backstage at the film's beginning.

Leslie Banks, who delivers the epilogue from the stage of the Globe just as he had spoken the induction, is meant to be Shakespeare himself. He seems pleased with his play and enjoys his direct rapport with the audience.

Production History   This film evolved during the dark days of World War II, a circumstance which may explain why war is shown as a picturesque pastime, a fantasy game. English audiences who had survived the blitz and the robot bombs could envision the real thing only too well.

The film is dedicated to the commandos and airborne troops of Great Britain, linking Agincourt with a modern battle against crushing odds.

Not surprisingly, *Henry V* became a box-office success not only in England but in America. It won numerous honors, including a special Academy Award.

Reviews and Studies   Collick, John. *Shakespeare, Cinema, and Society*. 1989. Pp. 47–51.

Crowther, Bosley. "Henry V." In Charles W. Eckert, ed., *Focus on Shakespearean Films*. 1972. Pp. 57–62.

Davies, Anthony. *Filming Shakespeare's Plays*. 1988. Pp. 26–37, 189–90.

Jorgens, Jack J. *Shakespeare on Film*. 1977. Pp. 122–35, 272–75, 321.

Manheim, Michael. "Olivier's *Henry V* and the Elizabethan World Picture." *Literature/ Film Quarterly* 11.3 (1981): 179–84.

Manvell, Roger. *Shakespeare and the Film*. 1971. Pp. 37–40.

Rothwell, Kenneth S., and Melzer, Annabelle H. *Shakespeare on Screen.* 1990. Item 172, pp. 93–95.

Purchase/Rental Inquiries   The Writing Company. See Appendix B for address.

❧ *10.2. Henry the Fifth.* 1979. British Broadcasting Company/Time-Life Television: The Shakespeare Plays. Color, 170 min. Producer: Cedric Messina. Director: David Giles.

CHORUS	Alec McCowen
KING HENRY V	David Gwillim
PRINCESS KATHERINE OF FRANCE	Jocelyn Boisseau
KING CHARLES VI OF FRANCE	Thorley Walters
LOUIS, DAUPHIN OF FRANCE	Keith Drinkel
HOSTESS QUICKLY	Brenda Bruce
PISTOL	Bryan Pringle
BARDOLPH	Gordon Gostelow
NYM	Jeffrey Holland
BOY TO PISTOL, BARDOLPH, AND NYM	John Fowler
ARCHBISHOP OF CANTERBURY	Trevor Baxter
BISHOP OF ELY	John Abineri
DUKE OF EXETER	Clifford Parrish
EARL OF WESTMORELAND	David Buck
EARL OF WARWICK	Rod Beacham
FLUELLEN	Tim Wylton
GOWER	Brian Poyser
MACMORRIS	Paddy Ward
JAMY	Michael McKevitt
QUEEN ISABEL OF FRANCE	Pamela Ruddock
CONSTABLE OF FRANCE	Julian Glover
MONTJOY	Garrick Hagon
ALICE, LADY-IN-WAITING TO PRINCESS KATHERINE	Anna Quayle

Pluses   A well-paced production, continuing the BBC's series of the English history plays with many of the same actors who appeared in one or both parts of *Henry IV*. Repeaters include actors playing the roles of Prince Hal, now Henry V; Hostess Quickly; Bardolph; Pistol; Prince John (Duke of Lancaster in *Henry IV,*

Part Two, but now duke of Bedford); the earl of Westmoreland; the earl of Warwick.

Minuses   Perhaps because Olivier's and Branagh's films have accustomed us to grand effects, a small budget can lessen the audience's rapport with *Henry V*. It is hard to believe in a battle of Agincourt fought by pedestrians in armor, wandering about an empty field.

Textual Cuts and Rearrangements   The Archbishop of Canterbury's explanation of King Henry's right to the French throne includes the "Salic law" argument but omits the genealogy (I.ii). Numerous scenes lose their opening or closing lines, and many passages are thinned. However, there is no systematic rooting-out of similes. The Archbishop's "honey bee" speech in the scene just mentioned, while often cut, is here retained (I.ii.187ff.).

King Henry's more disturbing lines—his capture and execution of the three traitors at Southampton (II.ii), his threats to the citizens of Harfleur (III.iii), and his order that his soldiers kill their French prisoners (IV.vi.37)—are retained, preserving the ambivalence in this play's view of power.

Settings   Small-scale studio sets, but trying hard. Characters enter and exit through round arches, giving a sense of unseen architecture beyond. The French court assembles in a sort of upholstered box—a sectional sofa, one might say. King Henry's addresses to Princess Katherine are paid in a courtyard surrounded by delicate gothic arches.

Costumes   The French and English are color-coded, with the French mainly in blues and greens, the English in browns and golds. Brocade and gilt take over for the last act, when the hostilities are done and each nation is putting its most splendid foot forward.

Interpretation of Roles   David Gwillim's King Henry often wears a puzzled expression, as if he were not sure what to do next. This tentative, experimental approach to the demands of kingship contrasts with the self-confidence of Olivier and Branagh but becomes an interesting alternative.

As the Chorus, Alec McCowen speaks the play's opening lines as he stands among the immobile figures of the English and French opponents. McCowen then enters the action, catching one of the tennis balls as King Henry tosses them about at the end of act one, and going on to join groups of French nobles or English soldiers as occasion arises.

Thorley Walters plays the French king as a person vigorously in command of his faculties, not losing them as in Olivier's film. Joceyln Boisseau's Princess Katherine is young, pretty, and bashful.

The Boar's Head gang diminishes during this film. Falstaff's death is reported (II.iii); Bardolph and Nym are hanged in France, Bardolph for theft (III.vi.101) and Nym for an unspecified reason (IV.iv.73). The Boy is among those killed by the French, "the cowardly rascals that ran from the battle," as Fluellen puts it (IV.vii.6). Pistol (Bryan Pringle) alone remains, though bested by Fluellen and forced to eat a leek (V.i).

Hostess Quickly, whose death is also reported (V.i.81), is last seen bidding the adventurers farewell (II.iv). Brenda Bruce, who played this role during both parts of the BBC's *Henry IV*, turns to the camera at the end of her speech, and her final "Adieu" is said to the audience.

Reviews and Studies   Bulman, J. C., and Coursen, H. R., eds. *Shakespeare on Television*. 1988. Extracts from reviews of this film, pp. 260–63.

Rothwell, Kenneth S., and Melzer, Annabelle H. *Shakespeare on Screen*. 1990. Item 182, pp. 98–99.

Purchase/Rental Inquiries   Ambrose Video; Filmic Archives; Insight Media; The Writing Company. See Appendix B for addresses.

&✿ **10.3.** *Henry the Fifth.* 1989. Samuel Goldwyn. Color, 138 min. Producer: Stephen Evans. Director: Kenneth Branagh.

KING HENRY V	Kenneth Branagh
PRINCESS KATHERINE OF FRANCE	Emma Thompson
CHORUS	Derek Jacobi
KING CHARLES VI OF FRANCE	Paul Scofield
HOSTESS QUICKLY	Judi Dench
DUKE OF EXETER	Brian Blessed
FLUELLEN	Ian Holm
ARCHBISHOP OF CANTERBURY	Charles Key
BISHOP OF ELY	Alec McCowen
PISTOL	Robert Stephens
BARDOLPH	Richard Briers
NYM	Geoffrey Hutchings
BOY TO PISTOL, BARDOLPH, AND NYM	Christian Bale
LOUIS, DAUPHIN OF FRANCE	Michael Maloney
CONSTABLE OF FRANCE	Richard Easton
ALICE, LADY-IN-WAITING TO PRINCESS KATHERINE	Geraldine McEwan

PRINCE JOHN, DUKE OF BEDFORD	James Larkin
MACMORRIS	Daniel Webb
JAMY	Jimmy Yuill
CONSTABLE OF FRANCE	Richard Easton
MONTJOY	Christopher Ravenscroft
SIR JOHN FALSTAFF	Robbie Coltrane

Pluses   Large-screen plenitude, with consistent characterization and a pace that is brisk but not hurried. An immediate hit with student audiences.

Minuses   Viewers of the film tend to express very few negatives.

Textual Cuts and Rearrangements   Cuts apparently aim at regulating the flow of the action. Complicated similes, for example, tend to disappear.

King Henry retains many of his sterner speeches, often presented as agonizing decisions which the king has no choice but to make. He orders the execution of the traitors, one of whom is a close friend (II.ii). He threatens the citizens of Harfleur (III.iii). (The soldiers listening to the threat, who by this time are familiar faces to the audience, look at one another in surprise as the king details the terrible things the soldiers will do when he, the king, loses control of them. When the governor surrenders, the king gives a brief "Whew," indicating it was all a bluff.) However, for this King Henry to order his soldiers to kill their French prisoners (IV.vi.37) would apparently be too much, and this line is omitted.

Several scenes are added or augmented. Bardolph's execution for theft takes place in the king's presence and with his immediate approval; Shakespeare's text leaves some wriggle room on this point. Bardolph stares reprovingly at the king while the noose is put round his neck. We then see the king's flashback to his days at the Boar's Head, laughing with Bardolph, Falstaff and the others.

Queen Isabel of France, who in Shakespeare's text appears only in the final scene, is cut entirely. Her lines about "God, the best maker of all marriages" (V.ii.359) are taken by King Henry.

Settings   Settings give a panoramic impression, but on closer inspection are often relatively concise.

The Battle of Agincourt does not cover as much acreage as it does in Olivier's version, and the field is partly hidden by the mist and drizzle that help make this battle, by comparison to Olivier's, less of a pageant. We have more blood, more mud, more sodden corpses.

The cavalry charge is not shown as such—another difference from Olivier's film that students immediately notice. Instead, we see the faces of the English longbowmen as they wait for the order to release their arrows, and we hear the galloping hooves coming closer and closer.

Student audiences are often divided about whether or not the battle scenes glamorize war. Certainly there is plenty of gore. But when the battle is done and King Henry walks over the field, to a swelling chorus of "Non Nobis Domine," the sense of triumph over incredible odds is undeniable.

Costumes   The characters' clothes give a fifteenth-century feeling, but they do not look like a costume party. Nothing is insistently scalloped, and the colors harmonize rather than contrast.

Interpretation of Roles   Branagh plays King Henry as essentially a serious person, serious about England's honor and about his duty as king. He seems relieved nevertheless when the battle is over and he can marry a pretty girl and go home.

Derek Jacobi as the Chorus opens the film, striking a match to show his own face and then throwing a switch to illuminate what we recognize as a film studio. (Properties that will be used later in the film are lying about.) Jacobi continues to form a bridge between the story and the audience, wearing a present-day black overcoat as he slogs through the rain with the English soldiers. Eventually, as he speaks the epilogue, Jacobi closes the doors on the tableau of the final scene. (We do not return to the film studio of the opening shots, however.)

The role of the duke of Exeter, here played by man-mountain Brian Blessed, is given more prominence than in other films of *Henry V*. Exeter becomes a joyous spirit of war. Eyes flashing, he brings Henry's message to the French court while dressed in full armor (II.iv). During the Battle of Agincourt, the camera follows Exeter in slow motion, bashing away, an ecstatic smile on his face.

Paul Scofield interprets the French king, Charles VI, as sane but sorrowful, apparently foreseeing his country's fall.

Emma Thompson's Princess Katherine is neither coy nor shy but angry at her position as a spoil of war. She attends the peace negotiation wearing a black veil; when her lady-in-waiting pulls it back, as if to display the merchandise, Katherine sits impassively. But she cannot help laughing at King Henry's attempts to speak French (V.ii.180), and once the ice is broken it is clear the two are in rapport. Audiences who have seen this husband-and-wife team in *Much Ado about Nothing* (22.3) here experience a kind of carryover glow.

Production History   This film became a box-office success in both England and America, winning numerous prizes as well as several Academy Award nominations.

Reviews and Studies   Branagh, Kenneth. *Henry V: A Screen Adaptation*. 1989.

Crowl, Samuel. *Shakespeare Observed: Studies in Performance on Stage and Screen.* 1992. Pp. 165–74, 189–90.

Kael, Pauline. Film review. *New Yorker*, 27 November 1989, pp. 104–5.

Klawans, Stuart. "Films." *The Nation*, 11 December 1989, pp. 724–26.

Purcell, Michael. "Playing the Game: Branagh's *Henry V.*" *Literature/Film Quarterly* 20 (1992): 268–75.

Tatspaugh, Patricia E. "Theatrical Influences on Kenneth Branagh's Film of *Henry V.*" *Literature/Film Quarterly* 20 (1992): 276–83.

Rothwell, Kenneth S., and Melzer, Annabelle H. *Shakespeare on Screen*. 1990. Item 182.2, pp. 99–100.

Willson, Robert F., Jr. "*Henry V*: Branagh's and Olivier's Choruses." *Shakespeare on Film Newsletter* 14.2 (1990): 1–2.

Purchase/Rental Inquiries   Filmic Archives. See Appendix B for address.

&. **10.4. *The Wars of the Roses: Henry the Fifth*.** 1991. The English Shakespeare Company. Color, 175 min. Producers: John Paul Chapple, Andy Ward. Director: Michael Bogdanov.

KING HENRY V	Michael Pennington
CHORUS	Barry Stanton
HOSTESS QUICKLY	June Watson
PISTOL	Paul Brennan
BARDOLPH; SIR THOMAS ERPINGHAM	Colin Farrell
NYM	John Dougall
BOY TO PISTOL, BARDOLPH, AND NYM	John Tramper
KING CHARLES VI OF FRANCE	Clyde Pollit
LOUIS, DAUPHIN OF FRANCE	Andrew Jarvis
PRINCESS KATHERINE OF FRANCE	Francesca Ryan
ARCHBISHOP OF CANTERBURY; CONSTABLE OF FRANCE	Hugh Sullivan
BISHOP OF ELY	Roger Booth
DUKE OF EXETER	Ian Burford
FLUELLEN	Sion Probert
MACMORRIS	Michael Cronin
GOWER	Michael Fanner
MONTJOY	Philip Bowen
ALICE, LADY-IN-WAITING TO PRINCESS KATHERINE	Ann Penfold

Pluses   Interesting as a contrast to other available films of *Henry V*, and as a continuation of the English Shakespeare Company's engrossing series of history plays, filmed as a live stage production in Swansea, Wales.

Minuses   Anachronisms can delight some members of the audience but alienate others.

Textual Cuts and Rearrangements   Cut are frequent, although the gist of the action comes through without impairment. References to King Henry's piety often disappear. The king does, however, pray to the "God of battles" (IV.i.289) with wry sincerity.

King Henry's more savage lines are retained. His order at Agincourt is not only spoken but echoed, as the text directs: "Then every soldier kill his prisoners;/ Give the word through" (IV.vi.37–38).

The opening observations of the Archbishop of Canterbury and the Bishop of Ely (I.i), letting the audience in on the political situation, are supplemented by a non-Shakespearean comment about the king's claim to the French throne by inheritance through the female line. "My lord, allowance of this female claim/ Upholds the right of Edmund Mortimer," exclaims Ely in proper iambic pentameter, preparing the audience for the Jack Cade rebellion still to come in *Henry VI*.

Settings   Specific places are created by properties carried on and off. King Henry addresses his court from behind a heavy, official-looking desk. The French courtiers are contrastingly frivolous, reclining on white lawn furniture or picnicking on a rug. The field of Agincourt is represented by a pile of sandbags, while machine-gun fire rattles in the distance.

Costumes   Historical periods are briskly mixed. English soldiers wear camouflage or olive drab; the French appear in white trousers with blue and red jackets. The English also possess the more modern weapons—automatic rifles, for example—while the French go into battle waving swords. This discrepancy complicates student reactions to the Battle of Agincourt. It seems less surprising when the English win.

Hostess Quickly (June Watson) as Pistol's newlywed bride wears a little pillbox hat, shiny blue dress, and white gloves, with a general effect of the 1950s (I.ii).

Interpretation of Roles   Michael Pennington portrays King Henry as a sneering, cynical monarch with little patience for niceties. On "There's for thy labor, Montjoy" (III.vii.158), he gives the French herald not a tip but one of the Dauphin's tennis balls, saved for the occasion.

King Henry's courtship of Princess Katherine (Francesca Ryan) becomes merely another of the wrap-up chores. "An angel is like you, Kate," drones the king, scarcely looking at the humiliated princess and laying special emphasis on her future role as a "soldier breeder" (V.ii.206).

Production History; Reviews and Studies   See the English Shakespeare Company's production of *Richard II* (25.3).

Purchase/Rental Inquiries   Films for the Humanities and Sciences. See Appendix B for address.

11 &❧ HENRY THE SIXTH, Parts One, Two, and Three*_____

&❧ 11.1. *Henry the Sixth, Part One.* 1982. British Broadcasting Company/
Time-Life Television: The Shakespeare Plays. Color, 185 min. Producer: Jonathan
Miller. Director: Jane Howell.

KING HENRY VI	Peter Benson
BISHOP OF WINCHESTER	Frank Middlemass
LORD TALBOT	Trevor Peacock
DUKE OF YORK	Bernard Hill
DUKE OF SOMERSET	Brian Deacon
EARL OF WARWICK	Mark Wing-Davey
DUKE OF GLOUCESTER	David Burke
EARL OF SUFFOLK	Paul Chapman
DUKE OF EXETER	Joseph O'Conor
CHARLES, DAUPHIN OF FRANCE	Ian Saynor
JOAN OF ARC	Brenda Blethyn
MARGARET OF ANJOU	Julia Foster
DUKE OF BURGUNDY	Antony Brown

Pluses   A vivid, well-acted interpretation.

Minuses   Problems with the film are essentially problems with the play itself—
lengthy, verbose, crowded with characters and events.

Textual Cuts and Rearrangements   Shakespeare's text is followed very closely.
A few redundant lines are cut. The first scene of act five, in which Henry VI's
advisors broach the subject of his marriage, has been deferred until after the
second scene of that act.

Several cuts concern Joan of Arc, rather surprisingly since this film is apparently making an effort not to downplay her role and to follow the characterization
familiar to Shakespeare's audience, that of a witch. (Joan's reputation has been

* Note: Because these three plays are staged or filmed as a unit, when they are staged or filmed at all,
I have kept sequential productions together rather than lumping together all the part ones, then all
the part twos, etc. (The situation is different with the two parts of *Henry IV*, since in this case the
first part is sometimes done by itself.)

thoroughly refurbished in the following centuries, of course, and students are surprised to encounter this earlier stereotype.) Charles the Dauphin's praise of Joan has lost a few lines (I.vi.6–10, 21–27), though quite a lot of praise remains. Some of Joan's observations to the English ambassador, Sir William Lucy, are omitted (V.vii.72–76, 87–88).

Just before Joan's capture, her conversation with her personal "fiends" takes place as in the text (V.iii), but we do not see these supernatural beings hanging their heads or otherwise following the stage directions. Joan appears to hold discourse with the empty air. Her part of the dialogue makes clear that she is dealing with demons, not blessed spirits; the line "my ancient incantations are too weak" (V.iii.27) is left intact, not altered as in the English Shakespeare Company's film (11.4). But the text's reference to the fiends as servants of "the lordly Monarch of the North"—Satan—has been omitted (V.iii.6). Perhaps the intent was to admit that Joan was seen as a witch, but not to rub it in.

Settings   The entire play takes place in a large, barn-like space, flexibly interpreted as interior or exterior, chapel or battlefield, as need requires. Wooden ramps, stairs, balconies and catwalks surround the central playing area. These are not tidily or symmetrically placed, but have a random, tossed-together appearance. Many of the doors, stair railings, etc., are painted in bright colors.

Costumes   Court dress seems authentic for the fifteenth century. Men wear turban-like padded rolls, draped with brocade; short coats of patterned velvet; slashed sleeves. Women wear elaborate headdresses and high-waisted gowns.

Armor is made of quilted fabric, but the effect is armor-like, and the actors' movements are not impeded by them. Shields (brightly painted) are obviously made of wood. Helmets are often topped with plumes, and some have modern-looking face guards, probably a useful precaution as the fighting is energetic. (The cast includes some twenty-odd fighting extras, so to speak, who fill the large space during battle scenes and proceed with an acrobatic variety that keeps the battles from becoming monotonous.) The armies are heraldically color-coded, blue predominating for the French and red for the English.

Interpretation of Roles   Henry VI is well played by the pale and ascetic Peter Benson, who gazes mildly about and, before saying anything, makes a point of glancing at his advisors (especially Gloucester) to be sure they approve. In the film's opening scene Benson doubles as a monk, singing in the funeral of Henry V, to the subsequent confusion of some viewers, but as Henry VI's character is rather monk-like, no great harm is done.

Lord Talbot, the English warrior hero, is played by Trevor Peacock with stern authority, dying gorily in battle beside his son (IV.vii).

Ian Saynor as Charles, the dauphin of France, is a surprisingly valiant-looking young man. In expressing his admiration for Joan of Arc, he makes weird dopey faces (I.ii), perhaps as a signal to the audience not to take him for a hero despite his outward appearance.

Joan of Arc, played by Brenda Blethyn, is meant to be seen as a witch, as mentioned above, yet she displays common sense and great confidence. The audience assumes she believes in her own image and is not a conscious phony. She speaks with an accent apparently meant to imply rural, non-courtly origins.

In the last act we meet Margaret of Anjou (Julia Foster), at this point in the tetralogy a young and inexperienced girl who so entrances the duke of Suffolk that he resolves to persuade Henry VI to marry her—in order that he himself might "rule both her, the king and realm" (V.v.108).

Production History   The so-called first tetralogy, the three parts of *Henry VI* and *Richard III*, were conceived, filmed, and presented to the television audience as a unit. All were directed by Jane Howell and used the same set and essentially the same cast. The three parts of *Henry VI* were broadcast in Britain and North America during 1983.

Reviews and Studies   Bulman, J. C., and Coursen, H. R., eds. *Shakespeare on Television*. 1988. Extracts from reviews of the three parts of *Henry VI* and *Richard III*, pp. 292–96.

Rothwell, Kenneth S., and Melzer, Annabelle H. *Shakespeare on Screen*. 1990. Items 186, 187, 193, pp. 103–5, 107–8.

Willis, Susan. *The BBC Shakespeare Plays*. 1991. Pp. 175–83.

Purchase/Rental Inquiries   Ambrose Video; Filmic Archives; Insight Media; The Writing Company. See Appendix B for addresses.

  11.2. *Henry the Sixth, Part Two*. 1982. British Broadcasting Company/ Time-Life Television: The Shakespeare Plays. Color, 185 min. Producer: Jonathan Miller. Director: Jane Howell.

KING HENRY VI	Peter Benson
MARGARET OF ANJOU, QUEEN TO HENRY VI	Julia Foster
EARL OF SUFFOLK	Paul Chapman
EARL OF WARWICK	Mark Wing-Davey
JACK CADE	Trevor Peacock

BISHOP OF WINCHESTER	Frank Middlemass
RICHARD PLANTAGENET, DUKE OF YORK	Bernard Hill
EDWARD PLANTAGENET	Brian Protheroe
RICHARD PLANTAGENET	Ron Cook
MARGERY JOURDAIN	Pat Keen
DUCHESS OF GLOUCESTER	Anne Carroll
DUKE OF SOMERSET	Brian Deacon
DUKE OF BUCKINGHAM	David Daker
LORD SAY	Derek Say
SIR HUMPHREY STAFFORD	Peter Wyatt
SIMPCOX	Derek Fuke
SIMPCOX'S WIFE	Gabrielle Lloyd
LORD CLIFFORD	Arthur Cox

Pluses and Minuses   See *Henry VI, Part One* (11.1), of which this film is a continuation.

Textual Cuts and Rearrangements   As in *Part One*, cuts are infrequent. The duke of York's genealogical justification of his claim to the throne (II.ii) is shortened, although the gist of it remains. The fifth scene of act four is omitted, with no harm done as the dialogue summarizes actions that the audience will find out about anyhow.

Setting   The same large, barn-like space, with its wooden scaffolding and numerous playing areas, continues from *Part One*. Again the space is frequently filled with fighters. This time they are English against English, rather than English against French. Jack Cade's rebels wave torches, burn great piles of books, set priests and soldiers alight, and march about with the severed heads of Lord Say and Sir James Cromer impaled on poles (IV.vii). There is plenty of room for all this. The Battle of St. Albans leaves the set strewn with so many corpses that the camera, lingering on them after the final words are spoken, travels from one bloodied tableau to another for a considerable length of time.

Costumes   The same types of garments, and in some cases literally the same garments, continue from *Part One*. Nobles wear velvets and brocades; the duke of York takes to wearing his white rose prominently in his hat. The common people—Cade and his rebels, or the apprentice Peter Thump and his friends—wear roughly woven tunics, stocking caps, and leather aprons.

Dress reflects the wearer's personality as well as his or her status, and personality is sometimes shown as changeable. When she is presented as his bride to Henry VI, Queen Margaret wears a light-colored embroidered gown, her blonde hair loose down her back; after Suffolk, her lover, is killed, she braids her hair and puts on a dark robe with fur trim (IV.ix). For the Battle of St. Albans she invents a form of military dress—a long skirt, but one in which she can move quickly; a jacket of the kind of quilted cloth that symbolizes armor in this film; wrist guards; and a sword.

Interpretation of Roles   Peter Benson continues to play Henry VI as pale and timid, lifing his hands to heaven and eschewing violence. The results of these pacifist impulses are bloody indeed. The king walks out of his own Parliament, distressed by the infighting of his lords, and so leaves the plot against Gloucester to proceed under the sponsorship of Queen Margaret (III.i). When the Lancastrians are defeated in battle, he sits down in such discouragement that it is all the queen can do to persuade him to get up and flee to London (V.ii.81).

Trevor Peacock's Jack Cade leads a band of ragged rebels armed with axes and cleavers which they use without hesitation. When one of his followers suggests "The first thing we do, let's kill all the lawyers," the viewer does not doubt that he means it. Neither the lower social order nor the act of rebellion is romanticized here, an attitude shared by Shakespeare's original audience.

The duke of York (Bernard Hill) becomes more prominent in this play, and so do his sons, particularly Richard—many bloodsoaked years later to become Richard III. When York justifies his claim to the crown to Salisbury and Warwick (II.ii), the sons appear as small boys playing in their father's garden. (One of them, presumably Richard, wears a metal brace on his leg.) Later, at the Battle of St. Albans, Richard (Ron Cook) is seen as a model of energy, of initiative, and, strange to say in view of later events, of family loyalty. He fights lustily, defends Salisbury "from imminent death" (V.iii.19), and generally does his share toward the Yorkist victory. Cook plays Richard with a slight limp and a small hump. Neither slows him down.

Production History; Reviews and Studies; Purchase/Rental Inquiries   See *Part One* (11.1).

૏ **11.3. *Henry VI, Part Three*.** 1982. British Broadcasting Company/ Time-Life Television: The Shakespeare Plays. Color, 200 min. Producer: Shaun Sutton. Director: Jane Howell.

HENRY VI	Peter Benson
QUEEN MARGARET	Julia Foster
RICHARD PLANTAGENET, DUKE OF YORK	Bernard Hill

EDWARD IV	Brian Protheroe
RICHARD, DUKE OF GLOUCESTER	Ron Cook
GEORGE, DUKE OF CLARENCE	Paul Jesson
LADY ELIZABETH GREY, LATER QUEEN TO EDWARD IV	Rowena Cooper
EARL OF WARWICK	Mark Wing-Davey
RUTLAND	Matthew David
EDWARD, PRINCE OF WALES, SON TO HENRY VI	Nick Reding
DUKE OF SOMERSET	Arthur Cox
DUKE OF EXETER	Derek Farr
DUKE OF NORFOLK	Peter Wyatt
EARL OF NORTHUMBERLAND	John Benfield
LORD RIVERS	Paul Chapman
LORD HASTINGS	David Daker
LORD STANLEY	Tenniel Evans
LOUIS XI OF FRANCE	Antony Brown
LADY BONA	Merelina Kendal
YOUNG RICHMOND	Tim Fuke

Pluses   Inventive and interesting. Scenes with Richard, duke of Gloucester (later Richard III), are useful to show as background for classes studying *Richard III*.

Minuses   Battles and long speeches may become tedious.

Textual Cuts and Rearrangements   The text is followed closely. The opening and closing lines of scenes sometimes disappear—the first 14 lines of the play are cut, for example. A few passages are thinned of their classical references, among them Clifford's dying reference to Phoebus and Phaeton (II.vi.11–13). George, later duke of Clarence, has been added to a scene with his brothers Edward and Richard (II.i), presumably to remind the audience of the identities of the surviving sons of the duke of York. Each of the text-authenticated brothers here contributes a few lines to George so that he seems part of the group.

Setting   The set is the same used in the two previous plays, but by this time a difference is apparent. The wooden scaffolding is now charred, splintered, and hacked, with few traces of the red and yellow trim that sparkled in *Part One*. Civil strife has literally weakened society's infrastructure.

When the action shifts to the more prosperous French court (III.iii), blue draperies cover the scarred walls.

As before, the set is stylized rather than realistic. The forest where Edward IV is rescued from captivity (IV.v) consists of the four-by-fours supporting one of the upper galleries.

During the Battle of Wakefield (V.v), audience and participants are startled by a blizzard of snowflakes, obviously made of torn paper. As the stage floor then turns white and the bodies lying about are partially covered with flakes, one assume that an actual snowfall is meant. The battle took place on May 4 of 1471, and no snow is mentioned by Holinshed, chief chronicler of these events and Shakespeare's source.

Costumes   Like the set, the characters' clothes have become drabber. Many are brown or gray; hats and headdresses tend toward black. By this time, of course, most of the characters are mourning for somebody. Queen Margaret keeps her black military uniform except when visiting the French court, when she wears a gown but retains the black in the form of a shawl wrapped around her head. Lady Grey, a widow when she meets Edward IV, wears a tasteful gray dress.

An exception to this sartorial reserve occurs near the end of the play, when Edward IV, feeling more secure on his disputed throne, goes in for red cloaks and other royal garments trimmed with gold. Lady Grey, who has refused to become Edward's mistress and is now his queen, joins him in this display.

Interpretations of Roles   Ron Cook's Richard of Gloucester now becomes a dominant figure. Small of stature, scuttling of gait, with a nasal cockney accent and sharp darting eyes, he is the opposite of kingly. Nevertheless he is in control. After the death of his father, Richard Plantagenet, duke of York (I.iv), Richard's family loyalty seems to evaporate, and he lets the audience in on his plan to destroy his brothers and their progeny and take the throne (III.ii.124–95; V.vi.68–94). Outwardly, of course, he remains his hearty, good-old-boy self.

The end of this play leaves Richard at obvious loose ends. The wars are over, or so it would seem; Edward is on his throne, and in the final scene (V.vi) his queen literally sits on it, admiring their baby son, while the surviving Yorkist nobles and the black-clad soldiers celebrate with a noisy, stamping circle dance. Richard pushes his way past the merrymakers and shoves through a pair of swinging doors, which close behind him for the film's final shot. *Richard III* (26.2) will open from that moment on the other side, with Richard coming through the doors toward the camera, while the music and dancing are faintly heard.

Tall and handsome Brian Protheroe plays King Edward IV as a self-confident monarch, regarding his brothers and other supporters with condescension. He announces his regal impulses as unarguable facts. His insistence on marrying Lady Grey so infuriates his ally the earl of Warwick (who is negotiating a strategic French marriage for King Edward when the news arrives) that Warwick switches over to the Lancastrians.

As the unfortunate King Henry VI, tossed on and off his throne as Lancastrian fortunes wax and wane, Peter Benson is consistently gently, meditative, unresisting. When Richard of Gloucester comes to the Tower of London to kill him, King Henry calmly lectures his assassin on his (Richard's) demonic nature, but puts up no resistance (V.vi).

Queen Margaret (Julia Foster) becomes everything her husband is not, passionate, grim, her mouth contracting to a small horizontal line. Like many of the characters, she has aged during the sequence of plays. The death of her son Edward, stabbed by the York brothers (V.v), seems to crush her; she collapses, begging for death. But by the end of the scene she has managed to stand erect. She will appear in *Richard III* as an emblem of vengeance.

Production History; Reviews and Studies; Purchase/Rental Inquiries See *Part One* (11.1).

ₐ 11.4. *The Wars of the Roses: Henry the Sixth: The House of Lancaster.* 1991. The English Shakespeare Company. Color, 150 min. Producers: John Paul Chapple, Andy Ward. Director: Michael Bogdanov.

KING HENRY VI	Paul Brennan
JOAN OF ARC	Francesca Ryan
CHARLES, DAUPHIN OF FRANCE	Andrew Jarvis
LORD TALBOT	Michael Fenner
DUKE OF GLOUCESTER	Colin Farrell
DUKE OF YORK	Barry Stanton
EARL OF WARWICK	Michael Cronin
EARL OF SUFFOLK	Michael Pennington
MARGARET OF ANJOU	June Watson
DUCHESS OF GLOUCESTER	Ann Penfold
BISHOP OF WINCHESTER	Clyde Pollit
DUKE OF SOMERSET	Sion Probert
MONTJOY	Philip Bowen
DUKE OF EXETER	Ian Burford
DUKE OF BURGUNDY	Jack Carr
SIMPCOX	Roger Booth
SIMPCOX'S WIFE	Jennifer Konko

Pluses   A brisk and innovative stage play, continuing the English Shakespeare Company's series of history plays. Filmed before a live audience.

Minuses   Textual changes can be confusing.

Textual Changes and Rearrangements   The three *Henry VI* plays have been realigned as two, focused on the House of Lancaster and the House of York, respectively. The dividing line is in the fourth act of Shakespeare's *Part Two*.

Scenes are frequently taken apart and their components put in different places. Minor characters are deleted, renamed, or combined. The result is coherent in itself, if sometimes confusing from the perspective of Shakespeare's text.

Settings   The bare stage with its black backdrop is converted into various locales with the addition of furniture, etc. An arched trellis supplies red or white roses for the adherents of Lancaster or York as they declare their loyalties (*Part One*, II.iv). Battlegrounds make use of the pile of anachronistic sandbags seen in earlier parts of this series.

Costumes   The English Shakespeare Company's history plays make use of anachronistic costumes which form a sequence, though not always an even one. Punk-rock hairdos and camouflage military uniforms are likely to show up at any point. Court dress, however, has moved fairly predictably along. King Richard II wore early-nineteenth-century brocade; his successors appeared in Victorian tailcoats; by *Henry VI* we have turned the corner of the century and find gentlemen out hawking in tweeds and ladies wearing fashions that progress from Gibson Girl ankle-length skirts to the flapper costumes of the Roaring Twenties.

Interpretation of Roles   King Henry VI is played by Paul Brennan with a wondrously vacuous expression, appropriate to this reluctant monarch who only wanted to be left alone with his books.

The image of Joan of Arc, here played by Francesca Ryan, has undergone a sea change since Shakespeare wrote the play. Audiences, whether English or otherwise, now see her as a sympathetic character. In this production, Joan's actions and speeches would seem to have been altered accordingly. It is even possible that her unseen guiding spirits are to be taken as good rather than evil; certainly they are effective when the dauphin, to test her, insists on a fencing match (*Part One*, I.ii). The dauphin takes away the Maid's heavy fighting sword and gives her a fencing foil, which she grasps awkwardly with both hands until her spirits, their presence indicated by an eerie, high-pitched sound, give her instructions. She then shifts the foil to her right hand and acquits herself well, visibly learning as she goes.

To capture Joan, the English literally throw a net over her. Her remark on this occasion, "My holy supplications are too weak," has been changed from Shakespeare's text, which reads, "My ancient incantations are too weak" (*Part One*, V.iii.27).

Andrew Jarvis plays the dauphin of France, as he did in the English Shakespeare Company's preceding play, *Henry V* (10.4). Historically, these are different persons. The earlier dauphin, Louis, died shortly after the Battle of Agincourt; his brother Charles, later Charles VII, was the oldest surviving son of Charles VI in the present play. The audience is spared these complications, but Jarvis is listed as "Charles" in the credits.

Margaret of Anjou, played by June Watson, progresses from a subdued French princess to a domineering queen of England, dazzling her naive husband, Henry VI, plotting against her Yorkist enemies, and conducting an affair with the earl of Suffolk (Michael Pennington). In the final scene of *The House of Lancaster*, we see Margaret holding to her bosom the severed head of Suffolk, just slain by pirates, and awaiting more bloodshed to come.

Production History; Reviews and Studies; Purchase/Rental Inquiries   See the English Shakespeare Company's production of *Richard II* (25.3), the first play in this sequence.

❧ 11.5. *The Wars of the Roses: Henry the Sixth: The House of York.* 1991. The English Shakespeare Company. Color, 178 min. Producers: John Paul Chapple, Andy Ward. Director: Michael Bogdanov.

HENRY VI	Paul Brennan
QUEEN MARGARET	June Watson
DUKE OF YORK	Barry Stanton
EARL OF WARWICK	Michael Cronin
EDWARD PLANTAGENET, AFTERWARD EDWARD IV	Philip Bowen
GEORGE, DUKE OF CLARENCE	John Dougall
RICHARD, DUKE OF GLOUCESTER	Andrew Jarvis
JACK CADE	Michael Pennington
LADY GREY, AFTERWARD QUEEN TO EDWARD IV	Ann Penfold
DUKE OF SOMERSET	Sion Probert
LORD SAY	Clyde Pollit
WILLIAM STAFFORD	Ben Bazell
LOUIS XI, KING OF FRANCE	Ian Burford
LORD RIVERS	John Darrell
EARL OF OXFORD	Michael Fenner
LADY BONA	Jennifer Konko

Pluses   Continues the English Shakespeare Company's stage rendition of English history. Filmed before a live audience.

Minuses   Textual jumpings-about can cause confusion.

Textual Cuts and Rearrangements   The story takes up where the previous film stopped in *Part Two*, as the Jack Cade rebellion gets under way (IV.ii). Numerous passages are cut, and the sequence of others are shuffled. The duke of Buckingham is omitted from this play (though he will appear in the same company's *Richard III*), and his lines are given to various other characters.

Settings   Most of the action occurs on a bare or almost bare stage, with a great deal of smoke for the battles. The court of Edward IV, the Yorkist victor, has a 1930s cocktail party motif, complete with piano player.

Costumes   Queen Margaret, head of the Lancastrian party, wears a military uniform—olive drab skirt and coat, complete with metals, and an officer's cap. Other military characters wear miscellaneous combinations of twentieth-century dress uniforms, camouflage fatigues, and red jackets with gold braid. At all times their red or white roses are helpfully evident.

Jack Cade goes about in his undershirt, emblazoned with the Union Jack. Lady Grey (Ann Penfold), the penniless widow whom Edward IV so outrages his advisors by marrying, wears clinging tea gowns of a 1930s cut.

Interpretation of Roles   The Jack Cade rebellion, though ultimately not a crucial factor in the dynastic struggle, is a memorable part of this play. Michael Pennington transforms himself into a convincing demagogue, eyes aglint, slaughtering such enemies of the people as a man who boasts he can read and write (*Part Two*, IV.ii). Cade rides on a cart pulled by his supporters and waves a bottle about as he speaks, so drunk he almost falls off (IV.vi). After he names himself "Lord Mortimer" and declares that anyone who addresses him as anything else is guilty of treason, a follower runs onstage shouting "Jack Cade"; one of Cade's followers promptly draws a pistol and shoots him.

Paul Brennan's Henry VI continues his convincingly inept career, smiling sweetly and clutching his prayer book.

The savagery of June Watson's Queen Margaret becomes an off-balance looniness that gives an almost comic light to the gore with which she is constantly surrounded.

The final scenes of the play focus on Richard of Gloucester, played by Andrew Jarvis. His awkward leapings-about (he wears a hump), his bald head and goggling eyes, the conviction with which he speaks Richard's lines about being isolated from the human race ("I have no brother, I am like no brother," *Part Three*, V.vi.80), make his actions believable as well as horrifying.

Production History; Reviews and Studies; Purchase/Rental Inquiries   See the English Shakespeare Company's film of *Richard II* (25.3).

12 ❧ HENRY THE EIGHTH

❧ 12.1. *Henry the Eighth.* 1979. British Broadcasting Company/ Time-Life Television: The Shakespeare Plays. Color, 145 min. Producer: Cedric Messina. Director: Kevin Billington.

KING HENRY VIII	John Stride
CARDINAL WOLSEY	Timothy West
QUEEN CATHERINE	Claire Bloom
ARCHBISHOP CRANMER	Ronald Pickup
DUKE OF NORFOLK	Jeremy Kemp
ANNE BOLEYN	Barbara Kellerman
STEPHEN GARDINER	Peter Vaughan
DUKE OF BUCKINGHAM	Julian Glover
THOMAS CROMWELL	John Rowe
CARDINAL CAMPEIUS	Michael Poole
BISHOP OF LINCOLN	David Dodimead
LORD SANDYS	Charles Lloyd Pack
LORD CHAMBERLAIN	John Nettleton
DUKE OF SUFFOLK	Lewis Fiander
EARL OF SUFFEY	Oliver Cotton
OLD LADY	Sylvia Coleridge
PROLOGUE	Tony Church
GRIFFITH	John Bailey
PATIENCE	Sally Home

Pluses   Visual beauty; excellent acting.

Minuses   Very few. Dissatisfaction with the film is likely to proceed from the disjointed construction of the play itself, now identified by scholars as a collaboration between Shakespeare and John Fletcher (1579–1625).

Textual Cuts and Rearrangements   Cuts are minor. The description of Queen Anne's coronation (IV.i) by the ubiquitous "three gentlemen" loses its society-column list of participants. The scene in the palace yard (V.iii), in which crowds of people struggle to catch a glimpse of the baby Elizabeth's baptismal procession, is cut entirely. The epilogue, which is not related to the content of the play, is cut. Several scenes lose their opening and/or closing lines.

Settings   *Henry VIII* was filmed on location at Leeds Castle, Hever Castle, and Penshurst. These stately homes, all near London and open to the public, are favorites with international visitors because of their beauty and their associations with history and literature. The film's settings thus give American audiences something to remember or to look forward to, as the case may be. The obviously full-sized, three-dimensional spaces give the film an authority that might well be lacking in a studio construction. During filming, the weather was often cold enough for the actors' breath to puff into clouds—another touch of non-studio authenticity.

Exteriors tend to favor courtyards and arched Tudor gateways where characters pause to converse. Interiors include long galleries with paneling and elaborate plasterwork, lighted by tall windows or, at night, banks of candles.

Costumes   Portraits by Holbein and his contemporaries would seem to be the inspiration here. The male silhouette emphasizes wide-shouldered power; the female, long-waisted grace. Fabrics are rich brocades, slashed to show contrasting colors underneath. Furs and jewels abound. Women's headgear include small round bonnets or, sometimes, the kind of "gable" hood that students liken to birdhouses.

Interpretation of Roles   John Stride surprises viewers because he does not present the ferocious, toad-like monarch familiar from legend. Instead, Stride's King Henry is young, handsome, gregarious and charming. When the film begins he is warmly affectionate toward Queen Catherine, and his attitude throughout the divorce proceedings is one of courteous regret.

Claire Bloom is both convincing and sympathetic as the devoted and high-principled Queen Catherine. She loves her husband, she has done no wrong, and she will be queen. Her defense of herself in court, or rather, her refusal to recognize the court's authority (II.iv), is moving and dignified. It also meets present-day standards of female assertiveness. That God is on her side, as the queen claims, would seem to be evidenced by her dying vision (IV.ii), in which angels dance against a gold background to welcome her to heaven.

If both the king and queen are blameless, then the fault for their break-up must fall on the third member of the triangle, Anne Boleyn, demurely played by Barbara Kellerman. Perhaps she will turn out to be a scheming hussy. But such does not appear to be the case, although students can argue persuasively that Anne's declaration that she does not want to be queen and her surprise at being made duchess of Pembroke (II.iii) are simply exercises in hypocrisy.

Nevertheless, we see little of Anne, considering her importance to the plot. She is not vilified, and no hint is given of her fate, beheaded on a charge of adultery only three years after her coronation. The reason for Shakespeare's and

Fletcher's discretion on this point, presumably, is that Anne was the mother of Queen Elizabeth I, whose glorious reign had not been long over when this play was presented in 1613.

To the rescue of the audience's need to find a scapegoat comes Cardinal Wolsey, played by Timothy West. West makes the most of the opportunities offered by the text. His Wolsey is proud, ambitious, his finger in every man's pie as the characters complain (I.i.52), and yet a complex and intelligent man. He is Queen Catherine's enemy because he favors the divorce; Anne's, because he wants the king to marry somebody else; and eventually the king's, because he turns out to have been embezzling a secret hoard to bribe his way into the papacy (III.ii). The audience rejoices at his fall, yet sympathizes when he makes his farewell to his secretary Cromwell, long a famous declamation piece (III.ii.428–57).

Production History   *Henry VIII* was one of the six films making up the first season of the British Broadcasting Company's project of filming the entire Shakespeare canon for television (1978–85). Reactions to *Henry VIII* were both positive and surprised. Little, apparently, had been expected of this seldom-produced play.

Reviews and Studies   Bulman, J. C., and Coursen, H. R. *Shakespeare on Television*. 1988. Extracts from reviews of this film, pp. 255–56.

Colley, Scott. "The Shakespeare Plays on TV: Season One." *Shakespeare on Film Newsletter* 4.1 (1979): 4.

Rothwell, Kenneth B., and Melzer, Annabelle H. *Shakespeare on Screen*. 1990. Item 196, pp. 110–11.

Purchase/Rental Inquiries   Ambrose Video; Filmic Archives; Insight Media; The Writing Company. See Appendix B for addresses.

13 ❧ JULIUS CAESAR* _____

❧ **13.1.** *Julius Caesar.* 1953. MGM. Black and white, 121 min. Producer: John Houseman. Director: Joseph L. Mankiewicz.

MARK ANTONY	Marlon Brando
BRUTUS	James Mason
CASSIUS	John Gielgud
JULIUS CAESAR	Louis Calhern
CALPHURNIA	Greer Garson
PORTIA	Deborah Kerr
CASCA	Edmund O'Brien
SOOTHSAYER	Richard Hale
OCTAVIUS CAESAR	Douglas Watson
LEPIDUS	Douglas Dumbrille
CICERO	Alan Napier
CINNA	William Cottrell
TREBONIUS	Jack Raine
LIGARIUS	Ian Wolfe
PUBLIUS	Lumsden Hare
LUCIUS	John Hardy
DECIUS BRUTUS	John Hoyt
METELLUS CIMBER	Tom Powers
PINDARUS	Michael Ansara
STRATO	Edmund Purdom
ARTEMIDORUS	Morgan Farley

Pluses   A sense of visual magnitude—crowd scenes, processions, imperial architecture, large-scale battles. Crisp photography and rapid pace. Well-known actors in their youthful glory.

Minuses   Very few.

Textual Cuts and Rearrangements   There is some cutting, and the narration incorporates such devices as an excerpt from Plutarch at the beginning and a later summary of events after Julius Caesar's assassination (IV.i).

___

* Note: For material related to Shakespeare's *Julius Caesar*, see Appendix A, "Analogues and Variations."

Text is often cut when replaced by action. In the final battle (V.ii-iv), Antony's soldiers ambush Cassius' troops as they ride through a rocky pass, and considerable dialogue, including the incipient quarrel between Antony and his ally (at the time), Octavius Caesar, is lost in the melee.

Other cuts streamline the action. Portia's scene with Lucius (II.iv) disappears, as does the lynching of Cinna the Poet (III.iii).

Brutus's discovery of Cassius' body is moved to a point just before his own suicide (V.v). In the final dialogue, Octavius Caesar's and Antony's lines are reversed, so that Antony's "This was the noblest Roman of them all," spoken over Brutus' body, ends the play.

Settings   Roman street scenes are lavish with squares and fountains; public places are filled with statues. A larger-than-life Julius Caesar peers down at Cassius and Brutus as the former gives his first hints about the assassination (I.ii).

Houses express the personalities of the people who live in them. Brutus has a quiet, meditative courtyard, where he receives the conspirators (II.i). Julius Caesar enjoys a grander living space, with a view of the city spread below. This same interior becomes ironic when Antony, Octavius, and Lepidus (the third member of the triumvirate) meet there, after the assassination of Caesar and the flight of Brutus and Cassius. Because the room is dignified and orderly, the audience has a fleeting sense that social stability will be restored. But the triumvirs' order of business, as it turns out, is drawing up a list of enemies to be killed (IV.i).

Costumes   Togas for civilians, helmets and breastplates for soldiers. Plebians wear roughly woven tunics. Antony manages to look a bit different from his colleagues; his toga is darker and is draped more simply.

Interpretation of Roles   James Mason's Brutus is deliberate, meditative, his eyes like great dark pools; he is convinced of his own nobility and thus convinces others. Meeting for the first time with the conspirators (II.i), he is calm and matter-of-fact rather than imperative, and step by step he takes the leadership away from Cassius, advising, among other things, that Mark Antony not be killed along with Caesar. The disastrous results of this and other of Brutus' advice seems to be noticed by nobody in the film, with the exception of the increasingly distressed Cassius. Sometimes, so great is Mason's hypnotic power, they are noticed by nobody in the audience either.

As Cassius, John Gielgud makes it clear that, time after time, his devotion to Brutus demolishes his common sense. When in act four the two quarrel and then make up, Cassius is so relieved that he goes along with Brutus' plan to challenge Octavius Caesar's and Antony's troops at Philippi, instead of remaining in place and forcing the enemy to come to them (IV.iii.213). The result will be defeat.

Gielgud's manner makes clear that he knows the decision was a bad one, but his need for his friend's approval will not permit him to start another quarrel.

Marlon Brando's Antony is brooding and intense. He is clearly a man who has his own private thoughts, however adroitly he behaves in public. On his first appearance (I.ii), when Caesar asks him to touch Calphurnia during his running of the Lupercalia race and thus relieve her "sterile curse," Brando's facial expression makes clear what he thinks ought to be done for this particular problem. Again, during his oration over Julius Caesar's body, Brando convinces the crowd that he is indeed a plain, loyal man who loved Caesar and has no desire to manipulate anybody. And as the crowd erupts in riot, Brando smiles a private, triumphant smile.

Louis Calhern's Caesar, like Mason's Brutus, believes implicitly in his own image of himself. He is invulnerable, unshakable, constant as the northern star (III.i.60). Often he is photographed from a low angle, towering above the camera. The viewer's sympathy is alienated, although student audiences usually will not go so far as to say he deserved his death.

Octavius Caesar, played by Douglas Watson, is youthful, but not startlingly so, and does not greatly contrast with Brando's Antony. Antony in fact seems younger than Octavius. Thus the film does not foreshadow this angle of the conflict in Shakespeare's *Antony and Cleopatra*, where part of Antony's bitterness at being dominated by Caesar springs from the fact that he is an experienced veteran and his rival is not.

Since student audiences enjoy seeing actors at various phases of their careers, a showing of Mankiewicz's *Julius Caesar* often entails some non-Shakespearean pauses for reminiscence. Brando is best known to the young generation for his portrayal of the aged Don Corleone in *The Godfather* (1972), often found on television movie channels. Brando's earlier image, though revolutionary at the time, seems to have faded in the popular consciousness. James Mason has appeared in so many films that it is hard to predict what students will mention, but *Lolita* (1962) and *The Verdict* (1982) are frequent choices. John Gielgud was recently seen as Prospero in Peter Greenaway's *The Tempest* (Appendix A, 29.E), and his list of Shakespearean and other significant roles is a lengthy one, but to many American moviegoers he is most familiar as the butler in *Arthur* (1981).

Production History   Mankiewicz's *Julius Caesar*, while not exactly a blockbuster, was well received at the box office and by the critics.

Reviews and Studies   Dick, Bernard F. *Joseph L. Mankiewicz*. 1983. Pp. 132–48.

Jorgens, Jack J. *Shakespeare on Film*. 1977. Pp. 92–105, 265–68, 318–20.

Manvell, Roger. *Shakespeare and the Film*. 1971. Pp. 86–91.

Rothwell, Kenneth S., and Melzer, Annabelle H. *Shakespeare on Screen*. 1990. Item 214, pp. 117–18.

Purchase/Rental Inquiries   Filmic Archives. See Appendix B for address.

𝕒 13.2. *Julius Caesar*. 1969. A Commonwealth United Production. Color, 117 min. Producer: Peter Snell. Director: Stuart Burge.

MARK ANTONY	Charlton Heston
JULIUS CAESAR	John Gielgud
BRUTUS	Jason Robards
OCTAVIUS CAESAR	Richard Chamberlain
PORTIA	Diana Rigg
CALPHURNIA	Jill Bennett
CASSIUS	Richard Johnson
CASCA	Robert Vaughan
CINNA	David Neal
PUBLIUS	Edward Finn
DECIUS BRUTUS	Derek Godfrey
METELLUS CIMBER	Michael Gough
ARTEMIDORUS	Christopher Lee
LEPIDUS	David Dodimead
CINNA THE POET	Peter Eyre
TREBONIUS	Preston Lockwood
CICERO	Andre Morrell

Pluses   An outgoing, energetic film, dominated by Charlton Heston's virile Antony.

Minuses   Extensive cutting.

Textual Cuts and Rearrangements   Cuts are so numerous that an audience familiar with the play sometimes feels lost. The plot has been plucked out of its matrix, leaving behind not only poetic similes but such introspective glimpses as Brutus' rationalization on the need to kill Caesar (II.i). Again, in the quarrel between Brutus and Cassius (IV.ii), Brutus upbraids Cassius for not sending him money for his troops but does not add, "For I can raise no money by vile means"; the audience thus loses this example of Brutus' assumption that other people will do the un-idealistic dirty work.

Some scenes have survived almost intact, however. The assassination scene (III.i) is one of these, although Ligarius has been left out altogether and Mark Antony enters abruptly, without first sending a servant. The scene is carefully thought out, the camera showing first one conspirator and then another as they swallow, exchange glances, and work themselves up for the deed. At one point during the killing, the camera sees Brutus through Caesar's dimming eyes.

Some non-textual interpolations are effective. The film begins with an eagle circling in the sky and connoting imperial grandeur; we then see that he is flying over a battlefield, where skeletons lie among broken chariot wheels. Calphurnia's dream (II.ii) is not described by Caesar but shown to the audience, Caesar's statue spouting large quantities of blood while Artemidorus' petition to Caesar (II.iii) is read as a voice-over.

Settings   Settings are often large-scale and detailed, well designed for the action that takes place in them. In the senate house, for example, the non-conspiring senators occupy boxed-in benches, like old-fashioned church pews, when the killing begins; they rise in horror, and their helplessness is emphasized by their being visually trapped in their places.

The battle takes place on rocky hillsides, where horsemen charge about and clouds of dust float in the air.

Costumes   The expected Roman togas are here done in bright colors, a useful touch as the characters become much easier to tell apart.

Interpretation of Roles   Charlton Heston's Antony is all shoulders and rugged cheekbones. Even when he manipulates the crowd at Caesar's funeral, he gives the effect of being as plain and sincere as he says he is.

As Caesar, John Gielgud is strangely un-imperial. He pays attention when people speak, and he seems willing (if not exactly eager) to please. He goes to the senate house, one feels, despite the omen of Calphurnia's dream, because he does not want to disappoint his companions.

Cassius, played by Richard Johnson in a fierce, dark beard, is taciturn and brooding. He does not seem dependent on Brutus' approval and gives way to him, apparently, because he recognizes Brutus' weightier public image. His methods of persuasion are ingenious. As he persuades Brutus to to join the conspiracy, standing beside a graffiti-covered wall, Cassius carves Brutus' name beside Caesar's — in larger letters.

Jason Robards's interpretation of Brutus is aided by a tidy row of spit curls across his forehead. Anyone who would wear his hair like that, student audiences reason, has got to be a phony, or at least seriously self-deceived.

As Octavius Caesar, Richard Chamberlain is supremely young and self-confident. "I do not cross you," he says on overriding one of Antony's decisions, "but

I will do so" (V.i.20). Antony appears so stunned at this impertinence that he is unable to argue.

Diana Rigg plays a loving and concerned Portia, but as her lines are severely cut she can hardly be blamed for not making much of the role.

Production History The film's box-office performance seems to have been disappointing, and critics were not greatly impressed.

Reviews and Studies Manvell, Roger. *Shakespeare and the Film.* 1971. Pp. 91–96.

Rothwell, Kenneth S., and Melzer, Annabelle H. *Shakespeare on Screen.* 1990. Item 226, pp. 121–22.

Purchase/Rental Inquiries Filmic Archives. See Appendix B for address.

❧ 13.3. *Julius Caesar.* 1979. British Broadcasting Company/ Time-Life Television: The Shakespeare Plays. Color, 180 min. Producer: Cedric Messina. Director: Herbert Wise.

BRUTUS	Richard Pasco
JULIUS CAESAR	Charles Gray
MARK ANTONY	Keith Michell
PORTIA	Virginia McKenna
CALPHURNIA	Elizabeth Spriggs
CASCA	Sam Dastor
CASSIUS	David Collings
CINNA	Darien Angadi
LIGARIUS	Anthony Dawes
OCTAVIUS CAESAR	Garrick Hagon
CICERO	Manning Wilson
SOOTHSAYER	Ronald Forfar
ARTEMIDORUS	Patrick Marley
CINNA THE POET	John Tordoff
DECIUS BRUTUS	Alex Davion
TREBONIUS	William Simons
POET	Reginald Jessop
LEPIDUS	Roy Spencer

Pluses A thorough treatment, recognizing the play's built-in ambiguities.

Minuses   Slow pace, talking heads, claustrophobically squeezed sets.

Textual Cuts and Rearrangements   Very few. Some seldom-heard lines are retained; we have not only Cinna the Poet, lynched by the mob after Caesar's assassination (III.iii), but the mysterious poet who visits Brutus in his camp (IV.iii) and whose function is never developed. Portia's claim that she can be trusted with secrets because she has given herself "a voluntary wound, here in the thigh" is not only retained, as it often is not, but is supported by a brief glimpse of a bloody gash (II.i), understandably horrifying Brutus and foreshadowing Portia's strange suicide by "swallowing fire."

The passage in which Brutus reacts to the news of Portia's death (IV.iii) is also retained in full. This option is an interesting one as it shows a facet of Brutus' character often obscured by textual cutting or editorial puzzlement. On patching up his quarrel with Cassius, Brutus mentions Portia's death, which he has just heard about, as an excuse for his short temper. Messala, entering with letters, then tells the same news; Brutus gives no sign that he already knows it and merely says, "Why, farewell, Portia." Some editors have assumed a textual problem, perhaps an incomplete revision, but Brutus may simply have seized an opportunity to display his stoicism, a much-esteemed Roman virtue.

The play's final lines are spoken in the correct sequence. Antony's eulogy of Brutus, "This was the noblest Roman of them all," is followed by Octavius Caesar's compulsive one-upmanship: "Within my tent his bones shall lie tonight" — emphasizing the "my."

Settings   The studio sets are simple. Rome has streets and buildings, rather small ones, but few people. Most of the time the screen is filled with faces. Battles take place off-camera and are indicated by distant shouting.

Costumes   Togas for the upper classes, rough tunics for the plebians, helmets and breastplates for the soldiers. For students who also watch the BBC's *Antony and Cleopatra* (2.2), where the characters are dressed to convey not the ancient world but the time of Shakespeare's audience, the shift can be disconcerting.

Interpretation of Roles   Charles Gray as Julius Caesar goes in for pomposity. He often closes his eyes, as if to shut out the possibility of dissent.

Brutus, played by Richard Pasco, is sleepy-eyed and slow-moving. David Collings's Cassius is contrastingly nervous, pacing about, gesturing. Whatever he may be saying, he keeps an eye on his hearer, ready to adjust his message if he senses negative feedback.

As Mark Antony, Keith Michell is middle-aged, paunchy, and soft about the chin. He nevertheless moves the crowd, delivering his oration over Caesar's body not with studied effect but as if the words had just occurred to him. His glee as the riot begins makes him resemble a comfortable-looking businessman who has just pulled off a daring deal. Later (IV.i), in his conversation with the very young Octavius Caesar (Garrick Hagon), Antony seems contrastingly shopworn. He reaches for a pitcher of wine.

Production History *Julius Caesar* was shown on British and American television in 1978 and 1979, respectively, during the first season of the British Broadcasting Company's series of the entire Shakespeare canon.

Reviews and Studies Bulman, J. C., and Coursen, H. R., eds. *Shakespeare on Television.* 1988. Extracts from reviews of this film, pp. 249–51.

Rothwell, Kenneth S., and Melzer, Annabelle H. *Shakespeare on Screen.* 1990. Item 233, pp. 124.

Willis, Susan. *The BBC Shakespeare Plays.* 1991. Pp. 197–99.

Purchase/Rental Inquiries Ambrose Video; Filmic Archives; Insight Media; The Writing Company. See Appendix B for addresses.

14 ✒ KING JOHN

✒ **14.1. *King John*.** 1984. British Broadcasting Company/ Time-Life Television: The Shakespeare Plays. Color, 155 min. Producer: Shaun Sutton. Director: David Giles.

KING JOHN	Leonard Rossiter
CONSTANCE	Claire Bloom
QUEEN ELINOR	Mary Morris
PHILIP THE BASTARD	George Costigan
KING PHILIP OF FRANCE	Charles Kay
DAUPHIN OF FRANCE	Jonathan Coy
BLANCHE OF SPAIN	Janet Maw
CARDINAL PANDULPH	Richard Wordsworth
ARTHUR, DUKE OF BRITAIN	Luc Owen
HUBERT DE BURGH	John Thaw
EARL OF SALISBURY	John Castle
EARL OF PEMBROKE	Robert Brown
LORD BIGOT	John Flint
PRINCE HENRY	Rusty Livingstone
CHATILLON	William Whymper
ROBERT FAULCONBRIDGE	Edward Hibbert
LADY FAULCONBRIDGE	Phillida Law

Pluses   An absorbing study of clashing priorities, shifting alliances, self-interest at odds with principle, bought friendship, and other universal patterns.

Minuses   Audiences need to have read the play beforehand, preferably in an edition with notes and family trees.

Textual Cuts and Rearrangements   The film follows the text very closely, and the few minor alterations may have been accidental. An exception occurs as young Arthur begs Hubert de Burgh not to put out his eyes with red-hot irons (IV.i). Some thirty lines of Arthur's plea are cut. This decision may have resulted from the unfortunately mechanical diction of the actor playing Arthur. Arthur's plea is successful even if truncated; Hubert has mercy, and Arthur then dies (speaking all of his lines, although in this scene there are not many of them) after falling from a prison wall in an escape attempt (IV.iii).

Settings   Studio sets, but with a shift in style as we cross the English Channel. Scenes in England are somewhat realistic. King John's palace is a gothic interior, figured pavements receding into dimly lighted bays, sturdy columns ornamented with geometric patterns. In the final scene, when the poisoned King John is brought out to die in the open air, we have a misty wood with real-looking trees, though leafless.

In France, by contrast, the settings are stylized. Surrounding the city of Angiers we find, instead of an outdoor landscape, a blue backdrop patterned with fleurs de lys. The city walls are of gray-painted cardboard, or they seem to be.

Costumes   Dress is lavish, encrusted with gold and brocade. The opposing sides are color-coded, red for the English and blue for the French. Soldiers generally wear chain mail. Faulconbridge, the Bastard, who by the end of the play seems to have become the chief English commander, wears an elaborate breastplate distinguishing him from the other military characters.

Women wear gowns with trailing skirts and flared sleeves, hats with barbettes, wimples that float in the breeze.

Interpretation of Roles   Leonard Rossiter is a wonderful King John, the cartoon of a Bad King, sneering, leering, and slumping as things get worse and worse. He does show some concern for others, even if it takes him awhile. On hearing of his mother's death, his first thought is for his own affairs — "How wildly then walks my estate in France!" (IV.ii.129). But later, in the midst of other pressing matters, he becomes pensive: "My mother dead!" (IV.ii.181).

That mother, Elinor of Aquitaine, is played by Mary Morris with a ferocious energy and, one senses, a deep enjoyment. Her rich voice growls, chuckles, and rages. (Students familiar with James Goldman's *Lion in Winter* are especially interested in following the later fortunes of Elinor.) Her life consists of aggrandizing her family, and she is not dismayed by obstacles. Her last surviving son, John, must not lose his throne, even to the claims of Arthur — her grandson by another son, Geoffrey, now dead, who had preceded John in birth order and thus would have a higher rank by the principles of primogeniture.

Constance (Claire Bloom), the mother of Arthur and widow of Geoffrey, is equally determined to get the kingdom, but in rhetoric and resources she is no match for Elinor, as the audience notes when the two meet (II.i). Her sorrow in defeat makes her a sympathetic character, particularly in her lament for her son — "Grief fills the room up of my absent child" (III.iv.93).

Luc Owen, who plays young Arthur, looks the part, sturdy and handsome. He is not adept with Shakespearean verse, a noticeable handicap since he is surrounded by actors who are.

The Bastard, Philip of Faulconbridge, renamed Richard when he is accepted as the illegitimate son of Richard the Lionhearted (another of Queen Elinor's deceased progeny), is acted very competently by George Costigan. It is a curious role. The Bastard is a fictional character with no historical basis, so that he may be bent to many purposes. In some ways he serves as a chorus, commenting on the action; Costigan looks into the camera on these occasions. Sometimes he becomes a court jester, hurling gibes at the French (III.i) while the other characters ignore him. But the Bastard also takes part in the action, becoming increasingly responsible and courageous as the play goes on, until at the end he is the staunchest of King John's retainers.

Production History   *King John* was shown on British television in November of 1984 and on American television in January of 1985, near the end of the British Broadcasting Company's project (1978–85) of filming the entire Shakespeare canon.

Reviews and Studies   Bulman, J. C., and Coursen, H. R., eds. *Shakespeare on Television*. 1988. Extracts from reviews of this film, pp. 310–12.

Rothwell, Kenneth S., and Melzer, Annabelle H. *Shakespeare on Screen*. 1990. Item 240, p. 128.

Willis, Susan. *The BBC Shakespeare Plays*. 1991. Pp. 207–8.

Purchase/Rental Inquiries   Ambrose Video; Filmic Archives; Insight Media; The Writing Company. See Appendix B for addresses.

15 ❧ KING LEAR*

❧ **15.1. *King Lear.*** 1953. TV/ Radio Workshops of the Ford Foundation. Black and white, 75 min.

A much-abbreviated version, with Orson Welles (King Lear), Alan Badel (the Fool), and Michael MacLiammoir (Mad Tom). Peter Brook was involved the project, but this is not the film generally referred to as "the Peter Brook *King Lear*" (see below, 15.3).

The subplot involving Gloucester and his two sons is here omitted. Gloucester becomes a noble who happens to feel sorry for King Lear. Mad Tom is a character in his own right, not an invention of the disguised Edgar. Edmund does not exist at all, and Oswald takes over his function as the illicit lover of both the sisters.

For students focused on Shakespeare's text, this *Lear* as an entirety is probably not a good choice. However, some of the scenes are useful for comparative analysis. Lear's conversation with Gloucester (IV.vi.95ff.) is a possible candidate. Welles sits on a beach, draped with seaweed, meditating on the realities of life.

The film is occasionally available from distributors.

❧ **15.2. *Karol Lear*** [King Lear]. 1970. Lenfilm. Black-and-white, 140 min. Russian with English subtitles.

A famous film, directed by Grigor Kozintsev and starring Yuri Yarvet as King Lear. Many outdoor scenes; wolfhounds and hawks; panoramic landscapes; crowds of people fleeing from armies. The story is set in a bleak, primitive era.

For classroom use, the film has disadvantages. The white-lettered English subtitles sometimes disappear in the snow, and the beautiful Russian sounds rumble along unintelligibly unless the instructor or some of the students happen to know the language. (The Russian text is Boris Pasternak's.) The visual quality is poor in videotape, so that indoor scenes tend to blur into shadows.

---

* Note: For films related to Shakespeare's *King Lear*, see Appendix A, "Analogues and Variations."

℘ 15.3. *King Lear.* 1971. Filmways (London). Black-and-white, 137 min. Producer: Michael Birkett. Director: Peter Brook.*

KING LEAR	Paul Scofield
GONERIL	Irene Worth
ALBANY	Cyril Cusack
CORNWALL	Patrick Magee
CORDELIA	Anne-lise Gabold
FOOL	Jack MacGowran
GLOUCESTER	Alan Webb
EDGAR	Robert Lloyd
KENT	Tom Fleming
REGAN	Susan Engel
EDMUND	Ian Hogg
OSWALD	Barry Stanton
BURGUNDY	Soren Elung-Jensen

Pluses   A much-discussed example of the "theater of cruelty," influenced by Jan Kott's writings in the 1960s. Useful for comparative analysis of individual scenes; contrasts with virtually any other film of *King Lear* that one might have on hand.

Minuses   Many students find Brook's negative worldview paralyzing and pointless. Others find the film amusing, though for reasons unlikely to have been intended.

Textual Cuts and Rearrangements   A large proportion of the text is cut, and much of what remains has been taken apart and reassembled. The opening dialogue with Kent, Gloucester, and Edmund disappears, and Lear's division of his kingdom proceeds in a jerky fashion. Cordelia does not thank her father for having "begot me, bred me, loved me" (I.i.96); she merely declines to join her sisters' flattery contest. This omission would seem to be part of a pattern, as evidence of human kindness is given short shrift. When Gloucester is blinded— Cornwall scoops out his eyes with a spoon—the lines of the servants trying to care for him are omitted (III.vii.98ff.).

Scenes begin and end abruptly, and speeches are often scattered about. Edmund's "Why brand they us/ With base? . . . with bastardy?" (I.ii.9) is delayed until after Lear has left Goneril's castle and is then spoken to Edgar, of all people.

* Note: Not all the actors seem to be listed in the credits. The king of France appears in the play, for example.

Despite the shortened text, the characters seem to run out of time and finish the story in a rush. Goneril does not trouble to poison Regan but kills her with remarkable efficiency by throwing her on the ground, after which she commits suicide by banging her own head against a rock.

What does remain of the text is often unintelligible, as the actors have a habit of turning away from the camera and mumbling.

Settings We find ourselves in a large, empty, and cold landscape. (Much of the film was shot in North Jutland, Denmark.) Civilization is at an early stage. Castles are small palisades, crowded with livestock as well as retainers. People get from place to place on small, shaggy ponies or in horse-drawn wagons, strange, cumbersome affairs like leather-covered school buses, though windowless.

Interiors include Lear's throne room, a round wooden hut, and several larger halls, sparsely furnished but equipped with fireplaces round which the characters gather. The sense of cold is pervasive. In the courtyard of Gloucester's castle, essentially a wooden fort, Kent is put into the stocks and Oswald, for an added touch of torture, removes the prisoner's boots and socks.

Costumes Roughly woven cloth, leather, furs. Edgar, who as Mad Tom becomes a Christ figure, wears a crown of thorns (III.iii). Soldiers wear cylindrical helmets that look like stovepipes, and Edgar and Edmund fight not with swords but with enormous battle axes.

Interpretation of Roles Paul Scofield's Lear is at the beginning of the film not physically feeble, a fact which may add to his desolation. He can move about and give orders, but his orders have little effect. He and his retainers gallop home from a hunting trip and swagger into Goneril's castle, but they are helpless when Oswald, obeying Goneril, treats Lear with disrespect. All Lear and his men can do is start a food fight (I.iv).

Lear's physical strength ebbs during the storm, when he and the Fool lie on the ground and get soaked (III.ii). He recovers somewhat when taken first into a barn and then in a wagon to Dover, but before Cordelia's soldiers can catch him they have to pursue him into the surf. His reconciliation with Cordelia (IV.vii) is greatly cut. At the end of the film, he has just enough strength to pick up Cordelia's dead body. He then dies, falling out of the camera frame and leaving a symbolic view of nothing.

Goneril (Irene Worth) is brisk and determined, striding about in a long fur cape, fiercely impatient with her mild husband, Albany. Her sister Regan (Susan Engel) is sexier—blonde, languid, confident that she can seduce Edmund or do anything else she likes.

Production History Peter Brook had directed Paul Scofield and Irene Worth in a Royal Shakespeare Company stage production of *King Lear* some years before this film was made. Many of the stage production's ideas are developed here. On its release, the film received mixed reviews from critics and did not win favor with the general public. Its prestige among critics and film historians seems to have grown during the intervening decades.

Review and Studies   Acker, Paul. "Conventions for Dialogue in Peter Brook's *King Lear.*" *Literature/ Film Quarterly*, 20 (1980): 219–24.

Berlin, Normand. "Peter Brook's Interpretation of *King Lear*: Nothing Will Come of Nothing." *Literature/ Film Quarterly* 5 (1977): 299–303.

Gilman, Todd. "The Textual Fabric of Peter Brook's *King Lear.*" *Literature/ Film Quarterly* 20 (1992): 294–300.

Manvell, Roger. *Shakespeare and the Film.* 1971. Pp. 133–52.

Mullin, Michael. "Peter Brook's *King Lear*: Stage and Screen." *Literature/ Film Quarterly* 8 (1980): 219–24.

Rothwell, Kenneth S., and Melzer, Annabelle H. *Shakespeare on Screen.* 1990. Item 259, pp. 135–36.

Wilds, Lilian. "One *King Lear* for Our Time: A Bleak Film Vision by Peter Brook." *Literature/ Film Quarterly* 4 (1976): 159–64.

Purchase/Rental Inquiries   The Peter Brook *King Lear* is currently unavailable in videotape or videodisk.

ᐇ 15.4. *King Lear.* 1977. New York Shakespeare Festival. Color, 120 min.

James Earl Jones plays King Lear in Joseph Papp's production for the New York Shakespeare Festival. Filmed in the Delacorte Theatre in Central Park. With Raul Julia as Edmund.

This film is currently not available.

ᐇ 15.5. *King Lear.* 1982. British Broadcasting Company/ Time-Life Television: The Shakespeare Plays. Color, 180 min. Producer: Shaun Sutton. Director: Jonathan Miller.

KING LEAR	Michael Hordern
FOOL	Frank Middlemass
GONERIL	Gilian Barge
REGAN	Penelope Wilton

CORDELIA	Brenda Blethyn
KENT	John Shrapnel
ALBANY	John Bird
CORNWALL	Julian Curry
EDMUND	Michael Kitchen
EDGAR	Anton Lesser
OSWALD	John Grillo
GLOUCESTER	Norman Rodway
KING OF FRANCE	Harry Waters
BURGUNDY	David Weston

Pluses   Roles are thoughtfully and convincingly created.

Minuses   The small sets and seldom-changing camera angles can make the viewer feel trapped.

Textual Cuts and Rearrangments   Very little cutting. Some of Mad Tom's and the Fool's songs are shortened (III.vi). The First Folio text of 1623 seems to predominate. Thus the play's closing lines, "The weight of this sad time . . . ," are here given to Edgar, rather than to Albany as in the earlier quartos. Also, following the Folio, Kent's conversation with an anonymous gentleman about Cordelia's return to the kingdom (IV.iii) has been cut.

Settings   Most of the action, especially in the early acts, takes place on a small platform of bare boards, painted black. Tables and other properties are brought on and off, but there is no solid distinction between one place and another. Lear's, Gloucester's, and Albany's castles are the same locale as far as this film is concerned.
  The action does shift to a semblance of the outdoors for the storm scene, where Mad Tom has taken shelter in a large drainpipe (III.iv). Later they move to a more commodious cottage (III.v).
  In the last act the set shifts from dark to light colors, and the characters converse inside or in front of white tents.

Costumes   Most of the men look so much alike that the audience has trouble telling them apart. Dark costumes are the rule, vaguely seventeenth-century, with white lace collars and short brown beards. Lear blends with his somber court and does not wear or carry kingly regalia. Kent achieves a different look on returning in disguise; when he "razes his countenance" he shaves his head.
  Edgar when pretending to be Poor Tom wears a loincloth and a crown of thorns, even adding stigmata holes in his palms. (They do not go all the way through.)

As the Fool, Frank Middlemass is disconcertingly put into whiteface clown makeup, with a broad-brimmed hat and a bedraggled feather. His face floats like a puzzled balloon over the other characters. The makeup eventually runs off during the storm, and the Fool then becomes a large, plump, middle-aged courtier.

Women's dresses are also monotone, in black, white, and shades of gray. To tie in with the overall effect, all three sisters are brunettes.

Interpretation of Roles   Michael Hordern becomes a Lear who is in control of his faculties at one moment, then in full rage at the next. The combination is perfectly plausible. The audience sympathizes with Lear's terror as he realizes what is happening to him.

Lear's retainers, the hundred knights whose riotous behavior so upsets Goneril and Regan, are in this film for the most part nonexistent. His one or two anonymous attendants are quite decorous. The only riotous persons, in fact, are Lear himself, when the mood is on him, and Kent. The viewer consequently assumes that Goneril and Regan are making their accusations up, just the sort of thing they would do.

Gilian Barge, as Goneril, is smooth to the point of oiliness. Penelope Wilton's Regan is contrastingly agitated, smiling or frowning, always working her face, managing to be both sly and shallow. She is delighted when her husband, Cornwall, pulls out Gloucester's eyes (III.vii). Wifely reflex takes over when Cornwall asks for help after the rebellious servant wounds him, and she goes to him at once.

In the opening scene, Cordelia (Brenda Blethyn) strikes the audience as prim and self-satisfied—an unattractive personality altogether. Rejecting her sisters' flattery game, she seems to look around for approval, and she has given no thought to the hurt that this rigid regard for the truth might do her father. When she returns in the last act, her emotions have loosened up.

Gloucester (Norman Rodway) is an image of upright loyalty to his king, and in this production he suffers for it even more than usual. After his eyes are put out (III.vii), he encounters the mad King Lear at Dover, and as they sit talking together the king, in a frantic phase, grasps Gloucester by the beard and even pummels his bleeding, bandaged eyes (IV.vi).

Production History   This *King Lear* was shown on British and American television during the autumn of 1982. The British Broadcasting Company's project of filming the entire Shakespeare canon had then been under way for three years.

Granada Television's *King Lear* (15.6), with Laurence Olivier, was shown in England in early 1983 and in the United States the following year. Viewers thus had a chance to compare two interesting and different productions within a short time.

Reviews and Studies   Bulman, J. C., and Coursen, H. R., eds. *Shakespeare on Television*. 1988. Extracts from reviews of this film, pp. 287–89.

Lusardi, James P., and Schlueter, June. *Reading Shakespeare in Performance: King Lear*. 1991. Compares this film with the Laurence Olivier *King Lear* (15.6).

Rothwell, Kenneth S., and Melzer, Annabelle H. *Shakespeare on Screen*. Item 267, pp. 139–40.

Wilis, Susan. *The BBC Shakespeare Plays*. 1991. Pp. 127–31.

Purchase/Rental Inquiries   Ambrose Video; Filmic Archives; Insight Media; The Writing Company. See Appendix B for addresses.

ᴥ **15.6. *King Lear*.** 1983. Granada Television. Color, 158 min. Producer: David Plowright. Director: Michael Eliott.

KING LEAR	Laurence Olivier
GONERIL	Dorothy Tutin
REGAN	Diana Rigg
CORDELIA	Anna Calder-Marshall
KENT	Colin Blakely
FOOL	John Hurt
EDGAR	David Threlfall
CORNWALL	Jeremy Kemp
ALBANY	Robert Lang
EDMUND	Robert Lindsay
GLOUCESTER	Leo McKern
KING OF FRANCE	Edward Petherbridge
BURGUNDY	Brian Cox
OSWALD	Geoffrey Bateman
LEAR'S KNIGHT	John Cording

Pluses   Distinguished acting by a cast experienced in Shakespeare. Strong narrative flow.

Minuses   Disconcertingly picturesque; the story may seem sugared over.

Textual Cuts and Rearrangements   Some cutting has been done to speed up the pace and, in some cases, to focus attention on the central characters.

The Fool's songs are shortened (I.iv, III.ii, III.vi), in some cases following the First Folio text rather than the early quartos. Edgar loses some of Mad Tom's references to devils (III.vi), as well as several speeches on finding himself assigned to lead his blinded father to Dover (IV.i).

Some familiar lines disappear, among them Albany's fear that humanity will begin to prey upon itself "like monsters of the deep" (IV.ii.49). Other lines are altered. Albany is told of Cornwall's death while Cornwall was "going to put out the eyes of Gloucester," rather than "the other eye of Gloucester" (IV.ii.72), thus losing an intangible degree of horror. Goneril says of Regan's sickness, "If not, I'll ne'er trust poison" rather than the text's "I'll ne'er trust medicine" (V.iii.96), as if the viewer would otherwise miss the point.

The final lines are spoken by Edgar, as in the Folio, rather than by Albany, as in the earlier quartos.

Settings   The film begins and ends in a large-scale studio facsimile of Stonehenge. Here Lear holds his court and divides his kingdom; here the troops of Albany and Edmund defeat Cordelia's army, just landed from France; and here in the final scene the bodies of Lear and Cordelia lie on the altar. Stonehenge would thus seem to have been relocated to the immediate vicinity of Dover.

Much of the action takes place on green, misty hills. In this film, the earth ironically shows herself as kinder than many of her human inhabitants. (The contrast with the bleak and snow-swept landscapes of the Kozintsev and Brook *King Lear*s is an interesting one.) Even the storm seems more of a spring shower. The mad Lear appears quite at home when he takes to the outdoors. He not only festoons himself with flowers (IV.vi) but snares a rabbit, rips it open, and eats some inner part of it appreciatively.

Costumes   A prehistoric period is suggested by the simple lines of the garments, but the concept allows for luxury. Capes are pinned with gold brooches, for example. Colors are pastel but nevertheless vivid, in contrasting tints. All three of the sisters have red hair.

Interpretation of Roles   Olivier plays Lear as an old man whom the audience instantly feels that it knows—the codger next door, one might say. He loves to be flattered. He greets his family and courtiers affectionately, yet insists on a great deal of kneeling and ground-kissing. When Cordelia refuses to join her sisters in hyperbolic praise, he chuckles and twinkles at her; surely she has not understood. Her stubbornness incites an answering stubbornness in him, so that the reader realizes that Lear and his daughters are much alike.

Goneril (Dorothy Tutin) is here the fretful, impatient sister, always in motion, striding up and down as she shouts about the outrages of Lear's hundred knights (I.iv) and, naturally, resembling her father. Being younger, she is able to keep her rages at a higher pitch; Lear tends to get tired. Her attitude toward Edmund is proprietary rather than seductive. Appropriately, she threatens him with "a mistress's command" (VI.ii.21). Toward her husband, Albany, she is energetically scornful.

Diana Rigg's Regan has built her personality upon another of her father's traits, the serene superiority with which both regard the people around them. This Regan has not inherited her father's rages—she never loses her temper—but she has left behind his humanity as well, and his ability to learn (however late) from experience. She watches with a pleased smile as Cornwall pulls out the eyes of Gloucester (III.vii). But when Cornwall is mortally wounded, he ceases to exist as far as Regan is concerned. She ignores his plea for help, walks out of the room without looking at him, and is next seen scheming to marry Edmund.

Anna Calder-Marshall brings to Cordelia's later scenes enormous helpings of love and reconciliation, to such an extent that the play's grimmer messages are almost washed away and even her and Lear's deaths seem immaterial. Some viewers find this effect saccharine, oversimplified, and untrue to the play's more complex intent. Students, however, impatient of bleak worldviews, generally prefer it.

The Fool is played by John Hurt in a manner more withdrawn than abrasive. The storm on the heath seems to do him in. He sits trembling as the others prepare to take King Lear to Dover, and when called to join them does not respond (III.vi). It is the last we see of him.

Colin Blakely's Kent adopts a cheerful, stalwart persona along with his disguise as Caius. When Cornwall has him put in the stocks, he pulls out a flask and offers Gloucester a drink (II.iii). His clean-shaven chin and rougher clothing do make him look different from his earlier self, and he occasionally adds a lower-class slump.

Edgar (David Threlfall) takes off most of his clothes and grimes his face to become Mad Tom, but he does not really change his appearance, and audiences sometimes find it odd that nobody recognizes him. His horror at his father's blinding, and his energy in caring for and revenging him, are very convincing and add, since Edgar is one of the survivors, to the film's upbeat assertion that things will improve.

As the villainous Edmund, Robert Lindsay seems strangely inert. Possibly his character is diluted by the film's pastel color scheme.

Production History Laurence Olivier was 75 when this film was made. For some years his health had not permitted stage work, although he continued to perform in films. *King Lear* marks his last appearance in a Shakespearean role before his death in 1989.

The film was shown on British television in 1983 and in the United States in January of 1983.

Reviews and Studies   Many reviewers of the Olivier *King Lear* have a great deal to say as well about the BBC *King Lear* (15.5), as the two are close in time and present interesting contrasts.

Bulman, J. C., and Coursen, H. R., eds. *Shakespeare on Television*. 1988. Extracts from reviews of this film, pp. 299–303.

Cook, Hardy M. "Two *Lear*s for Television." *Literature/ Film Quarterly* 14 (1986): 179–86. Reprinted in Bulman and Coursen (see above), pp. 122–29.

Lusardi, James P., and Schlueter, June. *Reading Shakespeare in Performance: King Lear*. 1991. Compares this film with the BBC's *King Lear* (15.5).

Rothwell, Kenneth S., and Melzer, Annabelle H. *Shakespeare on Screen*. 1990. Item 271, pp. 140–41.

Urkowitz, Stephen. "Olivier's *Lear*." *Shakespeare on Film Newsletter* 8.1 (1983): 1, 6.

Purchase/Rental Inquiries   Filmic Archives; Films for the Humanities and Sciences; The Writing Company. See Appendix B for addresses.

ɕ 15.7. *King Lear*. 1984. Bard Productions. Color, 182 min. Producer: Jack Nakano. Director: Alan Cooke.

KING LEAR	Mike Kellan
KENT	Darryl Hickman
GLOUCESTER	Charles Aidman
EDMUND	David Groh
EDGAR	Joel Bailey
FOOL	Vincent Caristi
GONERIL	Gela Jacobson
REGAN	Melora Marshall
CORDELIA	Kitty Winn
CORNWALL	Carl Strano
ALBANY	Sam Anderson
OSWALD	Daryl Anderson
KING OF FRANCE	Brian Kerwin
DUKE OF BURGUNDY	Bart Braverman

Pluses   Text is followed closely. Elizabethan staging.

Minuses   Uneven acting quality. Kent and Edmund are particularly wooden.

Textual Cuts and Rearrangements   There is some cutting but not a great deal. Kent does not receive information about an invasion from France (III.i). Transitional passages at the beginning or end of scenes sometimes disappear, among them Edgar's observations on the relativity of suffering (III.vi). The play's closing lines are given to Edgar, in accordance with the First Folio text.

Settings   The studio set consists of an Elizabethan-style stage. Numerous acting areas are connected by changes in level, and a balcony runs across the back of the stage.

Different places are indicated by furniture and props. In the opening scene, Lear and his throne are carried in, something like a Mardi Gras float, and the action then begins. Gloucester's castle is indicated by a lion's-head sculpture.

Costumes   Dress is colorful and expensive-looking; there seems no attempt to depict a primitive historical period. Instead, the costumes connote earthly vanity, a legitimate motif for this play. Lear's courtiers glitter in gold and silver cloaks. Goneril's servants wear color-blocked tunics and look a little like playing cards. Oswald is particularly grand, with a plumed hat. The Fool wears whiteface makeup and a harlequin costume in pink and green.

Interpretation of Roles   Mike Kellan's Lear seems at the beginning neither weak nor senile, but his anger is more irascible than cosmic. As the play progresses his dynamics do not change, and he ends up mumbling his lines and plodding about.

Goneril (Gela Jacobson) and Regan (Melora Marshall) share the trait of being sexually turned on by cruelty. Regan gets the most opportunity for this variety of thrill. She kisses Cornwall passionately when Gloucester is brought in for interrogation; she then plucks out a bit of Gloucester's beard, speaking her lines with difficulty as if in the throes of ecstasy. When Cornwall says to Gloucester, "Upon these eyes of thine I'll set my foot," Regan begins to giggle hysterically. She gets control of herself in time to come to Cornwall's rescue, seizing a battle-ax from the wall and slaying the servant, and she then helps Cornwall offstage in wifely fashion.

David Groh plays Edmund with smiling confidence. He feels certain the gods will stand up for bastards. After he maneuvers Edgar into running away (II.i), he points would-be pursuers in the wrong direction, and the viewer realizes that Edmund naturally doesn't want Edgar caught as he might be able to prove his innocence.

Production History   For other films in the Bard series, all of which use American actors and an Elizabethan style stage, see the general introduction, p. 5.

Reviews and Studies   This film seems to have attracted little critical attention.

Purchase/Rental Inquiries   Crest Video; Filmic Archives. See Appendix B for addresses.

❧ **15.8.** *King Lear.* 1988. Thames Television. Color, 110 min. Producer: Charles Warren. Director: Tony Davenall.*

KING LEAR	Patrick McGee
EDMUND	Patrick Mower
REGAN	Ann Lynn
ALBANY	Philip Brack
GONERIL	Beth Harris
CORDELIA	Wendy Allnutt
EDGAR	Robert Coleby
GLOUCESTER	Ronald Radd
KENT	Ray Smith

Pluses   Useful for comparative scene analysis.

Minuses   To a viewer who knows the play, the textual omissions are frustrating. Viewers coming to the play for the first time may benefit from this film's quick run through the plot but ultimately are being short-changed.

Textual Cuts and Rearrangements   The text is considerably shortened. The play's poetry and its verbal resonance suffers, as do nuances of character and motive. Gloucester acknowledges his paternity of Edmund, for example, but does not elaborate on the circumstances; Regan and Goneril confer briefly after their father banishes Cordelia but do not mention their perception that he had always loved her most (I.i)

The Fool loses many of his songs and jokes (I.iii), and in the storm scene has little to do but cling to Lear's knees and wail (III.iii). Mad Tom's songs and his description of the devils that haunt him are abbreviated (III.vi).

Many of Lear's most effective lines are cut, especially near the end. These include his greeting to Cordelia, "I am a very foolish fond old man" (IV.vii.59ff.)

---

* Note: The credits supplied in this film are incomplete. The film does have a Fool, an Oswald, France, Burgundy, etc. Charles Warren is listed as "executive producer" and Tony Davenall as "producer"; I have translated into the American idiom.

and, later, his description of Cordelia's voice as "ever soft, gentle and low" (V.iii.272).

Edgar's description of the view from atop the cliffs of Dover (IV.vi.ii) is cut, as is his explanation of how he cared for his father (V.iii). Discussions of action occurring elsewhere (armies approaching, letters being sent, etc.) frequently disappear.

Like most present-day productions, this one follows the First Folio text and gives the play's final lines to Edgar rather than to Albany as in the earlier quartos.

Settings   Small-scale studio sets which manage to convey a sense of different places. Interiors are comfortable, with figured carpets and many candles. The last scene takes place on a patch of grass, green and fresh although a battle has presumably just been fought there.

Costumes   Women's dresses have a medieval air, long-waisted with full skirts but no hoops or puffs. Men wear tunics and cloaks.

Interpretation of Roles   Patrick Magee's King Lear speaks so slowly that he can give viewers the impression that Lear has had a stroke. He tends to nod his head rhythmically while talking. When he goes completely mad and wanders about wreathed with green leaves, he is suddenly able to speak more briskly, and his energy level goes up generally.

Goneril and Regan are differentiated by their manner. Goneril (Beth Harris) speaks with rather pompous dignity; Regan (Ann Lynn) tends to twitch and smirk.

Gloucester's blinding (III.vii) takes on immediacy because much of it is seen from Gloucester's point of view. When he loses his second eye—"Out, vile jelly, where is thy lustre now?"—the screen goes momentarily dark.

Both Kent and Edgar remain quite recognizable while in disguise, a circumstance which student audiences find disconcerting.

Production History; Reviews and Studies   This film was made for English television and seems to have received little attention in the United States.

Purchase/Rental Inquiries   Filmic Archives. See Appendix B for address.

16 ❧ LOVE'S LABOR'S LOST _____

❧ 16.1 *Love's Labor's Lost.* 1985. British Broadcasting Company/ Time-Life Television: The Shakespeare Plays. Color, 120 min. Producer: Shaun Sutton. Director: Elijah Moshinsky.

BEROWNE	Mike Gwilym
PRINCESS OF FRANCE	Maureen Lipman
ROSALINE	Jenny Agutter
KING OF NAVARRE	Jonathan Kent
ARMADO	David Warner
MOTH	John Kane
JAQUENETTA	Paddy Navin
MARIA	Katy Behean
KATHERINE	Petra Markham
LONGAVILLE	Christopher Blake
DUMAIN	Geoffrey Burridge
BOYET	Clifford Rose
COSTARD	Paul Jesson
DULL	Frank Williams
NATHANIEL	John Burgess
HOLOFERNES	John Wells

Pluses   Pleasant mood throughout.

Minuses   Static tableaux; slow pace. The film, though amiable, is not very funny.

Textual Cuts and Rearrangements   Cuts are frequent, although the continuity of the plot is not harmed. Among the casualties is one of the play's most quoted lines, Armado's "Sweet smoke of rhetoric!" (III.i.63), a puzzling excision since the context is retained.

Especially at the beginning of the film, some scenes are shuffled about. On Navarre's mention of Don Armado (I.i.161), we zip forward to the next scene to observe this character for a few minutes; we then return to Navarre and his friends, and pick up the remainder of scene two after the matter of Costard's flirtation with Jaquenetta has been dealt with.

Settings   Much of the action takes place in Navarre's library, a pleasant Georgian interior, light and spacious and very tidy, decorated with globes and rococo inkstands. This is a reasonable site for the opening scene, in which Navarre and his friends vow to devote themselves to books and forswear the company of women. Don Armado's study is contrastingly cluttered, crammed with books, bundles of paper, and musical instruments.

Exteriors are indicated by rather vaguely painted backdrops. The princess of France and her ladies seat themselves on some sort of masonry floor which we assume, from the dialogue, to be the gateway of Navarre's estate (II.i). Out hunting, they again seat themselves, this time on a wall (IV.i), with what seems the silhouette of a tree on the backdrop.

Costumes   The characters wear eighteenth century dress, hardly reminiscent of Shakespeare's day but perhaps in keeping with a mood of verbose leisure.

In the opening scene, Navarre and his friends appear in powdered periwigs and pastel coats and breeches, with lace cravats and cuffs. Later, having vowed a life of scholarship, they wear black, with touches of white, and their own hair. Still later, on rejecting scholarship in favor of love, they resume the pastel colors, though not the periwigs.

The princess of France and her ladies are in flowing silks, with low necklines, pointed waists, and panniers.

Interpretation of Roles   Berowne, the most articulate of Navarre's friends and indeed the leading character, is played by Mike Gwilym with an appropriate edge of self-mockery. The scene in which his three friends have confessed themselves in love and he has taunted them, only to have his own love revealed (IV.iii), is one of the liveliest in the film. Unfortunately the scene is staged in a way that frustrates student audiences with their preference for common sense. The characters successively hide in various parts of the library, where they remain in plain view of the audience and of one another, so that the viewer is distracted from the fun by the strenuous effort required to suspend disbelief.

The princess of France (Maureen Lipman) displays beauty, poise, intelligence, and, in the "Nine Worthies" pageant of the last act, a tact and humanity that far surpasses that of Navarre and his jeering courtiers. On hearing that her father has died—an announcement that changes the tone of the play's final moments—she makes a convincing shift from gaiety to responsibility, leading her ladies as they tell their would-be lovers to defer their suits for a year and a day.

Rosaline (Jenny Agutter), Berowne's beloved, seems a rather pensive personality. The other two ladies do not develop as individuals, perhaps because many of their lines have been cut.

David Warner plays Armado with great flourish, posing, bragging, contending with Holofernes and his other pedantic rivals. His change of heart at the end, doing right by Jaquenetta after he has made her pregnant, seems plausible in that Warner's Armado is clearly unpredictable.

Jaquenetta (Paddy Navin) is not played as a trollop. While she is humbly born and intellectually unable to respond to Armado's witticisms, she dresses quietly and holds herself with dignity.

John Kane plays Moth, Armado's page. This casting is puzzling, since Kane is decidedly an adult, larger than Armado in fact, and not a precocious youth. The jokes about Moth as a "tender juvenile" (I.ii.8) are nevertheless not cut. Kane also persists in playing the infant Hercules in the "Nine Worthies" pageant, coming on stage on his knees so as to be short enough.

Production History   *Love's Labor's Lost* was next to last of the British Broadcasting Company's five-year project of filming all of Shakespeare's plays. It was shown on British television in January and on American television in May of 1985.

Reviews and Studies   Bulman, J. C., and Coursen, H. R., eds. *Shakespeare on Television.* 1988. Extracts from reviews of this film, pp. 312–13.

Maher, Mary Z. "Moshinsky's *Love's Labor's Lost.*" *Shakespeare on Film Newsletter* 10.1 (1985): 2–3.

Rothwell, Kenneth S., and Melzer, Annabelle H. *Shakespeare on Screen.* 1990. Item 283, p. 146.

Teague, Frances. "The Shakespeare Plays on TV: *Love's Labor's Lost.*" *Shakespeare on Film Newsletter* 10.1 (1983): 1–2.

Purchase/Rental Inquiries   Ambrose Video; Filmic Archives; Insight Media; The Writing Company. See Appendix B for addresses.

17 ❧ MACBETH*_____

❧ **17.1. *Macbeth*.** 1948. Republic Pictures and Mercury Films. Black-and-white, 89 min. Producer: Orson Welles. Director: Orson Welles.

MACBETH	Orson Welles
LADY MACBETH	Jeanette Nolan
MALCOLM	Roddy McDowell
BANQUO	Edgar Barrier
MACDUFF	Dan O'Herlihy
HOLY FATHER	Alan Napier
LADY MACDUFF	Peggy Webber
DUNCAN	Erskine Sanford
ROSS	John Dierkes
LENNOX	Keene Curtis
SIWARD	Lionel Braham
YOUNG SIWARD	Archie Heugly
FLEANCE	Jerry Farber
MACDUFF CHILD	Christopher Welles
SEYTON	George Chirello

Pluses   An innovative and interesting film, much discussed in the context of Welles's other work.

Minuses   For a student audience focusing on Shakespeare's *Macbeth*, this film can obscure more than it enlightens.

Textual Cuts and Rearrangements   Welles scarcely leaves one stone upon another. All is taken apart and reassembled. Quite a lot of the text is left out altogether, although the basic structure of the plot remains.

Chief among the novelties is a character named the Holy Father, in long braids and priestly garb, who leads religious services and speaks the lines of various of Macbeth's thanes, particularly Ross. In the final battle he is speared by Macbeth.

By comparison to the Holy Father, Welles's other departures from the text are less baffling. Macduff, for example, is reported as having fled to England before the murder of Banquo, rather than afterward. Macbeth personally supervises the

---

* Note: For films related to Shakespeare's *Macbeth*, see Appendix A, "Analogues and Variations."

113

murder of Lady Macduff and her children, who appear to live in Macbeth's castle, or perhaps next door.

Settings   Macbeth's castle is essentially a jumble of cliffs and rocks, with occasional tunnels for corridors. Outdoors, the landscape is mostly misted over.

The settings are large enough for numerous crowd scenes. Duncan has a large army, including riders on hardy little horses. Macbeth's banquet (III.v) is crowded with extra thanes.

Costumes   Mostly medieval. Macbeth wears a plaid, sometimes adding a fur cape. Banquo and other soldiers go in for helmets with sweeping horns. Women at the court wear long-waisted gowns and draped headdresses.

Interpretation of Roles   Welles glowers and roars and drinks. Student audiences often react with laughter to his portentous acting style; he recoils with bugged-out eyes, for example, from the ghost of Banquo (III.v). His voice, sometimes magical, tends to fade in and out of an imperfect soundtrack, and his words are thickened with a put-on Scots accent.

Jeanette Nolan's Lady Macbeth also speaks with a burr. Often she seems to be reciting her lines automatically, but her sleepwalking scene is compelling (V.i). She changes tone, sounding helpless one moment and coldly authoritative the next. As she tries to get her imaginary Macbeth to bed, she bumps into the real one, who kisses her; she wakes up, recognizes him, screams, and runs off. Shortly afterward we see her climbing to the top of a cliff, apparently wide awake. Then she leaps into a chasm.

The witches begin the film by taking from their cauldron a lump of clay and modeling it into a small human figure—Macbeth, as it turns out, in the power of his evil fate. When at the end Macduff decapitates Macbeth, it is the clay figure whose head we see falling off.

Production History   Welles shot *Macbeth* in less than four weeks, making ingenious use of a small budget. Much of the sound was later re-recorded. Like much of Welles's work, *Macbeth* has found more favor with film critics than with the public.

Reviews and Studies   Davies, Anthony. *Filming Shakespeare's Plays.* 1988. Pp. 83–99, 192–93.

Jorgens, Jack J. *Shakespeare on Film.* 1977. Pp. 148–60, 179–82, 322–23.

Manvell, Roger. *Shakespeare and the Film.* 1971. Pp. 55–61.

Rothwell, Kenneth S., and Melzer, Annabelle H. *Shakespeare on Screen.* 1990. Item 297, pp. 150–51.

Purchase/Rental Inquiries   NTA Home Entertainment. See Appendix B for
address.

&⁊ 17.2. *Macbeth*. 1954. Hallmark Hall of Fame. NBC Television. Black and
white, 103 min. Producer: George Schaefer. Director: George Schaefer.

MACBETH	Maurice Evans
LADY MACBETH	Judith Anderson
MACDUFF	Richard Waring
BANQUO	Staats Cotsworth
MALCOLM	Roger Hamilton
DONALDBAIN	Peter Fernandez
DUNCAN	House Jameson
FLEANCE	John Reese
LADY MACDUFF	Margot Stevenson
ROSS	Guy Sorel

Pluses   A famous acting pair in famous roles.

Minuses   Students accustomed to today's younger and more intimate and emotional Macbeths may react negatively to these dignified elders.

Textual Cuts and Rearrangements   The play has been shortened considerably.
Macbeth's second visit to the witches (IV.i) has been turned into a dream in which
it is hard to tell what is happening. Numerous passages not immediately relevant
to the action have disappeared. Lady Macbeth dies in her bed; Malcolm's reference
to the "fiendlike queen" who "by self and violent hands/ Took off her life"
(V.ix.35) is omitted.

Setting   The television studio becomes a surprisingly solid castle, with a courtyard and many arched doorways.

Costumes   Dress is not elaborate—capes and tunics, with touches of plaid.
Soldiers wear studded belts and breastplates.

Interpretation of Roles   Judith Anderson plays Lady Macbeth with stately
grandeur. She is not a vulnerable personality. In planning the murder of Duncan,
she seems personally quite capable of the night's great business (I.v.68). The
irony of this interpretation is effective in the sleepwalking scene, when, even

though she is sobbing, she still manages to sound as if she thinks she is in control.

Maurice Evans is more flustered, more outwardly wracked with guilt. When Macduff goes to waken Duncan, and Macbeth knows that the body will be discovered and that he must pretend to be surprised, a close-up shows him trying to control his rising panic (II.iii). Throughout the film he gives the impression that he prefers action, even if bloody and ultimately unsuccessful, to being alone with his thoughts.

Production History   Hallmark Greeting Cards sponsored numerous high-quality dramatic programs. (See *Hamlet*, 7.5.) This one aired on November 28, 1954.

Reviews and Studies   Bulman, J. C., and Coursen, H. R., eds. *Shakespeare on Television*. 1988. Extracts from reviews of this film, p. 240.

Coursen, H. R. "The Schaefer 1954 *Macbeth* Revisited." *Shakespeare on Film Newsletter* 14.1 (1989): 7, 12.

Griffin, Alice. "Shakespeare Through the Camera Eye, 1953–54." *Shakespeare Quarterly* 6 (1955): 65–66.

Rothwell, Kenneth S., and Melzer, Annabelle H. *Shakespeare on Screen*. 1990. Item 305, pp. 143–45.

Purchase/Rental Inquiries   The Writing Company. See Appendix B for address.

ੀ 17.3. *Macbeth*. 1970. British television. Color, 137 min.

Produced by Cedric Messina and directed by John Gorrie, with Eric Porter (Macbeth), Janet Suzman (Lady Macbeth), John Thaw (Banquo), John Woodvine (Macduff).

This production was shown on British television in 1970 and in the United States in 1975. It is not part of the BBC series "The Shakespeare Plays," which filmed the Shakepeare canon between 1978 and 1985, although there is some overlap in personnel.

At present this film is not available.

❧ 17.4. *Macbeth.* 1971. Columbia Pictures. Color, 140 min. Producer: Hugh Hefner. Director: Roman Polanski.

MACBETH	Jon Finch
LADY MACBETH	Francesca Annis
ROSS	John Stride
BANQUO	Martin Shaw
FIRST WITCH	Elsie Taylor
YOUNG WITCH	Noelle Rimmington
BLIND WITCH	Maisie MacFarquhar
DUNCAN	Nicholas Selby
MALCOLM	Stephan Chase
DONALBAIN	Paul Shelley
MACDUFF	Terence Baylor
SEYTON	Noel Davis
LADY MACDUFF	Diane Fletcher
LENNOX	Andrew Laurence
FLEANCE	Keith Chegwin
MACDUFF'S SON	Mark Dightam
PORTER	Sydney Bromley
DOCTOR	Richard Pearson

Pluses   Intense, absorbing, and fast-paced.

Minuses   Students can become so thoroughly imprinted with this film that they resist the thought of other interpretations or even of other actors.

Textual Cuts and Rearrangements   The text is set into a visual context of swift, often bloody action, where cruelty is taken for granted. In the opening scene, robbers plunder the dead left on the battlefield, bashing any who still stir. Men who supported the losing side are hanged, in wholesale lots. The thane of Cawdor's execution for treason takes place on camera.

The text is considerably shortened. The Porter admits Macduff and Lennox efficiently, with only a sample of devil-portering as a prelude (II.iii). Ross converses with Macduff after the murder of Duncan, but not with the mysterious "old man" (II.iv). Many passages are thinned, often removing descriptions and complex metaphors.

Textual rearrangements include Lady Macbeth's "The raven himself is hoarse," spoken not immediately after she reads Macbeth's letter about the witches' prophecy (I.v) but as she watches Duncan's arrival under her battlements, in the following scene. Numerous events are re-ordered. The Doctor's report to Macbeth on

Lady Macbeth's "thick-coming fancies" (V.iii.36) is followed by the conversation between Malcolm and Macduff (IV.iii)—a briefer conversation than in the text, since Malcolm's testing of Macduff (by pretending to be an unfit ruler) is cut.

In the final battle, numerous lines are cut, including Siward's insistence that his son died well if his wounds were on the front (V.ix.13). Macduff brings Macbeth's severed head to the new king Malcolm, as in the text's stage directions. This is not the end of the story, however. Polanski adds a sequel on his own. We see a familiar green hillside—the cave where Macbeth met with the witches. Donalbain, Malcolm's younger brother, rides into view, ties his horse, and disappears. The cycle of evil would seem to be starting over again.

Settings   The Macbeths change castles as they rise in the social scale. Inverness, their starter castle, is essentially a stockade, filled with livestock—chickens, squealing pigs, a pack of wolfhounds. Dunsinane is large and impersonal, with echoing, stony chambers and high ramparts.

Outdoors, Scotland is seen in lush, big-screen grandeur.

Costumes   Clothes are simple but do not make a point of being shaggy or primitive. Many are graceful—Lady Macbeth's flowing blue gown, for example.

Several scenes are memorable, if not notorious, because of the actors' lack of costumes. Lady Macbeth's sleepwalking scene, in which she walks about nude (V.i), occasioned some outcry when the film was released. The witches also go in for nudity. When Macbeth pays his second visit (IV..i), he finds not just the three witches of the text but a roomful, clad scantily if at all.

Interpretation of Roles   Jon Finch plays a youthful, clean-cut Macbeth. He does not look like a battle-scarred warrior. His intensity makes him nevertheless a believable figure, a successful general as the film begins and an obsessed murderer as it continues.

Francesca Annis, also young and beautiful, looks entirely like the innocent flower; nothing in her appearance makes one suspect the serpent. Evil thus becomes all the more horrifying. As Macbeth's power grows, hers seems to diminish, and by the end she is isolated. Even in death she is neglected. Having leapt or fallen into the castle courtyard, she lies on the pavement, where Macbeth's soldiers hurry past her as they desert to the enemy. Someone tosses a blanket over her body, but hastily, and her legs and bare feet stick out, pale and helpless.

Ross, who in Shakespeare's text is one of a number of almost interchangeable thanes, in this film acquires a special function. Played by John Stride with a sunny and charming smile, Ross becomes one of Macbeth's devoted henchmen. He is the mysterious third murderer when Banquo is killed (III.iii), later shoving the other two murderers into a pit. After his visit to Macduff's castle (IV.ii), he leaves the gate open and signals to the waiting soldiers that the coast is clear for the destruction of Macduff's family. Ross abandons Macbeth's cause only when a promotion he wanted goes to Seyton instead. Ross then joins Malcolm in England (IV.iii), looking as trustworthy as ever.

Production History   Polanski made this film shortly after his wife, actress Sharon Tate, was murdered by members of the Charles Manson gang in 1969. There has been considerable conjecture about possible links between this event and the film's violence and bloodshed.

Macbeth did very well at the box office.

Reviews and Studies   Berlin, Normand. "*Macbeth*: Polanski and Shakespeare." *Literature/ Film Quarterly* 1 (1973): 190–98.

Jorgens, Jack J. *Shakespeare on Film.* 1977. Pp. 161–74, 286–90, 323–24.

Leaming, Barbara. *Polanski: A Biography.* 1981. Pp. 116–33.

Polanski, Roman. *Roman by Polanski.* 1984. Pp. 331–41.

Rothwell, Kenneth S., and Melzer, Annabelle H. *Shakespeare on Screen.* 1990. Item 324, pp. 161–62.

Wexman, Virginia Wright. *Roman Polanski.* 1985. Pp. 78–88.

Purchase/Rental Inquiries   The Writing Company. See Appendix B for address.

≈ 17.5. *Macbeth*. 1979. Thames Television. Color, 120 min. Producer: Trevor Nunn. Director: Trevor Nunn (stage); Philip Casson (television).*

MACBETH	Ian McKellen
LADY MACBETH	Judi Dench
MACDUFF	Bob Peck
MALCOLM	Roger Rees
BANQUO	John Woodvine
FIRST WITCH	Marie Kean
SECOND WITCH	Judith Harte
THIRD WITCH	Susan Drury
LADY MACDUFF	Susan Drury
DUNCAN	Griffith Jones
DONALBAIN	Greg Hicks

* Note: This production should not be confused with a later Thames Television film of *Macbeth*, 1988 (17.9).

SEYTON	Greg Hicks
DAVID HOWEY	Doctor
FLEANCE	Zak Taylor
ROSS	Ian McDiarmud
PORTER	Ian McDiarmuc
MACDUFF CHILD	Stephen Warner
LENNOX	John Bowen

Pluses   Excellent acting; subjective, intimate approach.

Minuses   The camera is so constantly in the actors' faces that all sense of spatial context is lost and the audience can feel claustrophobically hemmed in. This effect can of course be seen as intentional, and as one of the strengths of the production.

Textual Cuts and Rearrangements   The text is followed closely. There are a few exceptions. Ross has his conversation with the Old Man (II.iv), but the details of the horses' breaking from their stalls is omitted. Hecate's exchange with the witches, generally considered a spurious passage anyhow, is cut (III.v).

Even Malcolm's description of the English king's miraculous curing power, usually omitted, is here retained (IV.iii.140–59).

Setting   The film begins with the actors sitting in a circle, where in fact they remain throughout the action, watching each scene whether or not they happen to be taking part in it. Because of the constant close-ups, however, the audience tends to forget they are there. (This was not the case in the stage production on which the film is based. The audience was constantly aware of the circle of watchers, and a sense of ritual, according to reviewers, became overwhelming.)

There are no sets as such. Occasionally, as in Macbeth's banquet (III.iv), the camera draws back and the circle of actors creates the impression of a room. At other times, when the action is outdoors, isolated figures walk through a mist.

Costumes   Modern dress, with a few exceptions. Macbeth wears a black leather jacket, black leather gloves (pulled on or off at dramatic moments), and slicked-back hair. Lady Macbeth, in a black gown, has her head tied in a scarf that makes her look disturbingly as if she plans to wash the windows. Most of the Scottish thanes wear black turtleneck sweaters, but occasionally one glimpses an Edwardian suit.

The cloth-of-gold robe which Macbeth wears when he is crowned becomes a kind of security blanket which he clutches when he feels threatened. It is the giant's robe that dwarfs its wearer (V.ii.21). Another symbol is the pair of puppet-like heads on a stick, part scepter and part jester's bauble, given Macbeth by the witches.

Interpretation of Roles   Ian McKellan and Judi Dench draw the audience into the minds and hearts of the Macbeths, a horrifying but electrifying experience.

Kneeling to invoke the evil spirits (I.v), Lady Macbeth is suddenly terrified of what she has begun, and has to force herself to continue. But the spirits do their work. After planning the death of Duncan, Lady Macbeth is then able to comfort Donalbain when he learns of it, tenderly stroking his cheek, while her undaunted hypocrisy makes the audience gasp.

When her husband sees Banquo's ghost, this Lady Macbeth's horror seems to indicate either that she sees it too, or that she knows what he must be seeing (II.iv). But later, isolated, she weeps bitterly in her sleepwalking scene (V.i).

Ian McKellan's possession by evil turns him into an automaton, and his agony is that he seems aware of the shift. From an intimacy with his wife so close that he will murder rather than lose rapport with her mind or her body (I.v), he comes to inhabit his golden coronation robe as a kind of shell, and although he tries to look at other people he does not seem actually to see them.

Many parts are doubled, sometimes with puzzling results. Ian McDiarmud plays a particularly timid Ross and also appears as the brash Porter (II.iii), but the change of makeup and costume makes confusion unlikely. Young Fleance (Zak Taylor), however, reappears after his escape, this time as a messenger who tells Macbeth that Birnam Wood is indeed coming to Dunsinane. The audience wonders if this is an hallucination of Macbeth's, when those he has tried to kill somehow return and mock him. Again, when we see David Howey as the doctor who watches over Lady Macbeth and pronounces pious sentiments (V.i and iii), the aura of evil intensifies more than may have been meant, as Howey has earlier played one of Banquo's murderers.

Production History   The 1976 Royal Shakespeare Company stage production on which this film is based won considerable acclaim. The film was shown on British television in 1979.

Reviews and Studies   Bulman, J. C., and Coursen, H. R., eds. *Shakespeare on Television*. 1988. Extracts from reviews of this film, pp. 248–49.

Mullin, Michael. "Stage and Screen: The Trevor Nunn *Macbeth*." In Bulman and Coursen, cited above, pp. 107–15.

Perret, Marion D. "Double, Double: Trevor Nunn's *Macbeth* for Television." *Shakespeare Bulletin* 10.3 (1992): 38–39.

Rothwell, Kenneth S., and Melzer, Annabelle H. *Shakespeare on Screen*. 1990. Item 322, p. 165.

Purchase/ Rental Inquiries   Films for the Humanities and Sciences. See Appendix B for address.

❧ **17.6. *Macbeth*.** 1981. Bard Productions. Color, 150 min. Producer: Jack Nakano. Director: Arthur Alan Seidelman.

MACBETH	Jeremy Brett
LADY MACBETH	Piper Laurie
MACDUFF	Simon MacCorkindale
MALCOLM	Richard Alfieri
BANQUO	Barry Primus
LADY MACDUFF	Mille Perkins
DUNCAN	Alan Oppenheimer
LENNOX	Franklyn Scales
PORTER	Jay Robinson
ROSS	Brad David Stockton
SEYTON	Johnny Crawford
DOCTOR	Alan Mandell
FLEANCE	Douglas Kaback
DONALBAIN	Michael Augenstein
MACDUFF CHILD	Elliott Jaffe

Pluses   Individual scenes are useful to show in class, to serve as a contrast to the same scene as done in other films or by the students.

Minuses   Supposedly dramatic effects become grotesque. The film is hard to watch all the way through, or for any length of time.

Textual Cuts and Rearrangements   Not extensive. A startling cut occurs when Macduff gets word of his family's murder (IV.iii). The first 160 lines of the scene are gone, and we don't know where we are (in England) or what is happening (Macduff is begging Malcolm to lead an army against Macbeth).

Settings   All the action takes place on an Elizabethan-style stage with several playing areas, stairways, and other aids to versatility.

Costumes   Macabeth wears a shaggy animal fur over his tunic and tights. Lady Macbeth, in blonde curls, favors low necklines. The large number of witches, some of them male, are in gossamer drapery, beclouded with dry ice.

Interpretation of Roles   Jeremy Brett's Macbeth tends to bounce around and to stand on the throne for his soliloquies (III.i). After he has been king for awhile, he loses his energy and discusses Lady Macbeth's illness with the doctor while lying prone on a couch (V.ii).

Piper Laurie plays Lady Macbeth with frequent fits of giggles. Of a voluptuous figure, her request that the evil spirits unsex her is not entirely convincing (I.v). The murder of Duncan puts her into peals of laughter, and at the sight of Macbeth's bloody hands she starts purring and pawing at him (II.ii). Her sleepwalking scene involves laughter as well; she kneels, chuckling, and flicks her fingers in her imaginary basin of water (V.i).

The horde of witches (really only six, but they fill the screen) materializes frequently to watch the action and writhe about on the floor. Macbeth loses his final fight to Macduff partly because he has two witches hanging onto his legs (V.viii).

Production History   Bard Productions, in association with the Shakespeare Video Society, uses American actors and a studio set designed as an Elizabethan stage. Bard videos have been shown on cable television. For other films in the series, see the general introduction, p. 5.

Reviews and Studies   Coursen, H. R., and Schleuter, June. *"Macbeth* on Television: Is the Bard Version Usable?" *Shakespeare on Film Newsletter* 13.1 (1988): 4, 8.

Purchase/Rental Inquiries.   Filmic Archives. See Appendix B for address.

🎞 **17.7. *Macbeth.*** 1982. Lincoln Center for the Performing Arts. Color, 148 min. Producer: Raymond Crinkley. Director: Sarah Caldwell.

MACBETH	Philip Anglim
LADY MACBETH	Maureen Anderman
ROSS	James Hurdle
MACDUFF	J. Kenneth Campbell
BANQUO	Fritz Sperberg
DUNCAN	Neil Vipond
LADY MACDUFF	Kaiulani Lee
MALCOLM	John Vickery
DONALBAIN	Eugene Pressman
PORTER	Roy Stevens

FLEANCE   William Morrison

SEYTON   Jarlath Conroy

Pluses   A filmed stage performance that uses a single set with ingenuity.

Minuses   Uneven acting quality, frequent slow pace.

Textual Cuts and Rearrangements   Cuts are not extensive. Most of the Porter's soliloquy is cut (II.iii). Hecate does not appear (III.v), nor does Malcolm explain the English king's curative powers (IV.iii). The list of ingredients for the witches' brew (IV.i) is shortened.

Setting   The stage is usually bare, though furniture is brought on and off. The witches have a pile of rocks. A catwalk across the back of the stage forms an upper level, frequently used.

The audience at Lincoln Center appears from time to time in the long shots.

Costumes   Colorful, more or less medieval but not specifically Scottish or primitive. Two of the witches wear full-skirted eighteenth-century dresses, with curly wigs; the third, black and masculine, is dressed for armed combat. Lady Macbeth appears in slender, regal gowns of red or black. Soldiers wear tunics, cloaks, high boots.

Interpretation of Roles   Philip Anglim plays Macbeth in a dazed and ponderous manner, frequently rolling his eyes. In some scenes this approach works well. He clearly expects Duncan to name him as heir to the throne (I.iv), and does a double-take when the winner turns out to be Malcolm. He seems paralyzed by the sight of Banquo's ghost, a chalky apparition on the upper catwalk (III.iv), and comes to another complete halt during his final fight with Macduff. Macbeth has beaten his opponent to the floor and presumably would have killed him had not Macduff explained why he, Macduff, is not of woman born (V.viii), whereupon Macbeth's gears freeze.

Maureen Anderman's Lady Macbeth is petite, intense, and focused in all her movements—quite different from Macbeth, whom she complements. She knows what she is doing, and the bloody consequences do not seem to surprise her. Even in her sleepwalking scene she is precise, washing her hands with brisk intensity (V.i). Her death is not shown onstage, but Malcolm's lines about her taking her life "with self and violent hands" (V.ix) are retained.

Production History   The stage version was presented at Lincoln Center for the Performing Arts, New York City, in 1981. This film was shown on cable television the following year.

Reviews and Studies   Bulman, J. C., and Coursen, H. R. *Shakespeare on Television*. 1988. Extracts from reviews of this film, pp. 274–76.

Charney, Maurice. "Shakespeare in NYC." *Shakespeare Quarterly* 33 (1982): 222.

Rothwell, Kenneth S., and Melzer, Annabelle H. *Shakespeare on Screen*. 1990. Item 333, p. 166.

Purchase/Rental Inquiries   Films for the Humanities and Sciences. See Appendix B for address.

🎬 **17.8. *Macbeth*.** 1982. British Broadcasting Company/ Time-Life Television: The Shakespeare Plays. Color, 150 min. Producer: Shaun Sutton. Director: Jack Gold.

MACBETH	Nicol Williamson
LADY MACBETH	Jane Lapotaire
BANQUO	Ian Hogg
DUNCAN	Mark Dignam
FIRST WITCH	Brenda Bruce
SECOND WITCH	Eileen Way
THIRD WITCH	Anne Dyson
MACDUFF	Tony Doyle
ROSS	Gawn Grainger
LADY MACDUFF	Jill Baker
SEYTON	Eamon Boland
LENNOX	John Rowe
FLEANCE	Alistair Henderson
MACDUFF CHILD	C. Mair
DOCTOR	John Woodnutt
PORTER	James Bolam

Pluses   An energetic production with almost the full text and with interesting, three-dimensional interpretations of many of the characters.

Minuses   Nicol Williamson's agonized and often incoherent Macbeth can elicit a negative response. However, students who have seen Williamson play a psychopathic killer in the film *Consenting Adults* transfer this personality to Macbeth, simplifying Shakespeare's play but increasing, for some reason, their own enjoyment.

Textual Cuts and Rearrangements   The few cuts are fairly standard ones. We do not have Hecate (III.v) or Malcolm's commendation of the English king's curative powers (IV.iii.139–58). A shuffle in the sequence of scenes (III.vi here follows IV.i) allows the audience to find out about Macduff's flight to England at the same time that Macbeth does. Some of the brief scenes during the final fight in Macbeth's castle have been rearranged, with a few lines cut. Macduff neither mentions "the usurper's cursed head" (V.ix.21) nor displays it.

Settings   Exteriors depend largely on mist and anonymous rolling terrain. The witches have apparently taken over a prehistoric stone monument, a dolmen, a horizonal slab supported on smaller stones. Interior scenes are configured with simple rectangular shapes which form various rooms and courtyards, often with a short flight of stairs to make entrances more dramatic.

Costumes   Costumes have a medieval air but do not call attention to themselves. Soldiers wear leather with metal studs. Lady Macbeth's long-waisted gown is snugly fitted through the torso, revealing her lithe silhouette.

Interpretation of Roles   Nicol Williamson played Macbeth in several earlier stage productions and here seems to have devoted himself to a search for previously unknown readings. Many of his lines are unintelligible—he squeaks, hisses, and moans, with much trembling and gasping. The audience is distanced rather than drawn in. The audience feels even more left out when Macbeth's emotion seems to have an invisible source, one that we are not privileged to see. The "airborne dagger" (II.ii), Banquo's ghost (III.iv), and the apparitions of the witches' prophecies (IV.i) are in this production seen only by Macbeth.

Jane Lapotaire plays Lady Macbeth with some curious twists, but for most viewers she remains plausible and interesting. On receiving Macbeth's letter about the witches' prophecy she flings herself on a fur-covered bed and writhes sexily about, kneading her woman's breasts while praying for the evil spirits to exchange their milk for gall (I.v.49). But she cannot overcome her fear of the evil she has invoked. She trembles as she pushes Macbeth through the murder of Duncan (II.ii); in trying to excuse to their guests her husband's behavior at the banquet, we hear desperation in her voice (III.iv). In her sleepwalking scene she smells her hand and cries out in agony (V.i). Her death takes place offstage, the film supplying no clues to the manner of it other than Malcolm's lines implying suicide (V.ix.36).

Minor roles in this production are carefully thought out and well acted. Lennox (John Rowe), one of the thanes, leaps so enthusiastically to the support of Macbeth in accusing Duncan's servants of the murder (II.iii.101) that the viewer assumes Lennox must suspect Macbeth and is trying to camouflage his thoughts until he can switch loyalties more safely. Lennox's later actions bear out this hypothesis. He abandons Macbeth only when it is clear that Malcolm's forces have gained strength, and even then he prudently pledges only so much of his lifeblood as will be needed for the cause (V.ii.29).

Seyton, Macbeth's confidential servant (Eamon Boland), is called by name during the last part of the play, but is here built up earlier. We see him spying on the conversation between Ross and Macduff (II.iv), and Macbeth says, "Seyton, a word with you" (III.i.44), instead of "Sirrah, a word with you." Seyton is the third murderer; after Banquo has been killed, he briskly stabs the other two (IV.ii). He then leads the attack on Macduff's wife and children, a scene of spine-chilling savagery in which the young son is tossed from one to another of the murderers and finally lands, skewered, on Seyton's sword.

Production History *Macbeth* was telecast in England and America in the autumn of 1983, part of the BBC's project of filming the entire Shakespeare canon.

Reviews and Comments Bulman, J. C., and Coursen, H. R., eds. *Shakespeare on Television.* Extracts from reviews of this film, pp. 296–99.

Mullin, Michael. "The BBC *Macbeth.*" *Shakespeare on Film Newsletter* 9.1 (1984): 2.

Rothwell, Kenneth S., and Melzer, Annabelle H. *Shakespeare on Film.* 1990. Item 336, p. 167.

Purchase/Rental Inquiries Ambrose Video; Filmic Archives; Insight Media; The Writing Company. See Appendix B for addresses.

ᶜ⃝ 17.9. *Macbeth.* 1988. Thames Television. Color, 110 min. Producer: Charles Warren. Director: Charles Warren.*

MACBETH	Michael Jayston
LADY MACBETH	Barbara Leigh Hunt
MACDUFF	Gary Watson
MALCOLM	David Weston
LENNOX	Brian Badcoe
ROSS	Tim Hardy
SEYTON	Frederick Pyne
DOCTOR	Jack Lynn

* Note: This film should not be confused with an earlier Thames Television production of *Macbeth*, made in 1979 and based on Trevor Nunn's stage version with the Royal Shakespeare Company (17.5).

Pluses   A capably acted, unpretentious *Macbeth*.

Minuses   Subdued, low-budget style may make some viewers restless.

Textual Cuts and Rearrangements   Cuts are infrequent and minor. The role of the bloody sergeant is cut, and Duncan gets the war news directly from Ross (I.ii). Banquo is dispatched by two murderers only, so we do not have the puzzle of wondering who the third one might be (III.iii). As usual in stage and film productions, there is no Hecate (III.v) and no mention of the English king as a healer (IV.iii).

Settings   The studio sets include rather perfunctory outdoor scenes, craggy rocks and withered trees, and small-scale interiors. Castles resemble log palisades.

Costumes   Capes, fur, and leather. The witches are in mummy-like rags. Lady Macbeth is partial to blue.

Interpretation of Roles   As Macbeth, Michael Jayston tends to be withdrawn and stern. In some of the opening scenes he stands so far from the other characters that the camera has to travel to find him. Toward the end he occasionally breaks into bitter laughter—his reaction, for example, upon hearing of Lady Macbeth's death (V.v). His head is eventually brought onstage at the end of a spear, still looking remote.

Barbara Leigh Hunt's Lady Macbeth has a careworn, fragile face with large eyes. She trembles as she urges the murder of Duncan (II.vii) and is devastated when Macbeth, on becoming king, immediately begins to drift away from her. She joins him after his conversation with Banquo, only to have his remark about wishing to keep "till supper time alone" addressed directly to her (III.i.44). Her sleepwalking scene is absorbing (V.i). We hear the voices she has used throughout the play—snarling one moment, whispering in childlike tones the next, and then an abrupt shift into a smiling false face (V.i).

Production History; Reviews and Studies   This film deserves to be better known.

Purchase/Rental Inquiries   HBO Video; The Writing Company. See Appendix B for addresses.

18 ♣ MEASURE FOR MEASURE _____

♣ 18.1. *Measure for Meassure*. 1979. British Broadcasting Company/ Time-Life Television: The Shakespeare Plays. Color, 150 min. Producer: Cedric Messina. Director: Desmond Davis.

DUKE OF VIENNA	Kenneth Colley
ISABELLA	Kate Nelligan
ANGELO	Tim Piggott-Smith
POMPEY	Frank Middlemass
CLAUDIO	Christopher Strauli
JULIET	Yolande Palfrey
LUCIO	John McEnery
MARIANA	Jacqueline Pearce
PROVOST	Alan Armstrong
ESCALUS	Kevin Stoney
MISTRESS OVERDONE	Adrienne Corri
BARNADINE	William Sleigh
ELBOW	Ellis Jones
FROTH	John Clegg
ABHORSON	Neil McCarthy

Pluses   A lucid interpretation of a play dealing with, among other timely topics, sexual exploitation.

Minuses   *Measure for Measure* is usually categorized among Shakespeare's "problem comedies." Consequently a film that is faithful to the text will disappoint viewers assuming that any comedy is going to be amusing in the usual way.

Textual Cuts and Rearrangements   Lines at the beginning or end of scenes occasionally disappear, and some passages are thinned of elaborate metaphor or seeming repetition.

Settings   The film begins and ends with a painted view of a medieval walled city bristling with towers. But the interior of the duke's palace, where we find ourselves as the action begins, is in a different style, with marble floors and neoclassical pilasters. Since there is nothing historical about the story, and Shake-

129

speare apparently placed it in Vienna only because this seemed an exotic locale, consistent architectural style is hardly a major matter.

A clear, pale light falls on many of the settings. The nunnery which Isabella is in the process of entering (I.iv) is a place of pale colors and simple, tranquil shapes. Light streams through high windows into Angelo's presence chamber, where he struggles to govern Vienna and to subdue the lust in his heart (II.ii). In the prison, by contrast, sunlight is replaced by candles, and strange shadows jump about as the candles sputter. The brothel of Mistress Overdone is similarly murky.

Costumes   Dress is sedate in color though elaborate in workmanship. The time is the early seventeenth century, approximately. Men wear cloaks, doublets, small lace collars, trunk hose, and stockings, and discuss affairs of state as if they were posing for a group portrait by Rembrandt.

Isabella wears her novice's habit throughout the film. The duke, disguised as Friar Lodovick, wears a brown Franciscan robe, but as he does not pull up the hood he remains perfectly recognizable.

Interpretation of Roles   Kate Nelligan has the perfect face for Isabella—clear eyed, high-cheekboned, the embodiment of moral principle. She is thus able to make convincing a dilemma which present-day students may at first have trouble grasping. If all she has to do to save her brother's life is sleep with Angelo, students think when they begin the play, why on earth doesn't she do it? The moral and personal objections become apparent slowly, but they do become apparent. The presence in the play of Angelo's discarded fiancée, eager to serve as Isabella's substitute under cover of darkness, may seem to short-circuit the debate although it does move the plot along.

As Angelo, Tim Piggott-Smith manages to convey both an intense spiritual struggle and a smooth-faced hypocrisy once he has yielded to his desire. "Who will believe thee, Isabel?" he asks when she threatens to expose him—his tone not angry but simply matter-of-fact (II.iv.153). His descent into villainy is so swift that it comes as no real surprise when he reneges on his promise and orders Claudio's execution anyhow.

Claudio (Christopher Strauli) makes his unavoidably wishy-washy role seem human. He tries to be noble and say the right thing, but it's his life. Juliet (Yolande Palfrey) makes more appearances than is the case in some productions, accompanying Claudio to prison (I.ii), quite pregnant, then turning up in the final scene holding a wailing bundle.

Mariana (Jacqueline Pearce) must persuade the viewer that she really is in love with the cold, hypocritical man who has earlier rejected her, and she succeeds surprisingly well. Her gaze as she looks at Angelo is tolerant, affectionate, yet realistic; she knows what her situation is and she chooses it nevertheless, pleading urgently for Angelo's life and even persuading Isabella to join her. (Isabella's acquiescence shows how far she has come from the high-principled absolutist of her early scenes.) This film suggests that Mariana's future, married to a man who becomes her husband only on the duke's order, may not be so bad after all. She has saved his life, and he is (or wants to be) a man of principle. As she starts to rise from her knees after making her successful plea, Angelo extends his hand to help her.

Kenneth Colley's strangely non-authoritative portrayal of the duke may be appropriate, since it was his laxity that allowed Vienna to get so out of hand to begin with. The audience tends to feel, however, that he does not have a clear game plan for his disguised return. His sudden proposal to Isabella, six lines from the end of the play, is disconcerting as he has shown no real signs of falling in love with her; he has stared at her a good deal, but he stares at everybody. Isabella in this production does choose to accept him, or so the audience assumes. She waits for a long moment, thinking it over, and then takes his hand.

Production History   *Measure for Measure* was produced in the first year of the British Broadcasting Company's five-year project of filming all of Shakespeare's plays. It was shown on British and American television in the spring of 1980, to considerable critical praise.

Reviews and Studies   Bulman, J. C., and Coursen, H. R., eds. *Shakespeare on Television*. 1988. Extracts from reviews of this production, p. 255.

Carr, Virginia. "The Shakespeare Plays." *Shakespeare on Film Newsletter* 4.1 (1979): 4.

Coursen, H. R. "Why *Measure for Measure?*" *Literature/Film Quarterly* 12 (1984): 65–69. Reprinted in Bulman and Coursen, cited above, pp. 179–84.

Rothwell, Kenneth S., and Melzer, Annabelle H. *Shakespeare on Screen*. 1990. Item 350, p. 173.

Willson, Robert F., Jr. "The BBC-TV *Measure for Measure* and Television Aesthetics." *Bulletin of the New York Shakespeare Society* 4.6 (1986): 23–25.

Purchase/Rental Inquiries   Ambrose Video; Filmic Archives; Insight Video; The Writing Company. See Appendix B for addresses.

19 ❧ THE MERCHANT OF VENICE*___

❧ 19.1. *The Merchant of Venice.* 1969. Precision Video. Color, 120 min.
Producer: Cecil Clarke. Director: Jonathan Miller.

SHYLOCK	Laurence Olivier
PORTIA	Joan Plowright
BASSANIO	Jeremy Brett
ANTONIO	Anthony Nicholls
GRATIANO	Michael Jayston
NERISSA	Anna Carteret
JESSICA	Louise Purnell
SALERIO	Barry James
SOLANIO	Michael Tudor Barnes
LORENZO	Malcolm Reid
ARRAGON	Charles Kay
MOROCCO	Stephen Greif
DUKE OF VENICE	Benjamin Whitrow
TUBAL	Kenneth Mackintosh
GOBBO	Denis Lawson
STEPHANO	Peter Rocca
BALTHASAR	John Joyce

Pluses   An energetic, skilled performance by Laurence Olivier. Shylock is interpreted as both strong and loving, in his own way.

Minuses   The actors look much alike, moustachioed gentlemen in somber garb.

Textual Cuts and Rearrangements   The role of Jessica, Shylock's daughter, is shortened and simplified. Jessica's elopement with Lorenzo takes place off camera; we do not see her leave Shylock's house (II.vi), although the event is discussed. She loses her lighthearted joking with the servant Launcelot Gobbo (III.v), and her other lines are frequently cut or thinned.

Early scenes at Belmont, when Portia's suitors are making their choice of the

---

* Note: For films related to Shakespeare's *Merchant of Venice*, see Appendix A, "Analogues and Variations."

gold, silver, and lead caskets (II.i, II.vii, and II.ix) are here run together, not alternated with events in Venice.

Launcelot Gobbo also has his part shortened. Cuts include Launcelot's practical joke on his father, old Gobbo (II.2), but as present-day audiences do not find this scene very funny, the loss is small.

Settings   It should be acknowledged that some students dislike the transplanting of Shakespeare's plays to any setting outside the Renaissance. The shift seems to them confusing or unnecessary, or both, and class discussion on this point can be useful. Objectors need to know that their view is valid and that they are not in the wrong; as with so many things Shakespearean, preferences vary and flexibility is the key. In this case, the late-Victorian/Edwardian age with its desperate insistence on order and permanence seems appropriate for *The Merchant of Venice*. It is through the characters' professed dependence on law and precedent, after all, that Portia is able to save Antonio.

Sets are solidly designed and crowded with novelty. Portia examines her suitors' pictures in a stereoscopic viewer. Lampshades are fringed, windows are draped. Inobtrusive servants hover.

The courtroom is in this film a small space, more like a hearing chamber, with a long table running down the middle. Portia sits across from Shylock and explains in conversational tones, not elocutionary ones, that "the quality of mercy is not strained" (IV.i.184).

Belmont is a substantial mansion, equipped with a pillared facade and sweeping lawns. The final scene, which in Shakespeare's text takes place at night, is here played in broad daylight. References to moonlight and the approach of dawn are not cut.

Costumes   Men wear tall silk hats, or, if younger and/or of slightly lower status, derbies. Waistcoats are much hung about with watch chains.

Shylock is well dressed in dark, expensive fabrics, with a skullcap over which his silk hat fits neatly.

Women wear bustles and trains. Neriessa is in a high-necked gray silk. Portia generally goes in for lower necklines and more frills. Returning from a ride with Bassanio, however, she wears a severe black riding habit.

Portia and Nerissa adopt academic gowns and hair-covering headgear for their appearance in court. In this disguise they look different from their usual selves, but, according to skeptical students, not different enough.

Interpretation of Roles   Laurence Olivier, in his early sixties when the film was made, plays Shylock as a strong, intelligent, and yet emotional man, of considerable dignity. He has no intention of truckling to his Christian enemies.

During his "hath not a Jew eyes" speech (III .i.59ff.), Salerio and Solanio draw back in fear.

This Shylock finds Jessica's elopement heartbreaking. Thanks to a textual cut (II.viii), the audience does not hear a description of Shylock's immediate reaction to the news, in which he seems to mourn equally the loss of his daughter and his ducats. Instead, we see him looking at a photograph of Jessica, in an ornate silver frame, clutching it to his bosom as he tells his friend Tubal of the efforts he has made to find her. Then, in a sudden fury, he dashes the photograph to the floor. A moment later, a memory of his late wife, Leah (III.i.121), sends him, weeping, to another framed photograph.

Shylock's decision to hold Antonio to his bond is in this film made a direct result of Jessica's desertion. Shylock now sees all Christians as in league to rob and mock him. In line with this interpretation, the earlier scene in which the bond is set up is played as a "merry sport," as Shylock claims (I.iii.145). He is, at the time, simply in a generous mood.

As Portia, Joan Plowright conveys warmth, but a warmth carefully meted out according to circumstance. In the courtroom, once Shylock has declined her invitation to show mercy, she traps him with swift efficiency and listens unmoved to his wail of anguish as he leaves the room.

Jeremy Brett gets about all that can be expected from the role of Bassanio, an essentially unremarkable young man. In this film he benefits from his contrast with Portia's previous suitors. The prince of Morocco (Stephen Greif) is the epitome of pomposity, while the prince of Arragon (Charles Kay) teeters on the brink of senility.

Jessica, played by Louise Purnell, has had her role simplified as well as shortened. Her story becomes a cautionary tale: Daughters should not abandon their fathers. Arriving at Belmont (III.ii), she hangs back from the group, so self-effacing that Portia has trouble remembering her name. Her costume shows no evidence of her alleged shopping spree in Genoa (III.i.109). Her husband, Lorenzo, seems fond of her and tries to cheer her up (V.i), but Jessica remains immersed in gloom. At the end of the film, the others enter the house and she is left standing alone. Suddenly we hear the Kaddish, the Jewish mourning prayer, sung as the credits begin to roll.

Production History　The film is based on a stage production at the National Theatre, London, in 1968. It was shown on British television in 1969 and in the United States in 1974.

Reviews and Studies　Bulman, J. C., and Coursen, H. R., eds. *Shakespeare on Television*. 1988. Extracts from reviews of this film, pp. 244–45.

Rothwell, Kenneth S., and Melzer, Annabelle H. *Shakespeare on Screen.* 1990. Item 367, pp. 180–81.

Schlueter, June. "Trivial Pursuit: The Casket Plot in the Miller/Olivier *Merchant.*" In Bulman and Coursen, cited above, pp. 169–74.

Purchase/Rental Inquiries   Viewfinders, Inc. See Appendix B for address.

❧ 19.2. *The Merchant of Venice.* 1980. British Broadcasting Company/ Time-Life Television: The Shakespeare Plays. Color, 160 min. Producer: Jonathan Miller. Director: Jack Gold.

SHYLOCK	Warren Mitchell
PORTIA	Gemma Jones
NERISSA	Susan Jameson
JESSICA	Leslee Udwin
ANTONIO	John Franklyn-Robbins
BASSANIO	John Nettles
GRATIANO	Kenneth Cranham
LORENZO	Richard Morant
SALERIO	John Rhys-Davies
SOLANIO	Alan David
PRINCE OF MOROCCO	Marc Zuber
PRINCE OF ARRAGON	Peter Gale
LAUNCELOT GOBBO	Enn Reital
TUBAL	Arnold Diamond
OLD GOBBO	Joe Gladwin
DUKE OF VENICE	Douglas Wilmer

Pluses   An interesting, well-acted, and visually harmonious film.

Minuses   Any choice an actor makes for the portrayal of Shylock will annoy proponents of other possible choices. Consequently, Warren Mitchell's gentle and ingratiating figure has its dispraisers.

Textual Cuts and Rearrangements   Cutting is functional and generally pain-less. Dialogue is thinned of elaborate and/or repetitive images, and scenes occasionally lost their introductory lines.

Settings   Studio sets, for the most part stylized. Venetian exteriors become a series of round archways and low flights of stairs, obviously made of plywood, red-brown in color. The picture-postcard details one associates with Venice are absent, though occasionally the plywood shows rippling watery reflections and thus suggests the presence of a canal just off-camera.

Portia's Belmont shifts to a more romantic mode. Here we find blue misty air, a gazebo with classical columns, and a special room set up to display the three caskets, each on its pedestal and about the size of a cake box. (It may be worth mentioning that American students seem convinced that the word *casket* can only mean a coffin, with or without a body inside, and some discussion of this point is useful when dealing with this scene, especially as one of these caskets happens to contain a skull.)

Costumes   Unlike the stylized sets, costumes are realistic and lavishly detailed, late sixteenth century in feeling. Most are quite colorful. The young men of Venice wear clothes that are puffed and slashed and brocaded. Shylock's garments are humbler, but not ragged.

At Belmont, Portia enjoys several changes of sumptuous costume. She is after all a lady richly left. Her judge's robes, and Nerissa's clerkly ones, are not a very effective disguise despite hats that cover their hair. Bassanio's and Gratiano's failure to recognize their newly wedded wives must be met with a strong suspension of disbelief.

Interpretation of Roles   Warren Mitchell's Shylock displays stereotyped Jewish mannerisms, over-gesturing, pushing his face within inches of the person he is talking to (Antonio, while arranging the fatal loan, ends up leaning backward so far that the viewer expects him to fall over), and smiling in a self-deprecating manner. But we come to understand why he does it. His "Hath not a Jew eyes" speech (III.i) takes place while Salerio and Solanio are tickling him, enjoying their superiority and the fact that they have forced Shylock to pretend to be amused at what is actually a kind of torture. On Shylock's "Shall we not revenge," however, the laughter stops.

Shylock as a victim of oppression so wins the audience's sympathy that it is a jolt, in the courtroom scene, to watch him take his knife, flick aside the cross hanging on Antonio's bare chest, and judiciously choose his spot. This mild person, like the story he is in, becomes more complex than we may have thought. Sympathy swings back to Shylock when he is defeated by Portia's ingenuity and when certain of the Christians cannot stop rubbing it in. On Portia's "Down, therefore, and beg mercy" (IV.i.363), Gratiano throws Shylock to the floor and holds a knife on him; when Antonio demands that Shylock convert to Christianity, Salerio puts a cross around Shylock's neck and forces him to kiss it.

Shylock's daughter Jessica (Leslee Udwin) treats Shylock quite as badly as the Christians do, if not worse, and student audiences are divided in their opinion of

her. On the one hand, Shylock has kept her at home and refused to let her join
the merrymaking of Venice (II.v), and after her elopement he seems as distressed
to have lost his ducats as his daughter (II.viii). On the other hand, perhaps he
does not deserve quite the punishment she gives him. Udwin sneers at Shylock
behind his back, at one point mouthing the words she knows he will say next—
"Fast bind, fast find" (II.v.54). She steals his money and jewels with no com-
punction at all. After she and Lorenzo have run away to Genoa and are living
high, she sells the turquoise given Shylock by Shylock's late wife and her own
mother, to buy a monkey (III.i.121). Students sometimes cite as evidence of
Jessica's irresponsible nature that, in this film at least, she turns up at Belmont
without any monkey.

Gemma Jones, with crisp diction and fragile, Botticelli-like beauty, plays
Portia as a person accustomed to a life of privilege. When news arrives at Belmont
of Antonio's troubles and Portia asks the amount of the debt, Bassanio is scarcely
able to choke out the sum—three thousand ducats. Portia is amazed that this is
all. Later, giving her "mercy" speech in the courtroom, Portia is icily and paradoxically dictatorial. She does not, as some Portias do, attempt a comradely appeal to Shylock's better nature.

Portia gives herself and her wealth to Bassanio (III.ii.149) with a flourish
which the audience understands to be rhetorical. One cannot imagine this Portia
dropping the reins. As Bassanio seems to be a young man in need of direction,
perhaps the match is a fortunate one.

Production History   *The Merchant of Venice* was shown on British and American
television in 1981, as the British Broadcasting Company undertook its third
season of filming the Shakespeare canon. The film evoked some debate as to
whether it was or was not anti-Semitic. Defenders of the film pointed out that
the producer, the director, the actor playing Shylock, and the actress playing
Jessica were all Jewish.

Reviews and Studies   Bulman, J. C., and Coursen, H. R., eds. *Shakespeare on
Television*. 1988. Extracts from reviews of this film, pp. 268–70.

Hallinan, Tim. "Miller on 'The Shakespeare Plays.' " *Shakespeare Quarterly* 32
(1981): 141–42.

Rothwell, Kenneth S., and Melzer, Annabelle H. *Shakespeare on Screen*. 1990.
Item 370, pp. 181–82.

Rothwell, Kenneth S. "The Shakespeare Plays." *Shakespeare Quarterly* 32
(1981): 398.

Purchase/Rental Inquiries   Ambrose Video; Filmic Archives; Insight Media;
The Writing Company. See Appendix B for addresses.

20 ❧ THE MERRY WIVES OF WINDSOR*⎯⎯⎯⎯⎯⎯⎯⎯⎯⎯

❧ 20.1. *The Merry Wives of Windsor.* 1981. Bard Productions. Color, 160 min. Producer: R. Thad Taylor. Director: Jack Manning.

MISTRESS PAGE	Gloria Grahame
SIR JOHN FALSTAFF	Leon Charles
MISTRESS FORD	Valerie Seelie Snyder
FORD	Lyle Stephen
PAGE	Bert Hinchman
MISTRESS QUICKLY	Dixie Neyland Tymitz
DOCTOR CAIUS	Joel Asher
JUSTICE SHALLOW	Philp Persons
SLENDER	Eugene Brezany
SIMPLE	Richie Levene
SIR HUGH EVANS	Richard Cordery
PISTOL	Lee Fishel
BARDOLPH	Lanny Broyles
NYM	Paul Aron Scott
ANNE PAGE	Lisa Barnes
FENTON	Addison Randall
ROBIN	Lucinda Dooling
HOST OF THE GARTER INN	William Nye
RUGBY	David Stifel

Pluses A colorful slapstick presentation.

Minuses Very few.

Textual Cuts and Rearrangements Dialogue is frequently pruned of jokes that have lost their appeal (or intellibility) for a present-day audience. Some of the plot's perplexing loose ends have been snipped off—for example, the undeveloped complications about visiting Germans and stolen horses (IV.iii). In acts four and five, the sequence of events with regard to inviting Falstaff to a rendez-

---

* Note: For films related to Shakespeare's *Merry Wives of Windsor*, see Appendix A, "Analogues and Variations."

vous at Herne's Oak has been rearranged. Young William Page's lesson in Latin (IV.i), not essential to the plot but charming as a picture of Elizabethan life, is omitted in this production.

The film is introduced by John Houseman, a producer long interested in Shakespeare. Houseman sketches the play's plot and mentions the legend that it was written at the request of Queen Elizabeth I, who wanted to see Falstaff in love. (Alert students may notice that Shakespeare has not exactly complied with this request, as *Merry Wives* shows Falstaff trying to get women to fall in love with him while he himself remains heart-whole.) Houseman also gives a brief farewell at the end of the film.

Settings   A bare thrust stage of Elizabethan design, with stairs, an upper level, and numerous exits and entrances, some of them doorways of the housefronts comprising the village of Windsor. The stage is a studio set only; there is no live audience.

Costumes   Brightly colored Renaissance costumes—full skirted gowns for women, doublets and trunk hose for men, with ruffs at the collars. Hats have elaborate plumes. Sir Hugh Evans, parson and schoolmaster, wears a black gown and carries a stack of books.

Ford's disguise is reasonably convincing, depending on a false moustache and huge cartwheel ruff. The revelers at Herne's Oak wear carnival-type half-masks, and Falstaff's antlers are clearly artificial and seem in danger of falling off.

Interpretation of Roles   Leon Charles's Falstaff is at the heart of this production and seems to be having a wonderful time. His misadventures do not permanently dismay him. Visiting Mistress Ford, he sits down on her embroidery, needle and all. On being thrown into the river along with the dirty laundry, he takes shelter, sneezing, at the Garter Inn, where a bevy of barmaids fetch a tub for him to soak his feet in. He bursts into song—"Hey nonny no"—during any pause in the action. At the end, it is clear that he can take a joke, especially as the fairies have not pinched him very hard, and he happily accepts Mistress Page's invitation to "laugh this sport o'er by a country fire" (V.v.242).

Gloria Grahame, as Mistress Page, projects convincing merriment and speaks her prose passages with facility. In verse lines, she becomes strangely slow and wooden.

Students occasionally need reassuring that, in Shakespeare's day, "Mistress" was a style of address used for married as well as unmarried women. Today's connotations of the word can make the family relationships in this play somewhat strange.

Mistress Quickly, an unmarried "Mistress" as it happens, is played by Dixie

Nyland Tymitz. Red-haired and buxom, she romps through her part, exchanging pinches with Falstaff and occasionally pouring herself a drink from his bottle. Her physical, slapstick approach to the play is in line with that of most of the other actors, who bump into one another, make faces, and occasionally speak in unison.

Anne Page (Lisa Barnes) seems more amused than annoyed by her miscellaneous collection of suitors. She delights Slender by pretending to be frightened at his mention of bears (I.i.287). When her successful suitor, Fenton, confesses that he was first attracted by her wealth, she flares into anger but is quickly pacified (III.iv).

Production History   The Bard series of videotapes uses American actors on an Elizabethan-style stage, with period costumes. Some of the films have been shown on cable television. For other titles in the series, see the general introduction, p. 5.

Reviews and Comments   Bulman, J. C., and Coursen, H. R., eds. *Shakespeare on Television*. 1988. Extracts from reviews on this film, p. 270.

Purchase/Rental Inquiries   Crest Video; Filmic Archives; The Writing Company. See Appendix B for addresses.

≥ **20.2.** *The Merry Wives of Windsor*. 1982. British Broadcasting Company/ Time-Life Television: The Shakespeare Plays. Color, 150 min. Producer: Shaun Sutton. Director: David Jones.

FALSTAFF	Richard Griffiths
FORD	Ben Kingsley
MISTRESS QUICKLY	Elizabeth Spriggs
MISTRESS FORD	Judy Davis
MISTRESS PAGE	Prunella Scales
PAGE	Brian Marshall
ANNE PAGE	Miranda Foster
WILLIAM PAGE	Crispin Mair
DOCTOR CAIUS	Michael Bryant
HOST OF THE GARTER INN	Michael Graham Cox Inn
SIR HUGH EVANS	Tenniel Evans
BARDOLPH	Gordon Gostelow
PISTOL	Nigel Terry

NYM	Michael Robbins
ROBIN	Lee Whitlock
SIMPLE	Ron Cook
RUGBY	John Joyce

Pluses   Mellow, pleasant, and visually winning.

Minuses   Occasional slow pace.

Textual Cuts and Rearrangements   Cuts are minimal. A few metaphors, classical allusions, and jokes disappear, as do Mistress Quickly's references to the Order of the Garter in her speech as the fairy queen (V.v.66ff.). In act four, scene three precedes scenes one and two, thus juxtaposing two of Falstaff's otherwise separate appearances. Mistress Page's observation that "wives can be merry and yet honest, too" (IV.ii.105) is moved from its usual place to the end of act three, scene three.

Settings   The set is a charming reconstruction of a Tudor village. Houses and rooms are based on several actual structures with Shakespearean associations, preserved in and around Stratford upon Avon. We have black-and-white exteriors, polished wood interiors, hand-hewn beams, small-paned windows, and heavy, carved furniture.

The village does not look like the real Windsor, which is hillier, and apparently aims instead at re-creating Shakespeare's Warwickshire memories.

Herne's Oak and the adjacent woods have a romantically misty, bosky quality.

Costumes   Elizabethan garments include farthingale skirts, laced bodices, embroidered doublets, and trunks with padding and slashes. Most of the characters are of the well-off middle class and dress accordingly. Mistress Page wears an unobtrusive white cap while Mistress Ford, a shade more *nouveau* and less secure, has a jaunty hat with a green plume.

The fairies in the "Herne's Oak" scene wear gauzy draperies and cone hats that remind American viewers of the Ku Klux Klan, presumably an unintended effect. Mistress Quickly's fairy-queen costume appropriately suggests Queen Elizabeth I. The stag's head worn by Falstaff is meant to seem a real one, although his face shows beneath it.

Interpretation of Roles   Richard Griffith's Falstaff raises two questions in student audiences. Why is he so gloomy, when the text suggests a jollier mood? And what is the relationship between this Falstaff and the charcter in the "Prince Hal" plays (the two parts of *Henry IV* and, in a retrospective way, *Henry V*)?

The second question, which has absorbed much scholarly ink over the centuries and which will not be solved in this paragraph, is particularly perplexing for students who have seen the BBC films of the relevant plays. Bardolph is played by Gordon Gostelow, who took the part in all three "Prince Hal" plays. But this *Merry Wives* gives us new actors for Falstaff, Mistress Quickly, Nym, Pistol, and Shallow. Mistress Quickly is particularly puzzling as she seems never to have met this crew before and there is no mention of the Boar's Head in Eastcheap. Students come up with various solutions. Occasionally they decide all this must have happened not during or after the crew becomes involved with Prince Hal, but before they do. Mistress Quickly at this point, they suggest, just happened to be living in Windsor as housekeeper to Dr. Caius.

The first problem mentioned above, Falstaff's gloom, might become explicable in the light of this film's apparent preference for quiet nostalgia. Viewers tend to feel that a little more fun would not be amiss, just the same.

As Mistress Quickly, Elizabeth Spriggs has a way of speaking ordinary lines with an air of weighty significance, insinuating behind-the-scenes knowledge and making her listeners (both in the film and in the audience) feel part of a privileged in-group.

The two wives, Mistress Page (Prunella Scales) and Mistress Ford (Judy Davis), enjoy a cheery friendship despite, or perhaps because of, their differences. Mistress Page is older, with a mellow, hospitable husband and two children; Mistress Ford's household consists only of her super-jealous husband. Mistress Page is easygoing, Mistress Ford a bit jumpy. Once Falstaff makes the mistake of beginning his career as a gigolo by sending both the wives identical love letters, they cooperate in thinking up ways to embarrass him.

Ben Kingsley (known to many students for his title role in *Ghandi*) acts the maniacally jealous Ford. Kingsley literally adds action to the plot, as he is constantly running.

Production History   *The Merry Wives of Windsor* was shown in Britain in December of 1982 and in the United States in January of 1983. It was part of the British Broadcasting Company's 37-play series of all Shakespeare's plays.

Reviews and Studies   Bulman, J. C., and Coursen, H. R., eds. *Shakespeare on Television*. 1988. Extracts from reviews of this film, pp. 290–92.

Roberts, Jean Addison. *"The Merry Wives of Windsor." Shakespeare on Film Newsletter* 7.2 (1983): 5.

Rothwell, Kenneth S., and Melzer, Annabelle H. *Shakespeare on Film*. 1990. Item 385, pp. 187–88.

Willis, Susan. *The BBC Shakespeare Plays*. 1991. Pp. 192–94.

Purchase/Rental Inquiries   Ambrose Video; Filmic Archives; Insight Media; The Writing Company. See Appendix B for addresses.

21 ❧ A MIDSUMMER NIGHT'S DREAM*

❧ 21.1. *A Midsummer Night's Dream.* 1935. Black-and-white, 132 min. Producer: Max Reinhardt. Directors: Max Reinhardt, William Dieterle.

PUCK	Mickey Rooney
BOTTOM	James Cagney
HERMIA	Olivia De Havilland
HELENA	Jean Muir
LYSANDER	Dick Powell
FLUTE	Joe E. Brown
THESEUS	Ian Hunter
OBERON	Victor Jory
TITANIA	Anita Louise
INDIAN BOY	Kenneth Anger
DEMETRIUS	Ross Alexander
QUINCE	Frank McHugh
HIPPOLYTA	Verree Teasdale
SNUG	Dewey Robinson
STOUT	Hugh Herbert
STARVELING	Otis Harlan

Pluses   An imaginative, briskly paced film, flooded with Mendelssohn's music.

Minuses   Poetic images are made visual, sometimes with confusing results for students focused on the plot.

Textual Cuts and Rearrangements   This film has numerous cuts, some of them apparently intended to simplify the action. There is no royal hunting party in IV.i, for example, during which the newly sorted-out lovers are found in the forest. The lovers simply awaken and join Theseus' and Hippolyta's wedding procession as it gets under way.

Other cuts purge the film of details a 1930s audience might have found unacceptable. Oberon and Titania, for example, do not accuse each other of extramarital affairs with Hippolyta and Theseus, respectively (II.i).

---

* Note: For films related to Shakespeare's *Midsummer Night's Dream*, see Appendix A, "Analogues and Variations."

The text has also been given some visual additions. When Puck plans to turn himself into a hound, a hog, a fire (III.i), we then see him doing so, although the hound is a German shepherd. Ballet numbers (a tradition in stage productions of this play) include a sequence in which the powers of night, dressed more or less as bats, contend with the white-clad powers of day.

Settings   Theseus is given not only a gorgeous palace but an entire seaport, into which he sails, armor-clad, in the film's opening scene. He has just won his victory over the Amazons. Lysander and Demetrius are among the returning Athenian warriors on the deck, both eager for a glimpse of Hermia as she stands with the crowd, everyone singing away, on the shore.

In the forest, magic takes over, with mists and unicorns. Fairies fly about in twinkling spirals. Arthur Rackham, a British artist whose illustrations of *A Midsummer Night's Dream* have been popular since their first appearance in 1908, may have influenced the gnarled trees and the goblin orchestra scattered among the beech roots (II.i).

Costumes   Dress fits the fantasy atmosphere. Titania's gown is hung with silvery threads, suggesting raindrops. The little Indian boy, the bone of contention between Titania and Oberon, is dressed like a miniature rajah, complete with plumed turban. Oberon's dark cloak billows behind him. The four lovers wear elegant courtly garments which somehow escape harm from the woodland brambles. The ass's head which Bottom finds himself wearing is solid and furry, hiding his face.

Interpretation of Roles   Mickey Rooney's Puck steals the show. He speaks his lines awkwardly, often laughing in a forced and artificial manner. But his body language and facial expressions do the job. He sparkles and bounces. He trots his pony along the forest lanes, climbs trees, imitates the lovers in all their woe, and cavorts in sheer zest for life. Rooney was in his early teens when this film was made. Student audiences remember him as a middle-aged horse trainer in *The Black Stallion* (1979) and as Elizabeth Taylor's friend in reruns of *National Velvet* (1944).

James Cagney, known for his gangster roles, plays a self-confident Bottom, as accustomed to rule in his sphere as Oberon and Theseus in theirs, who is only momentarily perturbed to find himself "translated" into an ass.

Titania (Anita Louise) is all blonde demureness, not overtly sexy; she lulls Bottom to sleep on her lap with no hint of further recreations.

The little Indian boy (Kenneth Anger) weeps piteously when Titania ignores him for Bottom, but on being immediately snatched up by Oberon (an action which in Shakespeare's text occurs later, and offstage), he is comforted. He is afterward seen riding with Oberon on Oberon's horse and wearing a version of

Oberon's crown, a twiggy Art Nouveau affair, enjoying his new life and missing Titania not at all.

Helena (Jean Muir) does not play her part for laughs and is simply woeful in her unrequited love for Demetrius. Hermia (Olivia De Havilland) is contrastingly brunette and fiery. Dick Powell and Ross Alexander are starry-eyed in love, even when they love the wrong person. Hippolyta, Theseus' captive Amazon bride, appears rather sulky at first but cheers up as the play progresses and laughs with the others when Bottom and his friends act "Pyramus and Thisby" as a wedding entertainment.

Until the last few minutes, when the courtly audience most discourteously sneaks away and robs the workingmen of their applause, the last act is a delight. Much of the humor of "Pyramus and Thisby" consists of stage mishaps and ingenious cover-ups. Pyramus is not quite sure which is his left side, "where heart doth hop," but works it out eventually. Peter Quince has to prompt often and audibly. Moon's little dog picks a fight with Lion. Comedian Joe E. Brown, as a deadpan Thisby, dances ludicrously onstage and is only temporarily flustered when, after some confusion in handing props about, he finds himself armed with two swords instead of one.

Production History   Despite its big-name cast and extravagant mounting, Reinhardt's film was a disappointment at the box office of the 1930s. It has found more appreciative audiences since.

Reviews and Studies   Collick, John. *Shakespeare, Cinema, and Society.* 1989. Pp. 87–93.

Jorgens, Jack J. *Shakespeare on Film.* 1977. Pp. 36–65, 252–58, 315–16.

Rothwell, Kenneth S., and Melzer, Annabelle H. *Shakespeare on Screen.* 1990. Item 392, pp. 190–91.

Watts, Richard, Jr. "Films of a Moonstruck World." In Charles W. Eckert, ed., *Focus on Shakespearean Films.* 1972. Pp. 47–52.

Purchase/Rental Inquiries.   This film is not available at the moment.

ᴥ **21.2.** *A Midsummer Night's Dream.* 1964. Rediffusion Network Productions. Color, but available in black-and-white. 111 min. Producer: Rediffusion. Director: Joan Kemp-Welch.

BOTTOM	Benny Hill
THESEUS	Patrick Allen
HELENA	Jill Bennett

LYSANDER	John Fraser
DEMETRIUS	Clifford Elkin
HIPPOLYTA	Eira Heath
EGEUS	Cyril Luckham
PHILOSTRATE	Tony Bateman
TITANIA	Anna Massey
OBERON	Peter Wyngarde
PUCK	Tony Tanner
QUINCE	Miles Milleson
FLUTE	Alfie Bass
SNUG	Arthur Hewlett
STARVELING	Bill Shine
SNOUT	Bernard Besslaw

Pluses   A cheerful and unpretentious production.

Minuses   Very few, if the audience does not require dazzling special effects.

Textual Cuts and Rearrangements   Cuts tend to come in slivers rather than chunks. The object seems to be to retain the gist of the plot. Cuts sometimes sacrifice laughs; when Flute, hoping for a macho role, asks, "What is Thisby, a wandering knight?" (I.ii), he is here allowed to say only, "What is Thisby?" Other cuts take out nuances of personality. Theseus' tactful though possibly ambiguous excuse when the lovers are found asleep in the woods, "No doubt they rose up early to observe the rite of May" (IV.i), is among the casualties.

Settings   Although this is a studio production, the sets are neither cramped nor inadequate. Theseus' palace includes a broad lawn for the wedding guests to dance over. The forest has a papier-mâché effect but seems sufficiently mysterious and magical. Titles are sometimes used to explain settings, e.g, "The Cottage of Quince the Carpenter" (I.ii).

Costumes   Ancient Greece is evoked with togas and long, pleated gowns, but the costumes have a 1960s air, stylish and dry-cleaned. Bottom's ass's head is charming, with big eyes and an innocent look. Like Reinhardt's 1935 version, this film includes a bevy of traditionally dressed ballet dancers, performing to Mendelssohn's music.

Interpretation of Roles   John Fraser and Clifford Elkin, in the often unrewarding roles of Lysander and Demetrius, stand out because of their youthful optimism and naïveté, bounding through the woods with an energy that student audiences find immediately sympathetic. Hermia and Helena are opposites in looks (small and dark versus tall and blonde, as Shakespeare's text suggests). Their quarrel scene is a spirited one (III.ii).

Benny Hill as Bottom barges confidently along, unperturbed by events, delivering his lines with impeccable comic timing.

The little Indian boy is here about ten years old and thus presents a problem. Are we meant to assume that Titania and Oberon have been quarreling ever since he was an infant? Or has Titania only recently got round to stealing him?

Hippolyta is here an enthusiastic bride, not at all a reluctant captive. The film's opening scene finds her and Theseus alone on a sofa, murmuring about their approaching marriage and somewhat annoyed to be interrupted by Egeus and his disobedient daughter.

In act five, the courtly audience's jibes at the workingmen who are attempting quite competently to entertain them strike a sour note with present-day viewers. The carping lines are indeed in the text, and it is clear that at least some of them are heard by the players, but the result seems discourteous nonetheless.

Production History   This film was shown on British television in the summer of 1964.

Reviews and Studies   Rothwell, Kenneth S., and Melzer, Annabelle H. *Shakespeare on Screen*. 1990. Item 404, pp. 194–95.

Purchase/Rental Inquiries   Filmic Archives. See Appendix B for address.

છ 21.3. *A Midsummer Night's Dream.* 1969. Royal Shakespeare Company. Color, 124 min. Producer: Michael Birkett. Director: Peter Hall.

THESEUS	Derek Godfrey
HIPPOLYTA	Barbara Jefford
LYSANDER	David Warner
DEMETRIUS	Michael Jayston
HELENA	Diana Rigg
HERMIA	Helen Mirren
OBERON	Ian Richardson
TITANIA	Judi Dench
PUCK	Ian Holm
BOTTOM	Paul Rogers
QUINCE	Sebastian Shaw
SNOUT	Bill Travers

FLUTE   John Normington
SNUG   Clive Swift
STARVELING   Donald Eccles
PHILOSTRATE   Hugh Sullivan
EGEUS   Nicholas Selby

Pluses   An unusual and interesting production.

Minuses   Unusual touches can be disconcerting.

Textual Cuts and Rearrangements   Cuts are surprisingly few.

Settings   "Athens" is here not a Greek city but an English country house, neoclassically serene in its landscaped park. The forest, adjacent to the park, has tangles of undergrowth, streams, and ponds. Water is especially important. Titania's speech about the cold, wet summer (II.i.88ff.), often cut, is here included. The fairies spend considerable time standing waist-deep in ponds, and the mortal lovers grow progressively muddier as the night goes on.

Costumes   For the fairies, costumes are minimal. Titania is almost nude, with strategically placed vines that seem to have got there by accident. She and most of the other fairies are painted a bluish-greenish-gray color that sometimes causes students to ask if they are meant to be zombies. Puck does after all mention "the graves, all gaping wide" (V.i.38).

Mortals appear in modern dress, or what was modern dress in 1969. Women wear miniskirts and boots, with long skirts for evening; men wear Edwardian suits, sometimes with lace collars. Bottom's ass's head is realistically furry and cannot be seen through.

Interpretation of Roles   Judi Dench as Titania is exuberant and sexy, despite her greenish-gray color, and she embraces Bottom with great enthusiasm (III.i). Diana Rigg plays Helena in a thoughtful, almost melancholy way, loving Demetrius even while she thinks he is mocking her. When she really has him, at the end of the play, she can scarcely believe her luck and keeps looking at him to be sure. Helen Mirren's Hermia, by contrast, leaps joyously about, kissing Lysander at every opportunity and refusing to believe his temporary rejection of her.

Titania's attendant fairies, young children, are left their natural color. Their acting is refreshingly free of artifice. The fairy who asks Puck his identity (II.i) seems genuinely curious. Later, when Titania roars with laughter at Bottom's witticisms, her fairies are pointedly not amused.

Peter Quince and his crew are workmen on the estate. They meet to discus "Pyramus and Thisby" during their lunch hour, where Quince glares balefully at Bottom as the latter attempts to take over the proceedings.

The play of "Pyramus and Thisby" is especially effective because of the courtly audience's appreciation of it. Some of the crueler gibes are cut, and many of those that remain are not heard by the actors. The applause is enthusiastic. Hippolyta, who is in a cheerful mood throughout the film, joins in with delight. Theseus not only shakes the actors' hands but gives them a purse of money.

Production History   As director of the Royal Shakespeare Company, Peter Hall had nurtured the talents of many of the actors in the cast. The film was shown on British and American television in 1969.

Reviews and Studies   Jorgens, Jack J. *Shakespeare on Film.* 1977. Pp. 51–65, 255–58, 316–17.

Mullin, Michael. "Peter Hall's *Midsummer Night's Dream* on Film." *Educational Theatre Journal* 27 (1975): 529–34.

Ochiogrosso, F. "Cinematic Oxymoron in Peter Hall's *A Midsummer Night's Dream.*" *Literature/ Film Quarterly* 11 (1983): 174–78.

Rothwell, Kenneth S., and Melzer, Annabelle H. *Shakespeare on Screen.* 1990. Item 405, pp. 195–96.

Purchase/ Rental Inquiries   Films for the Humanities and Sciences. See Appendix B for address.

&. 21.4. *A Midsummer Night's Dream.* 1982. British Broadcasting Company/ Time-Life Television: The Shakespeare Plays. Color, 120 min. Producer: Jonathan Miller. Director: Elijah Moshinsky.

TITANIA	Helen Mirren
OBERON	Peter McEnery
PUCK	Phil Daniels
LYSANDER	Robert Lindsay
DEMETRIUS	Nicky Henson
HERMIA	Pippa Guard
HELENA	Cherith Mellor
THESEUS	Nigel Davenport
HIPPOLYTA	Estelle Kohler
EGEUS	Geoffrey Lumsden
PHILOSTRATE	Hugh Quarshie
BOTTOM	Brian Glover
QUINCE	Geoffrey Palmer

SNUG   Ray Mort
FLUTE   John Fowler
SNOUT   Nat Jackley
STARVELING   Don Estelle

Pluses   Many beautifully composed scenes.

Minuses   Sometimes lacks comic bounce.

Textual Cuts and Rearrangements   Cuts are few and scarcely noticeable. In IV.i, Theseus does not boast about his hounds, and Egeus does not express perplexity at finding the young people in the woods. Bottom's reunion with his fellow actors (IV.ii) is deferred until after Theseus' speech about the effects of the imagination (V.i).

Settings   Theseus' palace is a marble-halled mansion, dwarfing its inhabitants, although the library where Theseus meets with Egeus and the young people seems a bit more human in scale. Peter Quince and his fellow artisans gather in a strangely solemn pub. In the dark, enchanted woods, a pond waits to entrap travelers. Titania sleeps not on a flower bank but in a large golden bed, complete with sheets and pillows.

The film's static effect may result from the director's use of seventeenth century paintings—works of Rembrandt and Frans Hals, for example—as a visual reference. Scenes tend to become tableaux rather than actions.

Costumes   The seventeenth century supplies velvet and ruffs. Titania wears flowing white. Puck, though bare-chested, has a little ruff around his neck. Bottom's ass's head consists only of ears; his face is clearly seen, and his companions' terror at his "translation" does not make a great deal of sense.

Interpretation of Roles   Helen Mirren glows as Titania, an exception to the gloom that often pervades the film. She is surrounded by child fairies and holds the little Indian boy, a small child, in her arms as she quarrels with Oberon. Another comical note is supplied by Cherith Mellor, who plays Helena with an engagingly awkward, schoolmarmish air.

Puck (Phil Daniels) and Oberon (Peter McEnery) seem enmeshed in a sadomasochistic relationship of some sort. Oberon can scarcely speak to Puck without grabbing him, sometimes in a wrestling hold, and Puck snarls in return, displaying Dracula-like fangs and speaking in an exaggerated cockney accent.

Bottom takes to his new life with equanimity. At one point (IV.i), it is hard to tell from the camera angle whether he is copulating with Titania or merely kneeling beside the bed. Something brings him to a point of ecstasy, at any rate. Perhaps it is Peaseblossom scratching his head.

In the quarrel of the four lovers (III.ii), lines are garbled by being spoken at the same time, but the effect is refreshingly lively. Inevitably, most of the lovers fall into the pond.

Back at court, "Pyramus and Thisby" comes close to becoming a stately ritual. Theseus and his courtiers sit on one side of a long table, facing the players across a large room. Their derogatory comments are for the most part either cut or unheard by the actors. Thisby comes on in a golden mask, giving an effect of formal distance. Moon sings his lines, although nobody listens to him, including his fellow actors.

The festivity ends abruptly with a clap of thunder as the lights go out. The fairies then appear and Puck, in the darkness, sits comfortably at the table for his parting words.

Production History   This film was shown on British television in 1981 and on American television in June of 1982. It was part of the British Broadcasting Company's 37-play series of Shakespeare's canon.

Reviews and Studies   Bulman, J. C., and Coursen, H. R., eds. *Shakespeare on Television*. 1988. Extracts from reviews of this film, pp. 282–84.

Rothwell, Kenneth S., and Melzer, Annabelle H. *Shakespeare on Screen*. 1990. Item 412, p. 198.

Warren, Roger. *Text and Performance: A Midsummer Night's Dream*. 1983. Pp. 67–73.

Purchase/Rental Inquiries   Ambrose Video; Filmic Archives; Insight Media; The Writing Company. See Appendix B for addresses.

❧ 21.5. *A Midsummer Night's Dream*. 1982. New York Shakespeare Festival. Color, 165 min. Producer: Joseph Papp. Director: James Lapine.

OBERON	William Hurt
TITANIA	Michele Shay
PUCK	Marcel Rosenblatt
BOTTOM	Jeffrey De Munn
HIPPOLYTA	Diane Venora
THESEUS	James Hurdle
PHILOSTRATE	Ricky Jay
EGEUS	Ralph Drischell
HERMIA	Deborah Rush

HELENA	Christine Baranski
LYSANDER	Kevin Conroy
DEMETRIUS	Rick Leiberman
QUINCE	Steve Vinovich
FLUTE	Paul Bates
STARVELING	J. Patrick O'Brien
SNOUT	Andreas Katsulas
SNUG	Peter Crook

Pluses   Fresh and lively, with inventive acting. "Pyramus and Thisby," in the last act, is outstanding.

Minuses   Occasionally stilted, lines spoken slowly and without conviction. Actors seem to be shouting at one another. The accoustics of an outdoor theater might have some bearing here.

Textual Cuts and Rearrangements   Not extensive. Theseus loses some of his lines, including "The lunatic, the lover, and the poet . . . :" (V.i.7ff.). Titania voluntarily gives the Indian boy to Oberon as her romance with Bottom gets under way, so that Oberon's description of this negotiation (IV.i) is naturally omitted. The courtiers' jeers at the players during "Pyramus and Thisby" are curtailed.

Settings   The Delacorte Theatre, outdoors with real grass and trees, in Central Park, New York City. The live audience is seen taking its seats at the beginning and is occasionally heard thereafter, supplying laughter and applause. Imaginative lighting and camera work, along with fog machines to enhance the magic of the woods, keep the setting from becoming monotonous.

Costumes   Modern dress, in an eclectic street-fashion sense. Hippolyta wears black leather and looks as if she might have arrived on a motorcycle. Theseus imitates an American Indian in fringed leather trousers. Hermia is a southern belle, all feminine frills. Helena, carrying a handbag even into the forest and equipped with white gloves and a fan, projects the kind of starched dignity one associates with female costume of the 1950s.

Peter Quince, as a frustrated artist, has a beret and scarf. His actors wear working clothes; Flute is in overalls, and Snout shows a tattoo of the ace of spaces. Bottom's ass's head consists of ears only, so that his face shows clearly.

Titania is almost nude, while her fairies resemble surreal hallucinations reminiscent of the paintings of Hieronymus Bosch. One is a sort of hairball with legs.

For the wedding festivities in the last act, the court changes into white and thus appears to have become a more coherent as well as more harmonious society.

Interpretation of Roles   Bottom deserves credit for much of the film's energy, from the moment he bounds onstage with a shoulder bag which turns out to contain a collection of false beards. He does not seem perturbed at being turned into an ass, insofar as the addition of a pair of ears can be said to effect such a transformation, and his lusty appreciation of the fairy queen is consistent with his untroubled self-esteem.

John Hurt as Oberon is for some reason not at his best. He speaks his lines mechanically and seems unconnected to the other actors onstage.

Demetrius and Lysander (Rick Leiberman and Kevin Conroy), in some productions almost identical, here are differentiated. Demetrius is a smug yuppy, while Lysander is almost a yokel, stumbling about.

Marcel Rosenblatt's Puck is something of a blight. She rushes about, interferes with the action, and spends a lot of time convulsed with un-funny laughter, kicking her heels in the air. Student audiences say there is somebody like her in every dorm.

The little Indian boy, a happy African-American of two or three years, dances about with the fairies and adds his bit of spontaneity.

Philostrate, master of the revels and often a minor figure, is acted with flair by Ricky Jay. He does juggling tricks and clearly feels responsible for the success of the duke's festivities.

"Pyramus and Thisby" is acted with a sheer fun that is especially appealing to student audiences. Everything goes wrong, and the actors manage to triumph nevertheless.

Production History   The stage production ran during the summer of 1982.

Reviews and Studies   Bulman, J. C., and Coursen, H. R., eds. *Shakespeare on Television*. 1988. Extracts from reviews of this film, pp. 284–85.

Rothwell, Kenneth S., and Melzer, Annabelle H. *Shakespeare on Screen*. 1990. Item 413, p. 199.

Purchase/Rental Inquiries   Films for the Humanities and Sciences. See Appendix B for address.

22 ❧ MUCH ADO
ABOUT NOTHING⎯⎯⎯⎯⎯⎯⎯

❧ 22.1. *Much Ado about Nothing.* 1973. New York Shakespeare Festival. Color, 120 min.

Produced by Joseph Papp, directed by A. J. Antoon; with Sam Waterston (Benedick) and Kathleen Widdoes (Beatrice).

The film (and the stage play which it records) has early- twentieth-century costumes and sets. Dogberry and his crew dash about in the manner of the Keystone Kops.

The stage play had moved from the Delacorte Theatre, outdoors in New York's Central Park, to the Winter Garden shortly before this film was shown on television in February of 1973. The television version drew a large audience, and ticket sales for the stage show plummeted.

The film is not available at the present time.

⎯⎯⎯⎯⎯⎯⎯⎯⎯⎯⎯⎯

❧ 22.2. *Much Ado about Nothing.* 1984. British Broadcasting Company/ Time-Life Television: The Shakespeare Plays. Color, 150 min. Producer: Shaun Sutton. Director: Stuart Burge.

BEATRICE	Cherie Lunghi
BENEDICK	Robert Lindsay
DON PEDRO	Jon Finch
HERO	Katherine Levy
LEONATO	Lee Montague
CLAUDIO	Robert Reynolds
ANTONIO	Gordon Whiting
DON JOHN	Vernon Dobtcheff
CONRADE	Robert Gwilym
BORACHIO	Tony Rohr
MARGARET	Pamela Moisciwitsch
URSULA	Ishia Bennison
BALTHAZAR	Oz Clarke
DOGBERRY	Michael Elphick

VERGES	Clive Dunn
FIRST WATCH	Gordon Kaye
SECOND WATCH	Perry Benson
FRIAR FRANCIS	Graham Crowden
SEXTON	John Kidd

Pluses   A thoughtful and visually elegant production.

Minuses   Benedick and Beatrice are so wary of each other that the play takes awhile to warm up.

Textual Cuts and Rearrangements   Cuts are not extensive. Dogberry's watchmen occasionally swap their lines around. Borachio substitutes "hear Margaret call me Borachio" for the text's "term me Claudio" (II.ii.44), thus clarifying the action and repairing what must have been an error in Shakespeare's text.

Settings   Studio sets achieve an effect of spacious luxury, befitting the characters and the plot. Much of the action takes place in a large courtyard planted with fruit trees, where accidental eavesdropping can occur without straining credibility. Gentlemen ponder in a book-lined library, and Hero's room is a pleasant bower.

Costumes   Women wear what one might call folk-dancing costumes, full skirts and embroidered blouses. Men have a great deal of gold ornament. Don John, the villain, is in black velvet. At the dance (II.i), revelers carry elaborate masks which conceal their faces and allow mistaken identities to propel the plot. Hero's wedding dress is of a pretty silver fabric, giving her an air of innocent happiness that becomes ironic when at the altar Claudio accuses her of unchastity.

Interpretation of Roles   Cheri Lunghi's Beatrice makes it clear that she has had an unsatisfactory romance with Benedick in the past—"Marry, once before he won it [Beatrice's heart] from me with false dice" (II.i.279). She regards him sourly as the play opens and proceeds with caution even after her friends' practical joke has led her to believe that he loves her. (The same joke, of course, is being played on Benedick.) The shock of Hero's misfortune jolts Beatrice out of her defensive posture and allows her to draw closer to Benedick. A demonstration of their alliance occurs as Beatrice is weeping for Hero in the chapel (IV.i). Benedick joins her and silently gives her a handkerchief. Without looking at the handkerchief or its owner—quite unconsciously, in fact—Beatrice accepts it and hands him the soggy one she has been using. It is a perfect moment.

Robert Lindsay plays Benedick in a variety of moods. On shaving his beard to conform to Beatrice's preference in masuline faces, he looks quite different, more flexible generally. His immediate response to Beatrice's request for him to kill Claudio, "Not for the wide world" (IV.i.290), is followed by a pause for reconsideration; if Beatrice thinks Hero has been wronged, then he will challenge his friend. By the end, all problems resolved, he is ready to let go and celebrate, and the kiss with which he stops Beatrice's mouth (V.iv.97) is a long and urgent one.

Hero (Katharine Levy) and Claudio (Robert Reynolds), the more bashful and conventional pair of lovers, take a back seat to Beatrice and Benedick, as is inevitably the case. Claudio is a somewhat stuffy young man, wooing Leonato's daughter for material advantage and then rejecting her on the mere appearance of scandal. This obtuse righteousness has the natural effect of enhancing Benedick's more agile intelligence, just as Hero's passivity—she will marry anyone her father tells her to—enhances Beatrice's independence.

Hero's attendant Margaret (Pamela Moisciwitsch) looks enough like Hero to make plausible the mistaken identity that occurs when Hero's affianced husband sees "her chamber window entered" (III.ii.113). The audience assumes the plausibility, in any case, since in this film the event occurs offstage. Margaret seems unaware throughout much of the ensuing action that she is the cause of her mistress's troubles, though she does weep penitently in the last act.

Dogberry (Michael Elphick) does not strike most viewers of this film as particularly funny, even though he seems to be saying his lines conscientiously. Perhaps this is the trouble.

Production History   *Much Ado about Nothing* was the third-from-last film to appear of the British Broadcasting Company's series of Shakespeare's entire canon. It was broadcast in Britain and America in the autume of 1984. The BBC had in fact made an earlier *Much Ado* in 1978, intended as the first of the series, and had even publicized the film when it was canceled for reasons never revealed.

Reviews and Studies   Bulman, J. C., and Coursen, H. R., eds. *Shakespeare on Television*. 1988. Extracts from reviews of this film, pp. 309–10.

Rothwell, Kenneth S., and Melzer, Annabelle H. *Shakespeare on Screen*. 1990. Item 432, pp. 206–7.

Purchase/Rental Inquiries   Ambrose Video; Filmic Archives; Insight Media; The Writing Company. See Appendix B for addresses.

🐦 22.3. *Much Ado about Nothing.* 1993. Samuel Goldwyn Company. Color, 111 min. Producer: Kenneth Branagh, David Parfitt, Stephen Evans. Director: Kenneth Branagh.

BENEDICK	Kenneth Branagh
BEATRICE	Emma Thompson
DON PEDRO	Denzel Washington
DOGBERRY	Michael Keaton
ANTONIO	Brian Blessed
CLAUDIO	Robert Shaun Leonard
DON JOHN	Keanu Reeves
BORACHIO	Gerard Moran
CONRADE	Richard Clifford
LEONATO	Richard Briers
HERO	Kate Beckinsale
MARGARET	Imelda Staunton
URSULA	Phillida Law
BALTHAZAR	Patrick Doyle
FRIAR FRANCIS	Jimmy Yiull
VERGES	Ben Elton
SEXTON	Teddy Jewesbury
GEORGE SEACOLE	Andy Hockley
FRANCIS SEACOLE	Chris Barnes
HUGH OATCAKE	Conrad Nelson

Pluses   A warmhearted, fast-moving comedy, exuberantly acted. Students recognize many members of the cast from non-Shakespearean roles, among them Denzel Washington (*Malcolm X*) and Michael Keaton (*Batman*). Kenneth Branagh and Emma Thompson have appeared together in *Henry V* (10.3) and in several non-Shakespearean films, among them *Dead Again*. Emma Thompson won an Academy Award for her role in *Howard's End* and has been recently seen in *The Remains of the Day*.

Minuses   Flaws are hard to find.

Textual Cuts and Rearrangements   Cuts are frequent but judicious. Many passages of dialogue are thinned, and the plot is streamlined.

Much of the early misunderstanding about Don Pedro's secondhand wooing of Hero has been eliminated. Only enough of this wrinkle remains to allow Claudio to jump temporarily to the conclusion that his superior officer has betrayed him (II.i). The action gives us a foreshadowing of the malignity of Don John, who deliberately tries to put his brother Don Pedro in a bad light, and of the gullibility of Claudio.

Margaret, one of Hero's waiting-women and a pawn in another of Don John's plots, has lost a great deal of her dialogue. She does not get to practice being witty in a Beatrice-like manner (III.iv), as the scene is cut entirely, nor is she sent about on errands (III.i, V.ii). She has a strong function in the plot nevertheless. In the text, Margaret's leaning out her window to bid goodnight to an unknown man is described as having happened offstage (III.iii.144ff.), but in this film her escapade is not only seen by the audience but is made more explicitly scandalous. The camera accompanies Claudio and his two companions as they see, framed in an upper window, Margaret engaged in strenuous standing-up sex with Borachio. She is nude, her dark hair is loose to her waist, and from the back she does look very much like Hero. Claudio's instant shock, horror, and grief is more understandable to the audience than it might have been without this ocular proof. He should have investigated further, audiences agree, but he is after all very young, and one can see why he didn't.

Another addition to Shakespeare's text is the return of Don John in the final scene, guarded and glowering. In the text his capture is merely reported (V.iv.126).

Textual rearrangements include some taking-apart and redistributing of the actions of Dogberry and the watch (III.iii). Claudio's vigil at the tomb of the supposedly dead Hero (V.iii) is moved so as to immediately follow his remorse on finding that Hero was falsely slandered (V.i).

Benedick does not shave his beard, so the joke about his using the hair to stuff tennis balls is cut (III.ii.45). Beatrice's claim to dislike beards is retained, however (II.i.30). Presumably by the end of the play she has become more tolerant in this regard.

Settings   The film was shot on location in northern Italy, during a heat wave that is almost palpable on the screen. Leonato's villa includes a garden with plenty of shrubbery for eavesdropping; a courtyard for parties and dancing; and a lush, surrounding landscape for picnics, crossed with grape arbors and punctuated with Italian cypresses.

In its darker depths the villa is supplied with a dungeon for malefactors, where Borachio and Conrade are chained, bloodied and rumpled, as Dogberry and other agents of justice interrogate them, and a tunnel used by Don John for scheming and escaping.

Costumes   Light, cool garments are in favor. Men wear military uniforms of a nineteenth-century cast, with short white jackets and blue facings. Women wear simple, billowing white dresses and sometimes carry parasols.

Costumes for the ball (II.i) include elaborate masks, so that identities are convincingly concealed.

Interpretation of Roles   Emma Thompson makes Beatrice a many-sided yet consistent character—genuinely merry, but with an edge of sadness, and always ready to make fun of herself as well as others. It is her voice that we hear reading "Sigh no more, ladies," later to be sung by Balthazar, as the film opens. When she overhears Hero and Ursula describing Benedick's love for her (III.i), she blossoms on the instant, swinging in exultant slow motion in the garden swing.

Kenneth Branagh's Benedick manages to make clear even in mid-bluster that his supposed hatred of women is a cover-up. His surprise at hearing of Beatrice's alleged affection, though played for laughs as he falls through a deck chair he has been trying to set up in the garden (II.iii), is succeeded by a joy that is partly relief. He doesn't have to pretend any more.

Only once, in the final scene, do the lovers' old personalities come back and threaten to trap them again. The practical joke is revealed as such (V.iv.74ff.). Beatrice and Benedick pause in dismay, partly at having been fooled and partly, one feels, at the prospect of having to resume their witty, scornful, and ultimately pointless postures. But they are rescued; each is handed a poem written by the other. Instead of giving the papers a quick glance, as in many productions, these lovers read the evidence eagerly, thoroughly, and with great approval, then smile at each other, and all is well.

Denzel Washington gives to Don Pedro, the commanding officer of Benedick and Claudio, a solidity that the role does not always elicit. He is upright, honorable, and, while Don John's deception is under way, concerned that his junior officers not be tricked into marrying trollops.

Michael Keaton plays Dogberry in a puzzling manner as some kind of psychopath. He squints his eyes, shows his teeth, sweats enormously, pummels the longsuffering Verges (Ben Elton), and gallops about on an imaginary horse.

Several minor characters are made more prominent than the text might suggest. Dogberry's watchmen, Oatcake and the two Seacoles, are workers on the estate and can be seen putting up decorations and playing musical instruments during the festivities. Antonio (Brian Blessed) becomes a spirit of hospitality, in the middle of all the jokes, enjoying a companionable alliance with Ursula, the older of Hero's waiting gentlewomen.

Hero's other gentlewoman, Margaret(Imelda Staunton), in this film appears only twice more after she is so sensationally glimpsed through the window. When Claudio rejects Hero at the altar and explains his reasons (IV.i.83), we see Margaret's horrified face in the crowd. She understands the situation, but just as we begin to wonder if she will have to courage to come forward and save Hero, the camera moves away from her and it is clear that she will not. She is forgiven, nevertheless. Conrade makes clear that she did not know about the plot (V.i.300), and in this film Leonato's line, "Margaret was in some fault for this" (V.ii.4), is accompanied by a hug.

Production History   The film opened at first-run theaters in the spring and summer of 1993. Critical and public acclaim followed.

Reviews and Studies   Branagh, Kenneth. *Much Ado about Nothing: Screenplay, Introduction, and Notes on the Making of the Movie.* 1993.

Canby, Vincent. "A House Party of Beatrice, Benedick and Friends." *New York Times*, 7 May 1993, p. C16.

Lane, Anthony. "The Current Cinema: Too Much Ado." *New Yorker* 69.12 (10 May 1993): 97–99.

Purchase/Rental Inquiries   As of this writing, this film is expected to become available in videotape during the spring of 1994.

23 ❧ OTHELLO*

❧ 23.1. *Othello.* 1952. Mogadar Films/ Mercury Productions. Black-and-white, 91 min. Producer: Orson Welles. Director: Orson Welles.

OTHELLO	Orson Welles
IAGO	Michael MacLiammoir
RODERIGO	Robert Coote
DESDEMONA	Suzanne Cloutier
EMILIA	Fay Compton
BRABANTIO	Hilton Edwards
LODOVICO	Nicholas Bruce
CASSIO	Michael Lawrence
BIANCA	Doris Dowling
MONTANO	Jean Davis
PAGE	Joan Fontaine

Pluses A famous film, celebrated as a work of cinematic art.

Minuses Not directly aligned with the needs of a class studying Shakespeare's *Othello*.

Textual Cuts and Rearrangements The text has been considerably metamorphosed. The beginning is the end; we see the funeral procession of Othello and Desdemona winding its way up a hill, while an iron cage, with Iago in it, is hoisted into the air. Presumably he is going to starve to death for his crimes. The story then goes back more or less to Shakespeare's opening scenes, with a good deal of cutting and a narrator to fill in the gaps.

Among the cuts: Desdemona's willow song (IV.iii.40ff.); almost all of Iago's soliloquies; Bianca's entrance after the attack on Cassio (V.i.74); and many others. Emilia's role is considerably shorn. We see her for the first time when she picks up Desdemona's handkerchief to give to Iago (III.iii). Emilia's part of the dialogue after the ships land in Cyprus has been cut, and her exchange with Othello at the beginning of IV.ii also disappears.

Settings The film was made on location in several places, including Rome and Venice. Many of the Cyprus scenes were shot in a centuries-old Arab citadel at

* Note: For films related to Shakespeare's *Othello*, see Appendix A, "Analogues and Variations."

Mogador, Morocco. We have thick-walled ramparts, vaulted crypts, and a splendid sense of spatial solidity. Except in dimly lighted scenes, the film is pleasant to look at, even when the poor sound quality or jumpy narrative sequences make it hard to tell what is happening in the story.

Costumes   Othello wears an armored breastplate and a majestic trailing cape. Desdemona is in Renaissance costume, with a filigreed mesh cap on her hair. During the stalking of Cassio (V.i), which takes place in a Turkish bath, the participants wear sheets and are hidden by clouds of steam.

Interpretation of Roles   Welles presents a believable Othello, an Othello so convinced of the correctness of his perceptions that he is incapable of wondering if he might be judging by flawed evidence. He rolls about the screen as if on little wheels, propelled by his unshakable faith in himself.

Michael MacLiammoir plays Iago as a practical person with a grudge, not as a satanic demon. The result is a flattening of his personality.

As Desdemona, Suzanne Cloutier seems to hide her emotions behind a beautiful but impassive face.

Production History   The film was beset by difficulties, mainly financial. Shooting was frequently interrupted and various actors dropped out, lured away by more profitable jobs. The Desdemona we see was in fact the third to attempt the role. The general public was not impressed with the final result, but it received the Grand Prize at the 1952 Cannes Film Festival and has been consistently appreciated by film critics and historians.

Reviews and Studies   Buchman, Lorne M. "Orson Welles's *Othello*: A Study of Time in Shakespeare's Tragedy." *Shakespeare Quarterly* 39 (1987): 53–65.

Collick, John. *Shakespeare, Cinema, and Society*. 1989. Pp. 93–98.

Davies, Anthony. *Filming Shakespeare's Plays*. 1988. Pp. 100–118, 193–94.

Jorgens, Jack J. *Shakespeare on Film*. 1977. Pp. 175–90, 290–94, 325–26.

MacLiammoir, Michael. *Put Money in Thy Purse; The Filming of Orson Welles' Othello*. 2nd revised edition. London: Methuen, 1978.

Rothwell, Kenneth S., and Melzer, Annabelle H. *Shakespeare on Film*. 1990. Item 453, pp. 215–16.

Purchase/Rental Inquiries   The Writing Company. See Appendix B for address.

23.2. *Othello.* 1955. Mosfilm. In Russian, with English subtitles. Color, 108 min.

Directed by Seri Yutkevich, with Sergei Bondarchuk as Othello and Irina Skobt-seva as Desdemona. Panoramic landscapes, swarms of extras. Othello dark and brooding, Desdemona blonde and fragile. Because of the lauguage, this film would hardly be a first choice for classroom use, but a brief excerpt can make an interesting contrast to whatever else is on the agenda. The Russian text is Boris Pasternak's.

This film is intermittently available from distributors.

23.3. *Othello: The Moor of Venice.* 1965. Eagle Films, Color, 166 min.

A well-known film based on Stuart Burge's stage production of *Othello*, starring Laurence Olivier (Othello), Maggie Smith (Desdemona), Frank Finlay (Iago), Joyce Redman (Emilia), and Derek Jacobi (Cassio). Critics who saw both the stage play and this film found the latter a pale reflection of the former, but it is never-theless a record of an important theatrical event.

This *Othello* is unavailable in videotape or videodisk as of this writing.

23.4. *Othello.* 1979. New York Shakespeare Festival. Color, 190 min.

A record of Joseph Papp's New York Shakespeare Festival production of *Othello*, with Raul Julia (Othello), Richard Dreyfuss (Iago), Frances Conroy (Desdemona). Staged at the outdoor Delacorte Theatre in Central Park.

At present this film is not available.

23.5. *Othello.* 1981. British Broadcasting Company/ Time-Life Television: The Shakespeare Plays. Color, 210 min. Producer: Jonathan Miller. Director: Jonathan Miller.

OTHELLO	Anthony Hopkins
DESDEMONA	Penelope Wilton
IAGO	Bob Hoskins

EMILIA	Rosemary Leach
BIANCA	Wendy Morgan
BRABANTIO	Geoffrey Chater
RODERIGO	Anthony Pedley
CASSIO	David Yelland
DUKE OF VENICE	John Barron
MONTANO	Tony Steedman
GRATIANO	Alexander Davion
LODOVICO	Joseph O'Conor

Pluses   A clear rendition of Shakespeare's text. Viewers are not in doubt as to where we are in the plot.

Minuses   Anthony Hopkins's nervous, wired-up rendition of Othello strikes many viewers as antithetical to the role.

Textual Cuts and Rearrangements   Cuts are few. All of II.ii is omitted, but as the scene is only a few lines long and consists of a herald telling everyone to celebrate, the loss is slight. Cassio's exchange with the musicians disappears (III.i), and other lines drop out from time to time.

Settings   Most of the film takes place in a sequence of rooms, a vista of receding interiors, with checkerboard floors and a seventeenth-century Low Countries feeling, reinforced by the costumes. As we get no sense of either Venice or Cyprus, the effect is disconcerting, as if the Turks were threatening Amsterdam. However, a strong light comes through the windows during the daylight scenes, and perhaps a Mediterranean ambiance is intended.

Specific sets include a dining room in which Cassio is made drunk (II.iii), and Desdemona's dressing room (IV.iii), where, very strangely, a skull sits beside a flickering candle. Student audiences greet the skull with whoops of joy and instantly identify it as Poor Yorick. As Desdemona sits contemplating it, humming the willow song to herself, the scene resembles George de la Tour's painting "La Madeleine au Miroir," but the reason for the association is not clear.

Costumes   Here the visual reference seems to be Rembrandt paintings. Dark-clad gentlemen wear little white ruffs at the neck. Bits of armor are sometimes added—a breastplate, a plumed helmet. Othello wears a white jacket and tights.

Desdemona's gowns, rich but not gaudy, continue the black- and-white scheme. Emilia is in black and gray, with a little ruff. Even Bianca wears an unobtrusive black dress. It does have a low neckline, however, and while Bianca is demure in her first appearance (III.iv), she does some strumpet-like shouting at Cassio when she decides she does not want to copy the embroidery of Desdemona's handkerchief (IV.i).

Interpretation of Roles   In this production, students are interested, as always, when they encounter actors they associate with other filmic contexts. Anthony Hopkins is known to Americans for *The Silence of the Lambs* and *The Remains of the Day*. Bob Hoskins is often seen in comedies—*Who Framed Roger Rabbit*, for example.

Anthony Hopkins here breaks tradition by wearing very light makeup. Dialogue about Othello's blackness consequently makes little sense, and student audiences are likely to see this choice as a cop-out. Hopkins also eschews the traditional calm, self- confident, soldierly Othello. He is constantly leaping about.

Bob Hoskins as Iago is even jumpier, forever giggling and grimacing. In his exchanges with Othello, the camera is more often on him than on Othello. The other characters seem to trust this Iago, rather paradoxically, because they do not take him seriously. He is an underling, part of their everyday scene. Desdemona collapses into Iago's arms as she begs his advice: "Alas, Iago,/ What shall I do to win my lord again?" (IV.ii.148). To cheer her up, Iago makes faces as if she were a child, imitating the call of the trumpet that happens at that moment to announce supper. Then, as Desdemona and Emilia leave, he adds a happy little tootle of his own, celebrating the success of his villainy.

Penelope Wilton plays Desdemona with dignity and strength rather than pathos. She calmly defends her marital choice to the Venetian senate (I.iii) and, on landing in Cyprus, overcomes her anxiety about any harm that might have befallen Othello's ship (II.i). When Othello accuses her of infidelity, she is angry rather than apologetic (V.ii); when he smothers her with a pillow, she struggles, reaching a hand toward his throat.

Rosemary Leach finds a workable interpretation of Emilia as a happy, bubbly person, greeting the other characters as old friends and eager to please her husband. In her earlier scenes, this jollity becomes a kind of shallowness. She can watch Desdemona's anguish at having lost the handkerchief without jumping in to explain that she herself picked it up (III.iv.24). Leach's face in these moments shows anxiety followed by a resolute compression of the lips. One assumes that Emilia fears her husband's anger but plans to get the handkerchief back and return it before things get any worse. By the final scene, however, Emilia has made her choice, and she tells the truth even though she literally dies for it.

Production History   *Othello* was shown on British and American television in October of 1981. It was the eighteenth of the British Broadcasting Company's series "The Shakespeare Plays," which filmed the 37-play Shakespeare canon between 1978 and 1985.

Reviews and Studies   Bulman, J. C., and Coursen, H. R., eds. *Shakespeare on Television*. 1988. Extracts from reviews of this film, pp. 277–79.

Rothwell, Kenneth S., and Melzer, Annabelle H. *Shakespeare on Film*. 1990. Item 472, pp. 223–24.

Purchase/Rental Inquiries: Ambrose Video; Filmic Archives; Insight Media; The Writing Company. See Appendix B for addresses.

ɜ❧ **23.6.** *Othello: The Moor of Venice*. 1985. The Bard Series. Color, 195 min. Producer: Jack Nakano. Director: Franklin Melton.

OTHELLO	William Marshall
IAGO	Ron Moody
DESDEMONA	Jenny Agutter
CASSIO	Deveren Bookwalter
BRABANTIO	Peter MacLean
EMILIA	Leslie Paxton
RODERIGO	Joel Asher
BIANCA	Eugenia Wright
LODOVICO	Philip Persons
MONTANO	Michael Hayward
GRATIANO	Arnold Markussen
DUKE OF VENICE	Jay Robinson
FRIEND TO BIANCO	Anna Dresden

Pluses   Lively pace and interesting touches.

Minuses   Uneven acting; occasional shrill and nasal voices.

Textual Cuts and Rearrangements   Cuts are not extensive. Roderigo's ambush of Cassio (V. 1) has been tightened up. Some of Emilia's dying lines disappear, and she is not laid beside her mistress on the bed (V.ii). No letters are mentioned as having been found in pockets, and Lodovico's dying instructions to Gratiano are cut.

Settings   Like the other Bard films, this one uses an Elizabethan-style stage for the entire action. The camera frequently shows only a part of it at a time, avoiding monotony. Playing areas include several levels on the main stage, stairs, an upper gallery, and various alcoves.

Costumes A Renaissance medley. Bright colors prevail, a kaleidescope of puffed sleeves and close-fitting breeches. Othello wears flowing white robes.

Interpretation of Roles William Marshall plays Othello with authority—an older man, accustomed to getting what he wants, unaccustomed to self-doubt. The passion of his jealousy seems alternately to rouse and to drain his strength. When he strikes Desdemona, he does so without a great deal of force, tapping her with the rolled-up letter from Venice; at "she can turn and turn," he embraces her and then flings her toward Lodovico (IV.i.253). In his sarcastic pretense that Emilia is a brothel keeper, he puts a purse into Emilia's hands rather than throw the coins on the floor in the manner of more vehement Othellos (IV.ii).

Ron Moody's Iago is not a lower-class, up-from-the-ranks noncommissioned officer, as this character is often played, but an older man of refined tastes who has somehow fallen behind. He has aquiline features and thinning hair; his statement of his age, "I have looked upon the world for four times seven years" (I.iii.311), is amended to "six times seven." This Iago's bitterness at losing the promotion he had expected seems a natural outcome of events. In orchestrating Othello's downfall he speaks quietly rather than emotionally, with precise gestures and an appearance of solemn regret for the bad news he feels it his duty to convey.

Jenny Agutter plays Desdemona as a strong, energetic person, not given to self-pity. "I hope you will not kill me," she cries to Othello, jumping from the bed and trying to embrace him (V.ii.35). Othello's physical strength is of course too much for her.

Emilia (Leslie Paxton) is here young and pretty. In the opening scenes she is somewhat sullen and resentful of her mistress. Students may remember that she has not been Desdemona's maid for long; she was given the job after Desdemona's and Othello's marriage, and perhaps she is as annoyed by her low rank as her husband is. Maybe she expected better things from her own marriage. Such an Emilia could plausibly have stolen the handkerchief and refrained from confessing, despite the grisly consequences—until the final scene, of course.

Deveren Bookwalter's Cassio is a cheerful womanizer. Immediately upon his arrival in Cyprus he picks up (or is picked up by) not only Bianca but an equally voluptuous friend (II.i). The two women are onstage during the revels that follow, and Cassio downs the fatal cup of wine in order to impress them (II.iii).

Production History Bard Productions, based in California, use an Elizabethan- style stage as a setting for films of Shakespeare plays. The films are sometimes seen on cable television. For other titles in the series, see the general intro-duction, p. 5.

Reviews and Studies   Bulman, J. C., and Coursen, H. R., eds. *Shakespeare on Television*. 1988. Extracts from reviews of this film, pp. 306–7.

    Cooke, Anne Jennalie. *"Othello." Shakespeare on Film Newsletter* 12.1 (1987): 1, 4.

    Rothwell, Kenneth S., and Melzer, Annabelle H. *Shakespeare on Screen*. 1990. Item 447, p. 225.

Purchase/Rental Inquiries   Crest Video; Filmic Archives. See Appendix B for addresses.

⁀ 23.7. *Othello.* 1988. Othello Productions, Inc. Color, 198 min. Producer: David Pupkewitz. Director: Janet Suzman.

OTHELLO	John Kani
DESDEMONA	Joanna Weinberg
IAGO	Richard Haddon Haines
EMILIA	Dorothy Gould
RODERIGO	Frantz Dobrowsky
CASSIO	Neil McCarthy
BRABANTIO	Stuart Brown
GRATIANO	John Whiteley
LODOVICO	Peter Krummeck
BIANCA	Gaynor Young
MONTANO	Martin Le Maitre
DUKE OF VENICE	Lindsay Reardon

Pluses   Well-thought-out, well-acted, an absorbing experience.

Minuses   Flaws in this film are few.

Textual Cuts and Rearrangements   There is considerable cutting, as is typical of a film based on a stage production. The jingling rhymes in which the duke of Venice tries to reconcile Brabantio to his loss are among the cuts (I.iii), as are Brabantio's sarcastic replies. Lengthy metaphors and classical allusions tend to disappear. The clown and the musicians are cut from the opening of act three. The final scene is considerably streamlined.

Settings   With the exception of the first act, which seems to have been filmed in a studio, the action takes place on the stage of the Market Theatre of Johannesburg, South Africa. (It does not appear to be a performance before a live audience.) The stage includes stairs, alcoves, and an upper level. The camera varies its angles and distances.

Costumes   Venetian senators wear academic robes. Cassio is somewhat dandified in green velvet, and in several scenes Desdemona wears a dress that echoes it in color and general effect. Bianca is in Turkish costume, with full-cut harem trousers. Othello wears a barbaric necklace, the main ornament of which turns out to be, when unfolded, the knife with which he kills himself.

Interpretation of Roles   Othello, played by John Kani, speaks English with a shade of hesitation and a soft Afrikaans accent. Student audiences take awhile to get used to him. His combination of slow speech and dignified bearing translates, unfortunately, into a comic convention, and some of his earlier speeches evoke laughter. On lengthier acquaintance, this Othello turns out to be a complex individual, trapped between the world he thinks he understands and the world of deceit and humiliation invented for him by Iago.

Iago (Richard Haddon Haines) appears energetic and sociable, cheerfully doing Othello's bidding even to the extent of carrying Desdemona's pet dog ashore. Entertaining Desdemona and the others as they await Othello's ship, he lets his hearers fill in the rhyming words as he improvises verses (II.i); everyone has a good time. After Othello demotes Cassio (II.iii), Iago regards Cassio with a look of deep sympathy. With his wife, however, the mask is off, and he jabs Emilia in the crotch as he calls her a "common thing" (III.iii.302).

Iago seems unable to keep his hands off Othello, demonstrating, for example, his invented story about Cassio wringing his (Iago's) hand by wringing Othello's (III.iii.421). (Iago does not, however, go so far as to kiss Othello on the lips when he claims that Cassio, in his sleep, kissed him.) The suggestion of an unconscious homosexual motive is not new to stagings of *Othello* but works well here.

Joanna Weinburg portrays Desdemona as affectionate and outgoing. When she defends her marriage to the Venetian senate (I.iii), she and Othello kneel before Brabantio to ask his pardon, and on taking leave she embraces several of the senators. The viewer remembers that some of them are members of her family, and others she must have known since a child. This Desdemona's blonde good looks and serene self-confidence are ironically turned to account by Iago, whose insinuations convert her natural manner into a semblance of promiscuity.

Emilia (Dorothy Gould) is here more fiery than is often the case. She tries, though in vain, to snatch the handkerchief back from Iago (III.iii.35), and she is not so much eager to please him as physically afraid of him. She speaks her diatribe on the rights of wives with bitter passion (IV.iii.86ff.).

Cassio's characterization is greatly clarified, particularly to women in the audience, by the fact that Neil McCarthy, who plays the part, is remarkably handsome. Bianca's pursuit of him seems quite natural. His physical resemblance to Desdemona adds plausibilty to Othello's assumption that these two are somehow joined and that he, Othello, is intrinsically alien.

Production History   The stage play on which this film is based was presented in Johannesburg, South Africa, under the direction of Janet Suzman. The film was shown on American cable television in the spring of 1992.

Reviews and Studies   Suzman, Janet. "*Othello* Goes to Market." *Punch* (26 August 1988): 49.

Purchase/Rental Inquiries   Films for the Humanities and Sciences. See Appendix B for address.

᾿᾽ **23.8. *Othello*.** 1990. Rockbottom Productions. Color, 120 min. Producers: James M. Swain, Katherine A. Kaspar. Director: Ted Lange.

OTHELLO	Ted Lange
IAGO	Hawthorne James
DESDEMONA	Mary Otis
CASSIO	Domenick Allen
EMILIA	Dawn Comer
BIANCA	Marina Palmer
RODERIGO	Stuart Rogers
BRABANTIO	David Kozubel
LODOVICO	Ben Schick
DUKE OF VENICE	John Sereme
MONTANO	Nelson Handel
OTHELLO'S PASSION	Darryl Wright
DESDEMONA'S PASSION	Crista Marcione
PRIEST	Thomas Whayne

Pluses   Interesting concepts, including the casting. Iago and Emilia are black, as well as Othello.

Minuses   Ideas are not always consistently executed.

Textual Cuts and Rearrangements   Cuts are numerous. We hear almost nothing of the Turkish threat to Cyprus (I.iii). Most of Iago's drinking songs are gone (II.i), as is Emilia's and Desdemona's conversation about men and love (IV.iii). Gratiano is cut from the play, along with his announcment that Brabantio has died of grief (V.ii).

Emilia, in an addition to the text, apparently has an impulse to confess her theft of the handkerchief while Othello is haranguing Desdemona about its whereabouts (III.iv). "Milord—" Emilia begins, but nobody listens, and by the time she has another chance she seems to have changed her mind.

The film begins with Othello's and Desdemona's wedding, a silent pantomime, watched by Iago and Roderigo. Also added is a ballet sequence on Othello's and Desdemona's wedding night. The dancers are described in the credits as "Othello's Passion" and "Desdemona's Passion."

Settings   Settings have a low-budget air about them. Many scenes were shot in front of large buildings of campus Georgian architecture. The Venetian senate (I.iii) meets on a wide stairway, imparting an interesting sense of urgency; all the participants would seem to be on their way someplace else. Cyprus scenes take place in a park with wide vistas, terraces, and hedges.

Costumes   Othello strides about Cyprus in a striped cloak, holding a scimitar. He wears leather gloves in later scenes, perhaps to hide the wound sustained in his and Iago's oath of vengeance; each cut his palm, then they pressed them together. Costumes are in general colorful. Desdemona wears a dramatic red gown, later a blue one.

The handkerchief is introduced early, in the interpolated wedding ceremony. Othello is seen handing it to Desdemona, so that it seems to become part of the contract. Later, Bianca hurls it at Cassio and then spits on it (IV.i). Since Othello is watching, the audience can feel his outrage. Cassio then picks up the handkerchief. He has it with him in the final scene, when he puts it reverently on the bed beside Othello's and Desdemona's bodies.

Interpretation of Roles   Ted Lange is believable as a happy bridegroom and a jealous husband. Because of the textual cuts, we do not see or hear much of his competence as a general. He acts with energy, twisting Iago's arm behind his back on "Villain, be sure thou prove my love a whore" (III.iii.359) and later dragging Desdemona across a courtyard as he tells her to fetch the handkerchief (III.iv). He kills Desdemona by strangling her, not by smothering her with a pillow, as the text is usually interpreted. He tries furiously to kill Iago in the final scene and is barely restrained by the other characters.

Hawthorne James's Iago speaks and behaves in an awkward, sincere manner that gains his victims' confidence. The fact that he is also black gives the film an interesting dimension. Othello's choice of Cassio for promotion becomes, for Iago, a betrayal of brotherhood. At the same time, Othello would seem to have an innate reason to trust Iago. Leaving aside temporary impulses like promoting the wrong person, their bond is that of outsiders, alert for exploitation by a power group they do not entirely understand.

Emilia (Dawn Comer), Iago's wife and the third black in this film, shares this bond and consequently seems to feel little loyalty to her mistress during the earlier scenes. Her change of heart may be less a matter of their personal relationship than of simple respect for the truth. Earlier, when she finds the handkerchief, she is delighted, dancing about as she offers it to Iago. His words about "a foolish wife" (III.iii.304) are spoken teasingly, and up to Emilia's discovery of Iago's villainy they seem to share a cheerful, sexy relationship.

Mary Otis portrays Desdemona as a woman of passion, strength, and common sense. Othello's strange behavior seems to fill her not so much with terror as with concern. Until her last moments, when she realizes that Othello seriously intends to kill her, she seems to assume that some mistake has been made and that everything will be cleared up.

Production History   The film was made in America and so far has not been distributed to movie theaters.

Reviews and Studies   Russo, Peggy A. *"Othello." Shakespeare Bulletin* 10.3 (1992): 40–41.

Purchase/Rental Inquiries   Rockbottom Productions. See Appendix B for address.

24 ❧ PERICLES

❧ 24.1. *Pericles, Prince of Tyre.* 1983. British Broadcasting Company/ Time-Life Television: The Shakespeare Plays. Color, 180 min. Producer: Shaun Sutton. Director: David Jones.

PERICLES	Mike Gwilym
GOWER	Edward Petherbridge
MARINA	Amanda Redman
THAISA	Juliet Stevenson
BOULT	Trevor Peacock
THE BAWD	Lila Kaye
ANTIOCHUS	John Woodvine
CLEON	Norman Rodway
DIONYZA	Annette Crosbie
CERIMON	Clive Swift
LYSIMACHUS	Patrick Ryecart
ANTIOCHUS' DAUGHTER	Edita Brychia
THAILARD	Robert Ashby
HELICANUS	Godfrey Patrick
ESCANES	Toby Salaman
SIMONIDES	Patrick Allen
LEONINE	Nick Brumble
THE GODDESS DIANA	Elayne Sharling
LYCHORIDA	Valerie Lush
PHILEMON	Edward Clayton

Pluses Persuasive acting; interesting visual details.

Minuses None, granted that this story is very strange when measured by modern narrative expectations, and that any film of it will consequently seem at many points ludicrous and baffling.

Textual Cuts and Rearrangements The text is followed almost exactly. Every now and then a word or line drops out, perhaps by accident.

Marina's age is altered; she is here said to be sixteen, rather than the text's fourteen, when she is captured by pirates and sold into a brothel (V.iii.8).

There are some additions. King Simonides translates the Latin mottoes on the shields of the knights who visit his court (II.ii). The court then applauds, whether in honor of the visitors or of their king's linguistic skill is uncertain.

A longer addition occurs when Marina tries, successfully, to dissuade Lysimachus from ravishing her (IV.vi). Much of her speech in the film is taken from George Wilkins's *The Painful Adventures of Pericles, Prince of Tyre* (1608), a work of prose fiction which may have been based on a performance of *Pericles* by Shakespeare's company. The additional text improves the scene, as Marina's plea is more developed and Lysimachus' change of heart consequently more plausible.

Settings   Pericles and his scattered family visit numerous places in the ancient Mediterranean world—Antioch, Tyre, Tharsus, Pentapolis, Ephesus, Mytilene. These locales appear as various configurations of sun-baked courtyards, narrow streets, market-places.

A beach, or rather a row of sand dunes with an ocean presumably on the other side, recurs whenever needed, as a place for shipwrecked characters to land, or as the site of the temple of Diana.

Interiors are generally spacious and solid-seeming. The brothel in Mytilene makes its intentions clear with a beaded curtain and a round sofa of the sort portrayed in Toulouse-Lautrec's paintings.

Costumes   Dress is adapted to a hot climate. Men wear loose tunics and cloaks; women, long gowns of simple design. Royalty is sometimes more impressively garbed, with gold collars or pearl embroidery, but in this film luxurious clothing is suspect. Cleon and Dionyza appear in elaborate black mourning gear as they pretend that Marina died of natural causes (IV.iii). (Dionyza has had Marina murdered, or thinks she has.) Earlier in the play, the incestuous King Antiochus and his daughter wear silks and velvets, much looped and puffed, emblematic of their own decadence (I.i).

Interpretation of Roles   The play's chorus, or narrator, is John Gower (1325?–1408), the English poet whose *Confessio Amantis* was among Shakespeare's sources for *Pericles*. Shakespeare's including him in this guise is a graceful acknowledgment, and the device of the narrator adds coherence to the story. As played by Edward Petherbridge, Gower makes clear to the audience that they are watching a tale, a work of the imagination, and not a slice of reality.

Mike Gwilym is physically suited to act Pericles, having a long jaw and a gloomy look, and does a good job with this difficult (perhaps because essentially so passive) role. When called upon to do something heroic, he does it, but most of the time he is in the grip of malignant fortune.

Marina (Amanda Redman) portrays a convincing combination of vulnerability, common sense, and virtue. Her mother, Thaisa (Juliet Stevenson), does not appear in many scenes but projects a youthful love for Pericles and a maternal love for the infant Marina. Since this is not a realistic play, audiences are not perturbed to find that Thaisa has not aged noticeably during the time her daughter was growing up.

Production History *Pericles* was shown on American television in June of 1984, near the end of the British Broadcasting Company's project (1978–85) of filming the entire Shakespeare canon.

Reviews and Studies Bulman, J. C., and Coursen, H. R., eds. *Shakespeare on Television*. 1988. Extracts from reviews of this film, pp. 307–9.

Rothwell, Kenneth S., and Melzer, Annabelle H. *Shakespeare on Screen*. 1990. Item 482, pp. 228–29.

Willis, Susan. *The BBC Shakespeare Plays*. 1991. Pp. 194–96.

Purchase/Rental Inquiries Ambrose Video; Filmic Archives; Insight Media; The Writing Company. See Appendix B for addresses.

25 ❧ RICHARD THE SECOND

❧ 25.1. *Richard the Second.* 1978. British Broadcasting Company/ Time-Life Television: The Shakespeare Plays. Color, 180 min. Producer: Cedric Messina. Director: David Giles.

KING RICHARD II	Derek Jacobi
HENRY OF BOLINGBROKE, AFTERWARD KING HENRY IV	Jon Finch
JOHN OF GAUNT	John Gielgud
QUEEN TO RICHARD II	Janet Maw
DUCHESS OF YORK	Wendy Hiller
DUKE OF YORK	Charles Gray
EARL OF NORTHUMBERLAND	David Swift
HENRY PERCY, NICKNAMED HOTSPUR	Jeremy Bulloch
DUCHESS OF GLOUCESTER	Mary Morris
BISHOP OF CARLISLE	Clifford Rose
AUMERLE	Charles Keating
THOMAS MOWBRAY, DUKE OF NORFOLK	Richard Owens
DUKE OF SURREY	Jeffrey Holland
SIR JOHN BUSHY	Robin Sachs
SIR JOHN BAGOT	Damien Thomas
SIR HENRY GREEN	Alan Dalton
SIR PIERCE OF EXTON	Desmond Adams
LORD ROSS	David Dodimead
LORD WILLOUGHBY	John Flint

Pluses   Excellent acting. Emphatic sense of conflict, even without battle scenes as such, and of political rivalries.

Minuses   Faults in this film are hard to find.

Textual Cuts and Rearrangements   Cuts are not extensive. The opening lines of scenes occasionally disappear. An example is II.ii, in which we do not hear the queen's intuition of "some unborn sorrow, ripe in fortune's womb."

The early part of IV.i, in which the courtly opponents hurl challenges at each other, has been omitted; the audience thus misses the echo of the Bolingbroke/

Mowbray quarrel in the play's opening scene, an echo which suggests that the reign of the new Henry IV will not bring an end to discord.

A puzzling cut, since the line forms a link with the plays that follow, occurs at the beginning of V.iii. In this film King Henry does not ask for news of his "unthrifty son"—Prince Hal.

The ending is further tidied, and the implications of a bloody future further softened, by the omission of lines describing the capture of rebels (that is, of persons still loyal to Richard II) and the dispatching of their severed heads to sundry destinations.

Settings Sets are small and somewhat stylized. Outdoor scenes have painted backdrops or take place at night. Richard's palace interior has a raised throne and a few slender columns. Later, his prison cell includes a crucifix to emphasize the idea of Richard as a sacrificial victim.

Horses are brought in occasionally, but we see only their heads, there apparently being no space to ride them. They function as stage properties. Bolingbroke stands in front of a gray horse, creating a heraldic effect, as he greets his new allies against the king (II.iii).

The queen and her ladies walk in a charming cloistered courtyard when they overhear the gardeners talking "of state" (III.iv).

Costumes Costumes are sumptuous. Richard is clothed in gold brocade; his nobles wear velvets and furs. Bolingbroke looks menacingly comfortable in his black armor.

The queen wears flowing gowns and an elaborate fillet headdress that hides her hair. In this worldly accoutrement she nevertheless looks young and undeserving of hardship.

Interpretation of Roles As the poetic, self-centered, and impractical Richard, Derek Jacobi is consistently convincing. His earlier speeches roll from his tongue while he glances round at his listeners, certain of their approval. As his power melts away he is astonished, discovering that without his crown he has essentially no self. He weeps as Northumberland harasses him to read a list of his supposed crimes (IV.i.269). In his final scene in prison, Richard surprises himself by becoming a man of action, seizing a pike from his murderers and killing two of them (V.v). Exton's mortal blow comes from behind.

Jon Finch's dark, quiet Bolingbroke is contrastingly withdrawn, focused not on his companions but on his objectives. When he is banished from England he says farewell in tones of subdued threat (I.iii); when he returns with an army, he greets the flattery of his followers with an ironic shrug (II.iii.19).

The duke of York, helpless in the changing events and distressed by both his nephews, the incompetent Richard and the usurping Bolingbroke, yearns for a stable, peaceful realm. Charles Gray manages to convey York's deep sense of principle despite the fact that York ends up supporting whoever is in power and thus appears, inevitably, wishy-washy.

As John of Gaunt, John Gielgud has only a few scenes. These are memorable, however, in particular his paean to England — "This royal throne of kings, this sceptred isle" (II.i.40ff.) — one of the most familiar passages in the play.

Janet Maw, Richard's queen, is quite young and yet not a child. This casting represents a workable compromise with history. At the time of his murder (1399), Richard's beloved first queen, Anne, had been dead for five years, and he was betrothed to the French princess Isabel, a child under ten. Shakespeare's lines are clearly meant to be spoken by a grown woman, and in fact the playwright seems to have invented something of a generic queen.

Northumberland, eager to help Bolingbroke win the throne and equally eager to share in the spoils, is played by David Swift with bustle and energy. His son Henry Percy, to figure more largely in the first part of *Henry IV* under his nickname of Hotspur, is played by Jeremy Bulloch as a rather modest, well-mannered youth.

Production History   *Richard II* was presented during the first season of the British Broadcasting Company's ambitious project of filming the entire Shakespeare canon. It was shown on British television in December of 1978, and in the United States in March of 1979.

Reviews and Studies   Bulman, J. C., and Coursen, H. R., eds. *Shakespeare on Television.* 1988. Extracts from reviews of this film, pp. 253–55.

Rothwell, Kenneth S., and Melzer, Annabelle H. *Shakespeare on Screen.* 1990. Item 492, p. 234.

Willis, Susan. *The BBC Shakespeare Plays.* 1991. Pp. 201–3.

Purchase/Rental Inquiries   Ambrose Video; Filmic Archives; Insight Media; The Writing Company. See Appendix B for addresses.

ᑫ 25.2. *The Tragedy of King Richard II.* 1982. Bard Productions. Color, 172 min. Producers: Jack Nakano, Jack Manning. Director: William Woodman.

KING RICHARD II	David Birney
HENRY OF BOLINGBROKE, AFTERWARD KING HENRY IV	Paul Shenar
DUKE OF YORK	Peter MacLean

DUCHESS OF YORK	Nan Martin
QUEEN TO RICHARD II	Mary Joan Negro
EARL OF NORTHUMBERLAND	John Devlin
HENRY PERCY, NICKNAMED HOTSPUR	Nicholas Hammond
THOMAS MOWBRAY, DUKE OF NORFOLK	Jeff Pomerantz
JOHN OF GAUNT	John McLiam
BISHOP OF CARLISLE	Logan Ramsey
AUMERLE	Deveren Bookwalter
DUKE OF SURREY	William H. Bassett
SIR PIERCE OF EXTON	Alvah Stanley
SIR JOHN BUSHY	Jay T. Loudenback
SIR JOHN BAGOT	Michael Cummings
SIR HENRY GREEN	William Gamble

Pluses   Colorful, energetic, with the underlying brutality clearly indicated.

Minuses   Acting is sometimes uneven.

Textual Cuts and Rearrangements   A few scenes disappear entirely. Without the duchess of Gloucester's conversation with John of Gaunt (I.ii), we miss the dynastic background. Elsewhere, lists of names have been shortened and a few substitutions made. Surrey addresses "Sir Pierce of Exton" instead of "My lord Fitzwater" in IV.i, allowing the audience to become aware of Exton's existence before he suddenly emerges as the murderer of King Richard.

Some minor characters are cut. The queen has only one lady-in-waiting in the garden scene (III.iv), and they listen to the conversation of two gardeners rather than three.

Henry IV begins his reign with a dispersal of severed heads, as in the text (V.vi). His mention of his "unthrifty son," Prince Hal, is also retained (V.iii).

Settings   The Elizabethan-style stage has numerous acting areas, with two stairways curving toward the main stage and an upper passage connecting them. Camera angles and distances vary considerably and the effect is dynamic rather than static.

Costumes   Costumes are colorful and make an attempt at period accuracy, but the effect is somehow perfunctory. Everything seems to have scallops.

Interpretation of Roles   David Birney's King Richard shows a great deal of physical vigor. He seldom languishes about. The poetry present in his lines is not slighted, but Birney does not beome rapt in it, and, although he does show fear on appropriate occasions, he shouts and snarls at his captors without succumbing to self-pity. In his final scene, the Christ image takes over; Richard has whipped off his prisoner's gown to flail at his attackers, and when he is speared (from a grille in the ceiling of his cell), he falls, wearing only a loincloth, arms outstretched.

As Bolingbroke, Paul Shenar lets violence come close to the surface. He explains the justice of his cause (II.iii.112) with the air of a man going through a necessary preamble before getting down to business. His condemnation to death of Richard's followers Bushy and Green (III.i), an action quite outside any pale of law, delineates the process of might making right. Bolingbroke strikes the chained prisoners in the face, then yanks them about by the hair; when at last he tells Northumberland to "see them dispatched," we hear screams and blows from offstage.

The duke of York, who in the scene just described looks sorrowfully at his staff of office while the audience realizes that he is a hostage as well, is played by Peter MacLean. For student audiences, MacLean's performance is unfortunately undercut by his hair. It is bluish-white in color, set in deep waves, and it remains immaculate throughout the action—giving him, in today's visual idiom, an air of superficiality which does not seem to have been intended.

John Devlin, as Northumberland, is brutal not only to his enemies but to his allies. He hits people on the shoulder as he talks to them; when his son, Harry Percy, is slow in kneeling before Bolingbroke, Northumberland shoves him to the ground (II.iii.40).

Production History   This Bard Production film was taped in 1981 at KCET, Public Television for Southern California, in Los Angeles. It was sponsored by the Shakespeare Video Society and the Santa Barbara Gazebo Theatre One, Inc. For other films in the Bard series, see the general introduction, p. 5.

Reviews and Studies   Rothwell, Kenneth S., and Melzer, Annabelle H. *Shakespeare on Screen*. 1990. Item 494, p. 235.

Purchase/Rental Inquiries   Crest Video; Filmic Archives. See Appendix B for addresses.

❧ 25.3. *The Wars of the Roses: Richard the Second.* 1991. The English Shakespeare Company. Color, 145 min. Producers: John Paul Chapple, Andy Ward. Director: Michael Bogdanov.

KING RICHARD II	Michael Pennington
HENRY OF BOLINGBROKE, AFTERWARD KING HENRY IV	Michael Cronin

HENRY PERCY, NICKNAMED HOTSPUR	Andrew Jarvis
DUKE OF YORK	Colin Farrell
DUCHESS OF YORK	Ann Penfold
EARL OF NORTHUMBERLAND	Roger Booth
AUMERLE	Philip Bowen
QUEEN TO RICHARD II	Francesca Ryan
JOHN OF GAUNT	Clyde Pollit
EARL OF WESTMORELAND	Ben Bazell
SIR JOHN BAGOT	Paul Brennan
SIR JOHN BUSHY	Sion Probert
SIR HENRY GREEN	Michael Fenner
EARL OF SALISBURY	Ian Burford
THOMAS MOWBRAY, DUKE OF NORFOLK	Jack Carr

Pluses   A well-produced film of an ingenious, gripping stage play. Acting is energetic and convincing.

Minuses   Actors shifting from one role to another, within the same film or within this company's series of Shakespeare's history plays, can confuse viewers.

Textual Cuts and Rearrangements   The text is frequently cut, presumably in order to streamline the action. Information is seldom repeated, and the audience must be alert. Some of the poetry is sacrificed.

Aumerle's attempt to join a plot against Henry IV is omitted (V.ii and V.iii). The duchess of Gloucester's discourse on the sons of Edward III as "seven vials of his sacred blood" (I.ii. 12) also disappears.

Setting   The stage is essentially bare. An upper level has been constructed with scaffolding. Furniture is carried on and off to indicate various locations. On camera, figures tend to appear in isolation against a black backdrop.

Costumes   During the seven *Wars of the Roses* films (see "Production History," below), costumes move from the early nineteenth century to the present day. Here, at the beginning of the series, King Richard wears luxurious Regency garb—white knee breeches, brocade jackets, elaborate neck linen, curled sideburns. Ladies wear full skirts, with bonnets and shawls for outdoors. Military figures show quantities of gold braid.

Among student audiences, most viewers find these anachronisms amusing and interesting. Others express a preference for authentic period costumes of King Richard's actual era, the late fourteenth century.

Interpretation of Roles   Michael Pennington dominates the play as King Richard. His habitual expression, a blend of grimace and smirk, is well suited to the self-deceived monarch. Every movement shows that he expects to be looked at, and he is. He reacts with snarls and sarcasm, rather than pathos, to finding himself "unkinged." In prison, he throws his food at the keeper, then snatches the murderers' daggers away from them. Exton then enters and shoots Richard with a pistol.

As Bolingbroke, Michael Cronin at first seems overmatched. He has a pudding face and a stiff, perpendicular carriage. But he turns these traits to advantage. His stolid countenance demonstrates confidence and power while Richard writhes about.

John of Gaunt, played by Clyde Pollit, is brought onstage in a wheelchair for his farewell scene (I.iii). Later, he plays the small role of the groom who visits Richard in prison (V.v), leading viewers to wonder for a moment if Richard is now subject to hallucinations of people he mistreated earlier in his career.

Francesca Ryan plays the queen as a smiling, complaisant woman who assumes happiness is her right and cannot understand why her world has turned against her.

Production History   The English Shakespeare Company, led by Michael Bogdanov and Michael Pennington, first presented *The Wars of the Roses*, a twenty-hour cycle of Shakespeare's history plays, in Bath in 1987. The production later went on tour, visiting Australia and the United States among other places.

The cycle was staged, usually, within two-and-a-half or three days, thus creating an intense experience for theatergoers.

The film of *Richard II* and the six others was made before a live audience in the Grand Theatre, Swansea, Wales.

Besides *Richard II*, first of the sequence, the cycle of *The Wars of the Roses* includes *Henry IV, Part One* (8.3), *Henry IV, Part Two* (9.3), *Henry V* (10.4), *Henry VI: The House of Lancaster* (11.4), *Henry VI: The House of York* (11.5), and *Richard III* (26.3). The three parts of *Henry VI* have been reconfigured into two parts.

Shakespeare's other English history plays, *King John* and *Henry VIII*, are not included in this cycle because they do not concern the Wars of the Roses, and the time periods (early thirteenth century and early sixteenth century, respectively) do not link up.

Reviews and Studies   The following material deals with stage presentations of *The Wars of the Roses* rather than with the films.

Crowl, Samuel. *Shakespeare Observed: Studies in Performance on Stage and Screen.* Pp. 142–64, 187–89.

Fisher, James. "The Wars of the Roses." *Shakespeare Bulletin* 6.4 (1988): 14–17.

Jackson, Macd. P. *"The Wars of the Roses*: The English Shakespeare Company on Tour." *Shakespeare Quarterly* 40 (1989): 208–12.

McElroy, Bernard. "Shakespeare on Stage: The Plantagenets in Chicago." *Shakespeare Quarterly* 39 (1988): 495–500.

Purchase/Rental Inquiries   Films for the Humanities and Sciences. See Appendix B for address.

26 ❧ RICHARD THE THIRD*

❧ 26.1. *Richard the Third.* 1955. London Film Productions. Color, 138 min. Producers: Alexander Korda; Laurence Olivier. Director: Laurence Olivier.

KING RICHARD III	Laurence Olivier
LADY ANNE	Claire Bloom
DUKE OF CLARENCE	John Gielgud
DUKE OF BUCKINGHAM	Ralph Richardson
JANE SHORE	Pamela Brown
LORD HASTINGS	Alec Clunes
KING EDWARD IV	Cedric Hardwicke
ELIZABETH, QUEEN TO EDWARD IV	Mary Kerridge
LORD STANLEY	Laurence Naismith
DUCHESS OF YORK	Helen Haye
EARL OF RICHMOND, AFTERWARD HENRY VII	Stanley Baker
DUKE OF NORFOLK	John Phillips
LORD RIVERS	Clive Morton
LORD DORSET	Douglas Wilmer
LORD GREY	Dan Cunningham
ARCHBISHOP	Nicholas Hannen
LORD LOVEL	John Laurie
SIR RICHARD RATCLIFFE	Esmond Knight
SIR WILLIAM CATESBY	Norman Wooland
SIR JAMES TYRREL	Patrick Toughton
SIR ROBERT BRAKENBURY	Andrew Cruikshank
EDWARD, PRINCE OF WALES	Paul Hudson
YOUNG DUKE OF YORK	Andy Shine

Pluses   Students respond to this film's exuberance and especially to Olivier's demonic Richard.

Minuses   The film's visual style, which almost seems to turn history into an animated cartoon, disturbs some viewers.

Textual Cuts and Rearrangements   The film begins with the closing scenes of *Henry VI, Part Three,* thus emphasizing Richard's ambition to get the crown

* Note: For films related to Shakespeare's *Richard III,* see Appendix A, "Analogues and Variations."

and clarifying the fact that to do so, by the principles of primogeniture, he must eliminate his older brothers and their children. In adding these scenes, Olivier follows a quite sensible stage tradition in effect since the eighteenth century.

Richard's courtship of Lady Anne (I.ii) is split into two segments in this film, and the coffin she accompanies is provided with the wrong corpse. While in Shakespeare's text she mourns her father-in-law, Henry VI, here the deceased is named as her husband (actually her betrothed), the Lancastrian heir Prince Edward.

The film cuts many lines and passages, though most of these changes do not alter the action. George, duke of Clarence, is killed quite briskly in this film (I.iv), with no opportunity for the murderers to discuss the claims of conscience. The parade of ghosts appearing before Richard on the night before the Battle of Bosworth Field is shortened to the more prominent of his victims (V.iii), and Richard and his opponent Richmond do not speak their symmetrical orations before their respective armies.

The role of Queen Margaret, in Shakespeare's text the last of the Lancastrian warriors, is omitted.

King Edward IV's mistress, Jane Shore, has here been added to the cast and is played by Pamela Brown. Mistress Shore appears wordlessly in numerous scenes — at King Edward's coronation, in the Tower of London when Hastings is released, and in the king's bedchamber as he is dying. After Hastings becomes her protector, she waves a farewell to him as he rides unknowingly to his death in the Tower (III.ii).

In this film, King Richard is not killed by Richmond personally, as in Shakespeare's text (V.v). Instead, he is done in by a miscellaneous mob of soldiers. This interpretation more nearly accords with historical fact. (It might be added that in this play, as in his other history plays, Shakespeare has compressed the sequence of events and made other alterations. His depiction of Richard is considerably blacker than that of present-day historians, but Shakespeare was following the current Tudor political stance. Shakespeare's Richard is also irresistible theater.)

Settings   London of the 1480s here becomes a toy village, all tidy streets and arched cloisters. Snow falls picturesquely.

Costumes   Contrasting colors add to the liveliness of the general effect. Ladies wear tall conical hats with scarves drifting from the tops. Richard appears at first in black, an ominous figure, but he then follows his resolve to "entertain a score . . . of tailors" (I.ii.256) and becomes even more hypocritical, in a visual sense.

Interpretation of Roles   Olivier's Richard reaches a peak of villainous joy when, after his show of pious modesty has tricked the Lord Mayor of London into supporting his claim to the crown, he slides jubilantly down a bell rope to the courtyard below (III.vii). His cousin and henchman the duke of Buckingham approaches; Richard holds out a hand to him; as Buckingham prepares to kiss it, Richard lowers his hand and thus forces Buckingham to his knees.

Richard's vitality seems to ebb once he has achieved his goal. He goes on killing people—the little princes, the duke of Buckingham—but though he can force himself to make an effort the zest is gone.

Ralph Richardson plays Buckingham as a cheerful second-in-command, following orders and enjoying the reflection of Richard's power. It is believable that he would discover too late that Richard can turn against him as well (IV.ii).

As Lady Anne, Claire Bloom has the difficult task of succumbing to Richard's blandishments, in a scene (I.ii) which today's audiences find a strain to credibility; how could anybody marry a man who had killed her husband and father-in-law? The solution proposed in this film is that Lady Anne finds Richard's ruthlessness sexually attractive. She seems mesmerized, almost to the point of swooning.

Lady Anne in Shakespeare's text is not seen after she is summoned to Westminster for Richard's coronation (IV.i.32), but in this film Richard drags her with him as he literally ascends to the throne, climbing a flight of stairs. There is no throne for the queen, and after he lets her go she collapses. Richard does not seem to notice.

Production History   Olivier's *Richard III* was a definite success in movie theaters. It was also shown on American television in March of 1956.

Reviews and Studies   Brown, Constance. "Laurence Olivier's *Richard III.*" In *Focus on Shakespearean Film*, ed. Charles Eck. 1972. Pp. 131–45.

Davies, Anthony. *Filming Shakespeare's Plays*. 1988. Pp. 65–82, 191–92.

Jorgens, Jack J. *Shakespeare on Film*. 1977. Pp. 136–47, 275–79, 322.

Manville, Roger. *Shakespeare and the Film*. 1971. Pp. 47–54.

Rothwell, Kenneth S., and Melzer, Annabelle H. *Shakespeare on Screen*. 1990. Item 503, pp. 239–40.

Purchase/Rental Inquiries   Filmic Archives. See Appendix B for address.

ఇ 26.2. *Richard the Third.* 1983. British Broadcasting Company/ Time-Life Television: The Shakespeare Plays. Color, 230 min. Producer: Shaun Sutton. Director: Jane Howell.

KING RICHARD III	Ron Cook
LADY ANNE	Zoë Wanamaker
QUEEN MARGARET	Julia Foster
DUKE OF BUCKINGHAM	Michael Byrne
KING EDWARD IV	Brian Prothero
GEORGE, DUKE OF CLARENCE	Paul Jesson
LORD HASTINGS	David Dakar
DUCHESS OF YORK	Annette Crosbie
ELIZABETH, QUEEN TO EDWARD IV	Rowena Cooper
EARL OF RICHMOND, AFTERWARD	
KING HENRY VII	Brian Deacon
JANE SHORE	Anne Carroll
LORD STANLEY	Tenniel Evans
SIR RICHARD RATCLIFFE	Anthony Brown
LORD LOVEL	Oengus MacNamara
SIR WILLIAM CATESBY	David Burke
SIR ROBERT BRAKENBURY	Derek Farr
LORD DORSET	Alex Guard
DUKE OF NORFOLK	Peter Wyatt
PAGE TO KING RICHARD	Rusty Livingstone
CORPSE OF KING HENRY VI	Peter Benson
LORD RIVERS	Peter Chapman
LORD GREY	Arthur Cox
YOUNG DUKE OF YORK	Jeremy Dimmick
EDWARD, PRINCE OF WALES	Dorian Ford
SIR JAMES TYRELL	Mark Wing-Davey

Pluses   A thoughtful film, useful in the classroom as it follows the text and brings out the potential complexity of many of the characters.

Minuses   Can be slow going.

Textual Cuts and Rearrangements   Most of the text is retained, even the formal lamentation of the children of Clarence (II.ii). All the ghosts turn up to curse Richard and bless Richmond (V.iii).

Settings   *Richard III* follows the BBC's films of the three parts of *Henry VI*, also directed by Jane Howell, and uses the same barn-like set, though by this time it has become faded and splintery, knocked about by the earlier Wars of the Roses.

Costumes   Somber colors are in vogue for this production. Courtiers wear dark cloaks with touches of fur. Soldiers are in black armor.

Interpretation of Roles   Ron Cook plays King Richard in a low key, his face impassive, tending to mutter rather than orate. He seems to view his murders merely as practical solutions. His end is appropriately violent. After Richmond impales him on a spear, Richard runs up it, like a human shish kebab, the spear tip protruding from his back, in a vain attempt to kill Richmond with his own somewhat shorter sword. Other soldiers rally to the kill. By the time Richard dies, he has been skewered by so many shafts that he cannot fall over. He remains in a kneeling position, propped up by the spears, and gazes at the survivors from dead but only half-closed eyes (V.ii).

Zoë Wanamaker, as Lady Anne, shows a fiery temperament which makes her a sympathetic character to modern audiences but also lessens the plausibility of her acceptance of Richard's suit. When he offers her his sword and suggests that she kill him, she grasps the sword eagerly but somehow cannot bring herself to use it (I.ii).

As Queen Margaret, the last Lancastrian, Julia Foster becomes a symbol of the carnage not only of this play but of the preceding *Henry VI* plays. After the concluding lines of the text we hear hysterical laughter; the camera then shifts to Margaret, seated surreally on a pile of corpses, cradling the newly dead Richard in her arms.

Production History   *Richard III* was shown on British television in January of 1983, following the three parts of *Henry VI*. American television showed the tetralogy, at two-week intervals, in March and April of 1983. The British Broadcasting Company's project of filming Shakespeare's entire dramatic canon was then in its fourth year and would conclude in 1985.

Reviews and Studies   Bulman, J. C., and H. R. Coursen, eds. *Shakespeare on Television*. 1988. Extracts from reviews of this film, pp. 292–96.

Rothwell, Kenneth S., and Melzer, Annabelle H. *Shakespeare on Screen*. 1990. Item 513, p. 244.

Willis, Susan. *The BBC Shakespeare Plays*. 1991. Pp. 183–86.

Purchase/Rental Inquiries   Ambrose Video; Filmic Archives; Insight Media; The Writing Company. See Appendix B for addresses.

 26.3. *The Wars of the Roses: Richard the Third.* 1990. The English Shakespeare Company. Color, 194 min. Producers: John Paul Chapple, Andy Ward. Director: Michael Bogdanov.

KING RICHARD III	Andrew Jarvis
LADY ANNE	Francesca Ryan
QUEEN MARGARET	June Watson
KING EDWARD IV	Philip Bowen
LORD STANLEY	Michael Cronin
CORPSE OF HENRY VI	Paul Brennan
ELIZABETH, QUEEN TO EDWARD IV	Ann Penfold
DUKE OF BUCKINGHAM	Michael Pennington
LORD HASTINGS	Roger Booth
GEORGE, DUKE OF CLARENCE	John Dougall
LORD RIVERS	John Darrell
LORD GREY	Ben Bazell
LORD DORSET	John Tramper
DUCHESS OF YORK	Susanna Best
EARL OF RICHMOND, AFTERWARD KING HENRY VII	Charles Dale
SIR JAMES TYRELL	Jack Carr
EDWARD, PRINCE OF WALES	Simon Rance
YOUNG DUKE OF YORK	William Turner
SIR ROBERT BRAKENBURY	Colin Farrell
SIR RICHARD RATCLIFFE	Stephen Jameson
SIR WILLIAM CATESBY	Sion Probert

Pluses   An inventive, engrossing film, appealing to about 95 per cent of student viewers. This film is the conclusion of a series of history plays, but it can be shown on its own.

Minuses   Anachronisms disturb some viewers.

Textual Cuts and Rearrangements   The film begins with a non-Shakespearean introduction by actor Barry Stanton, who gives a brief sketch of the principle characters, stressing their family connections and political alignments, as the camera lingers on each. The characters meanwhile are enjoying a cocktail party complete with mellow jazz and smiling conversation. A coffin occupied by the pale corpse of Henry VI lies in the middle of the floor.

Shakespeare's text is augmented on a few other occasions, easily identified as interpolations. Many of these evoke a chuckle from the audience. The death of

Edward IV, for example, is announced by a newsboy shouting the headline "King Dies—Shuffles Off Mortal Coil."

Cuts occur from time to time. Queen Margaret's and Queen Elizabeth's symmetrical bewailing of various deceased Richards and Edwards (II.ii) has disappeared; Clarence's daughter and the duchess of York are missing from the group which attempts to visit the captive princes in the Tower of London (IV.i); the ghosts who curse Richard do not use the occasion to bless Richmond (V.iii).

Other passages are thinned, usually in order to speed the action. A few cuts are puzzling. The young Prince of Wales does not announce his ambition to "win our ancient right in France again" (III.i.92), a line full of ironic poignancy, especially when the history plays have been staged as a series.

Settings   Furniture and properties are carried onstage to establish various locales. The determinedly anachronistic time period begins in the 1930s and reaches to the present day. Stanley talks to Sir Christopher (IV.v) by means of a surreptitious telephone call, expressing perfectly Stanley's role as a double agent. By the fifth act, King Richard III has a computer on his desk. The earl of Richmond's victory speech, at the conclusion of the Battle of Bosworth Field, becomes a televised press conference. Technicians apply the royal makeup, "God Save the King" is played, and the studio camera lingers on Richmond's lapel, where a white rose and a red have been carefully pinned.

Costumes   Richard's rise to power is signaled by his change from a gangsterish zoot suit to gray chalkstripes. Queen Margaret, widow of Henry VI, wears her officer's uniform from the earlier plays and now looks entirely insane.

An attempt at middle-class normalcy characterizes the court of Edward IV. Queen Elizabeth wears soft, frilly dresses and surrounds herself with dainty furniture and vases of flowers. Her youngest sons, the little princes, appear in sweaters, immaculate but casual.

The Battle of Bosworth Field brings in the mixed military uniforms to which viewers of *The Wars of the Roses* have grown accustomed—camouflage fatigues, World War I wide-brimmed helmets, and so on. But in this case the smoke suddenly clears to reveal two knights in armor, one in gold and the other in black, fighting with broadswords. We have come full circle, and we have shifted (at least for the moment) from contemporary complexity to the reassuringly simple realm of myth. The fighter in gold—the earl of Richmond, soon to become Henry VII—manages to remove his opponent's visor and reveal the face of Richard. Then he cuts Richard's throat.

Interpretation of Roles   Andrew Jarvis makes Richard the most dazzling of his many roles in this seven-play series. His grotesque appearance and awkward manner fully fit the part. He lurches about the stage, bald head gleaming, long arms waving, a knife or pistol frequently in his hand. At the beginning of the play, however, before Richard is strong enough to reveal his true self, his awkwardness takes the guise of plain-spoken sincerity. Those who are taken in by this deception come to regret it.

Among these trusting souls is, of course, Lady Anne, played by Francesca Ryan. She is suspicious during Richard's declarations of love, but she forces herself, presumably from a sense of justice, to consider the possibility that he means what he says: "I would I knew thy heart" (I.ii.192). After the marriage she appears resigned to her fate. Although Shakespeare's text does not indicate her presence onstage when Richard tells Catesby to "rumor it abroad/ That Anne, my wife, is very grievous sick" (IV.ii.50–51), in this production she is standing not far from her husband, quietly, dressed in black. Catesby bows to her, then takes her roughly by the arm and pulls her offstage. She makes no protest.

Production History; Reviews and Studies; Purchase/Rental Inquiries   See the English Shakespeare Company's *Richard II* (25.3).

27 &❧ ROMEO AND JULIET*

&❧ **27.1. *Romeo and Juliet.*** 1936. Metro-Goldwyn-Mayer. Black-and-white, 126 min.

Directed by George Cukor, with Norma Shearer (Juliet), Leslie Howard (Romeo), John Barrymore (Mercutio), Basil Rathbone (Tybalt).
This film is currently unavailable.

&❧ **27.2. *Guiliete e Romeo/Romeo and Juliet.*** 1954. Verona Productions. Color, 138 min. Producers: Sandro Ghenzi, Joseph Janni. Director: Renato Castellani.

ROMEO	Laurence Harvey
JULIET	Susan Shentall
CHORUS	John Gielgud
JULIET'S NURSE	Flora Robson
FRIAR LAWRENCE	Mervyn Johns
PARIS	Norman Wooland
BENVOLIO	Bill Travers
TYBALT	Enzo Fiermonte
MERCUTIO	Aldo Zollo
CAPULET	Sebastian Cabot
LADY CAPULET	Lydia Sherwood
PRINCE OF VERONA	Giovanni Rota
MONTAGUE	Guilio Garbinetti
LADY MONTAGUE	Nietta Zocchi
FRIAR JOHN	Thomas Nicholls
ROSALINE	Dagmar Josipovich

Pluses   Beautifully photographed, briskly paced.

Minuses   Poetry sometimes sacrificed to other considerations.

* Note: For films related to Shakespeare's *Romeo and Juliet*, see Appendix A, "Analogues and Variations."

Textual Cuts and Rearrangements   Many of the numerous changes in the text might be defended as clarifying the action, adding to the characters' motivation, or underlining the irony of the plot.

Mercutio's "Queen Mab" speech (I.iv) is omitted, as are many familiar lines from the lovers' balcony scene (II.ii). Juliet does not encounter Paris in Friar Lawrence's cell (IV.i), and Romeo does not mention or visit an apothecary in Mantua (V.i). The ending is greatly simplified. We do not hear of Lady Montague dying of grief (V.iii.211), Friar Lawrence's explanation is cut, and neither of the newly reconciled fathers offers to raise a golden statue to commemorate the other's child.

At several points the director adds characters or dialogue. Rosaline, the mysterious lady whom Romeo loves at the play's beginning, is not only present at the Capulet's feast but speaks to Romeo—"Put on your mask, and leave this place at once."

Friar John's explanation of why he was unable to deliver Friar Lawrence's letter to Romeo (V.i) becomes a story in itself and is moved to an earlier point, preceding Juliet's taking the potion. The audience sees Friar John enter Mantua, where, as he walks down a street, he is called to hear the last confession of a dying man. "But this is plague," he remarks, having presumably been trained by Friar Lawrence in medical matters, and as he lingers beside the patient's bed the rest of the household run away, lock the doors, and board up the windows.

Settings   Narrow streets, ancient romanesque buildings, crooks and crannies, shot in several locations in northern Italy. The beauty and solidity of the settings add a special dimension to the film.

Interpretation of Roles   Laurence Harvey plays Romeo competently, but variations in fashion since the 1950s work against him for a present day audience. His hair is too elaborately coiffed, and he is simply too old. Except when he is in rapid motion, as when he runs through the streets of Verona to Juliet's tomb (V.iii), it is hard to believe in him as an impulsive lover.

Susan Shentall's blonde Juliet has a beautiful but stony face, appropriately expressionless when she hides her love for Romeo from her parents (III.v). But she remains distant from the audience as well.

The Nurse, Flora Robson, seems to be trying to bring an air of respectability to the proceedings. Some of her bawdier lines are cut. Her personality makes it quite plausible that she would urge Juliet to forget Romeo, now in disgrace after all, and marry Paris instead (III.v).

Aldo Zollo's Mercutio suffers from the textual cuts, which have removed the playful dimension of his personality and left him to fight Tybalt hastily and grimly (III.i).

Production History   This film won the Grand Prize at the Venice Film Festival in 1954, and fared reasonably well at the box office.

Reviews and Studies   Jorgenson, Paul A. "Castellani's *Romeo and Juliet*: Intention and Response." In Charles W. Eckert, ed., *Focus on Shakespearean Films*. 1972. Pp. 198–15.

Manvell, Roger. *Shakespeare and the Film*. 1971. Pp. 97–100.

Rothwell, Kenneth S., and Melzer, Annabelle H. *Shakespeare on Screen*. 1990. Item 538, pp. 252–53.

Walker, Roy. "In Fair Verona." In Charles W. Eckert, ed., *Focus on Shakespearean Films*. 1972. Pp. 115–21.

Purchase/ Rental Inquiries   Films for the Humanities and Sciences. See Appendix B for address.

🏿 **27.3.** *Romeo and Juliet*. 1968. Paramount. Color, 139 min. Producers: Anthony Havelock-Allan, John Brabourne. Director: Franco Zeffirelli.

ROMEO	Leonard Whiting
JULIET	Olivia Hussey
TYBALT	Michael York
MERCUTIO	John McEnery
FRIAR LAWRENCE	Milo O'Shea
JULIET'S NURSE	Pat Heywood
VOICE-OVER CHORUS	Laurence Olivier
BENVOLIO	Bruce Robinson
CAPULET	Paul Hardwick
LADY CAPULET	Natasha Parry
PRINCE OF VERONA	Robert Stephens
MONTAGUE	Antonio Pierfederici
LADY MONTAGUE	Esmerelda Ruspoli
PARIS	Roberto Bisacco

Pluses   For student audiences, this remains the most popular film version of this play—energetic, visually lush, filled with music.

Minuses   Loss of poetry and plot details.

Textual Cuts and Rearrangements   Viewers are divided as to whether this film's added spectacle compensates for the subtracted text.

Juliet's speech beginning "Gallop apace, you fiery-footed steeds" (III.ii) and her frightened imaginings, before she swallows the potion, of waking alone in the tomb (IV.iii.30ff.) are among the omissions. On finding Juliet's supposed corpse (IV.iv), the nurse spends no time or words trying to wake her mistress; she simply screams. The family's lengthy lamentations and Friar Lawrence's visit, both of which follow in the text, disappear from the film.

In some cases, a quick glimpse of an action substitutes for omitted text. We do not have Friar John's explanation of being detained in his attempt to deliver Friar Lawrence's letter to Romeo (V.ii). Instead, Friar John simply sets out for Mantua on a donkey. After Juliet's supposed death, Romeo's servant Balthasar leaves Verona on a galloping horse, and we see him pass the friar and his donkey on the road. Romeo thus receives the false news and takes immediate action.

Paris does not come to mourn at Juliet's tomb, and Romeo consequently does not kill him. When Romeo enters the tomb and sees Juliet, his line "Her beauty makes/ This vault a feasting presence full of light" (V.iii.85) is cut, although much of the passage is retained.

The final scene cuts a great deal of the text and substitutes an elaborate funeral procession, in which the lovers' bodies are carried through the square as bells toll and the city mourns.

Setting   Lavish landscapes, streets and gardens like picture postcards. We have a sense of Verona as a city. The Capulets' house is substantial, with its various parts fitting together in the viewer's memory.

Costumes   The Renaissance costumes are often made up in subdued colors, though rich in texture and detail, harmonizing with the softness of the scenery.

Interpretation of Roles   Olivia Hussey's Juliet dominates the film. Only fifteen at the time, she transmits an intense, sensual passion that is entirely believable, even if Hussey is not the more complex and highly verbal Juliet of Shakespeare's text. She giggles with joy when she embraces Romeo and sobs like a hurt child when she finds his body. Her small-scale brunette beauty, almost unearthly, is that of neither child nor woman.

Leonard Whiting, then sixteen, brings an answering urgency to his Romeo. After the balcony scene (II.i), when he swarms up the wall to embrace Juliet during much of the dialogue, he is so buoyed by joy that he runs through the fields, leaping down a dark hillside, on his way to meet Friar Lawrence at dawn.

Michael York plays Tybalt with graceful ferocity. He enjoys the fight with Mercutio and clearly does not intend to kill him. It is Romeo's intervention that puts off Tybalt's timing and causes the fatal thrust (III.i).

John McEnery's Mercutio leans toward the manic depressive—a tack that disturbs some viewers but that others find entirely plausible. Students sometimes say they know someone just like him. In his "Queen Mab" speech, Mercutio ends up babbling incoherently, running down a dark Verona street, until Romeo manages to calm him down: "Peace, Mercutio, peace!/ Thou talk'st of nothing" (I.v.95). His death is taken by his friends as just another joke (III.i). They laugh at his puns, then applaud his final spasms, enjoying the show.

Pat Heywood gives a happy, bawdy performance as Juliet's nurse. Being the target of sexy gibes in the street delights her (II.iv), but she then remembers her dignity and tries to straighten her expression.

Juliet's parents provide her, in this film at least, with a home life of chilly and perhaps only nominal affection. They are distant from each other as well. Capulet's warning to Paris about the bad effects of a too-early marriage (I.ii.13) apparently springs from experience; as he speaks, he glances across the courtyard, where Lady Capulet sees him and at once closes her window.

Production History   This film was a great success when released in 1968, often playing for months at first-run theaters.

Reviews and Studies   Deats, Sara Munson. "Zeffirelli's *Romeo and Juliet*: Shakespeare for the Sixties." *Studies in Popular Culture* 6 (1983): 60–67.

Jorgens, Jack J. *Shakespeare on Film.* 1977. Pp. 79–91, 261–65, 318.

Levenson, Jill. *Shakespeare in Performance: Romeo and Juliet.* 1987. Pp. 104–123.

Loney, Glenn, ed. *Staging Shakespeare: Seminars on Production Problems.* 1990. Pp. 239–70. Edited transcript of question-answer session on the filming of Zeffirelli's *Romeo and Juliet.*

Pursell, Michael. "Artifice and Authenticity in Zeffirelli's *Romeo and Juliet.*" *Literature/ Film Quarterly* 14 (1986): 173–78.

Rothwell, Kenneth S., and Melzer, Annabelle H. *Shakespeare on Screen.* Item 552, pp. 257–58.

Purchase/ Rental Inquiries   Filmic Archives. See Appendix B for address.

෴ 27.4. *Romeo and Juliet.* 1978. British Broadcasting Company/ Time-Life Television: The Shakespeare Plays. Color, 170 min. Producer: Cedric Messina. Director: Alvin Rakoff.

CHORUS:	John Gielgud
CAPULET	Michael Hordern
ROMEO	Patrick Ryecart

JULIET	Rebecca Saire
JULIET'S NURSE	Celia Johnson
FRIAR LAWRENCE	Joseph O'Conor
PRINCE OF VERONA	Laurence Naismith
MERCUTIO	Anthony Andrews
TYBALT	Alan Rickman
LADY CAPULET	Jacqueline Hill
BENVOLIO	Christopher Strauli
PARIS	Christopher Northey
PETER	Paul Henry
BALTHASAR	Roger Davidson
MONTAGUE	John Paul
LADY MONTAGUE	Zulema Dene

Pluses   Follows the text and has many innovative touches.

Minuses   Slow pace. Central characters lack magnetism.

Textual Cuts and Rearrangements   Cuts are infrequent. Romeo does not describe the apothecary (V.i.35ff.) but simply turns up at his shop. In the final scene, Romeo does not ask Balthasar to hand him a mattock and wrenching iron (V.iii.21), access to the tomb being easy in this setting. Friar Lawrence's explanation is substantially cut (V.iii.119ff.).

Occasional visual additions work well. In the opening fracas in the marketplace, we hear a woman's scream and find that a baby has been injured—an innocent victim foreshadowing those to come.

Settings   A studio set, the streets and squares of Verona on a small and cardboardy scale, but less claustrophobic than it might have been. The actors move frequently from place to place, thus breaking up the static effect of the long passages. The interior of the Capulet house is marbly and luxurious.

Costumes   Traditional and effective Renaissance wear—brocades, plumes, gold chains.

Interpretation of Roles   Juliet (Rebecca Saire) is small and pale; Romeo (Patrick Ryecart) is jowly and a bit lethargic. They are remarkably undemonstrative, gazing at each other but seldom touching. Students nevertheless find them convincing, once they get used to them. Juliet, students suggest, is too shy to have had other boyfriends; Romeo has protected his ego by falling in love with women like Rosaline, who are guaranteed to reject him so that he doesn't really get his hopes up. When Romeo and Juliet find each other, of course they fall in love.

Celia Johnson plays Juliet's nurse as old and almost feeble. She speaks slowly, and everyone waits patiently for her to finish. When she says she is too tired to tell Juliet about her meeting with Romeo (II.v), in this film she is not teasing her mistress but simply stating a fact.

Juliet's family is here interpreted as a warm and happy one. Lady Capulet (Jacqueline Hill) embraces Juliet when she speaks to her. Capulet, twinklingly played by Michael Hordern, beams at her indulgently. His sudden insistence that she marry Paris (III.v) thus comes as a jolt, but it might be accounted for on the supposition that Capulet wants a wedding to balance the sorrow of Tybalt's death—and that, benevolent or not, he is accustomed to getting his way without argument.

Production History   *Romeo and Juliet* was presented during the first year of the British Broadcasting Company's project of filming the entire Shakespeare canon. It was shown on British television in December of 1978, and in the United States in March of 1979.

Reviews and Studies   Bulman, J. C., and Coursen, H. R., eds. *Shakespeare on Television*. 1988. Extracts from reviews of this film, p. 253.

Rothwell, Kenneth S., and Melzer, Annabelle H. *Shakespeare on Screen*. 1990. Item 563, pp. 261–62.

Purchase/Rental Inquiries   Ambrose Video; Filmic Archives; Insight Media; The Writing Company. See Appendix B for addresses.

๊ **27.5.** *Romeo and Juliet.* 1982. Bard Productions. Color, 165 min. Producer: Jack Nakano. Director: William Woodman.

ROMEO	Alex Hyde-White
JULIET	Blanche Baker
JULIET'S NURSE	Esther Rolle
MERCUTIO	Dan Hamilton
BENVOLIO	Fredric Lehne
FRIAR LAWRENCE	Alvah Stanley
TYBALT	Norman Snow
CAPULET	Peter MacLean
LADY CAPULET	Penelope Windust
BALTHASAR	Michael Cummings

PARIS   Marco Barricelli
PRINCE OF VERONA   William H. Bassett

Pluses   Visually interesting. Well-choreographed fights.

Minuses   The acting is sometimes wooden, especially Juliet's.

Textual Cuts and Rearrangements   Opening and closing lines of scenes sometimes disappear, and passages are often thinned. Romeo's visit to the apothecary
is cut; instead, the apothecary silently appears while Romeo is describing him
(V.i.37ff.) and hands him the vial of poison. Many lines are cut in the final scene,
including most of Friar Lawrence's explanation.

Settings   The studio set is designed to resemble an Elizabethan stage, with
numerous acting levels. Camera angles keep the effect from becoming monotonous.

For the opening scenes the stage becomes a marketplace, with a tavern in one
corner. At the Capulet's feast, the stage is hung with garlands. Friar Lawrence's
cell is indicated with a desk and shelves of flasks for his chemical experiments.
For the Capulets' orchard, we have rows of potted trees.

The Capulet family tomb is seen both as an interior, occupying the main
stage, and as an exterior, where Romeo tries to get in; the camera has apparently
gone round backstage.

Costumes   Costumes are festive. Men wear tights with codpieces in contrasting
colors. Juliet has at least three outfits including, for the final scenes, a white
wedding gown with a little cap.

Interpretation of Roles   Blanche Baker's Juliet is a misfortune generally. She
speaks slowly, with little inflection, as if someone had wound her up. However,
she is irrefutably beautiful, with high-piled blonde hair and a daughterly resemblance to Lady Capulet, played by Penelope Windust.

Alex Hyde-White's Romeo is more expressive and more energetic. No goody-
goody, he deals with his frustrated love for Rosaline by drinking with Benvolio
at the tavern (I.i). His swordfights with Tybalt and Paris are acrobatic, all over
the stage, with extraordinary timing.

As Juliet's nurse, Esther Rolle uses her rich voice to create a calm, dignified,
nurturing presence.

Production History   Bard Productions sets its Shakespearean films in an Elizabethan-style stage and uses, for the most part, American actors. For other films
in the series, see the general introduction, p. 5.

Reviews and Studies   This film seems to have attracted little scholarly attention.

Purchase/Rental Inquiries   Crest Video; Filmic Archives. See Appendix B for addresses.

➤ *27.6. Romeo and Juliet.* 1988. Thames Television. Color, 180 min. Producer: Francis Coleman. Director: Joan Kemp-Welch.

ROMEO	Christopher Neame
JULIET	Ann Hasson
JULIET'S NURSE	Patsy Byrne
CAPULET	Laurence Paune
LADY CAPULET	Mary Kenton
FRIAR LAWRENCE	Clive Swift

Pluses   An attractive production, well acted, with a very full text.

Minuses   This film has few flaws other than the limited visual effects resulting from a small budget.

Textual Cuts and Rearrangements   Friar Lawrence's lines "The gray-ey'd morn smiles on the frowning night" (II.iii.1) are given to Romeo at the end of the preceding scene, comprising one of the few textual shifts in the film.

With this type of minor exception, the film precisely follows the text. The dialogue between the servant Peter and the musicians who come to the Capulets' house on the assumption they are to play for a wedding, almost always cut, is here retained (IV.v.102ff.). In the final scene, Friar Lawrence gives his entire explanation of what has happened, even though the audience already knows it (V.iii.229ff.). The film's credits are incomplete and give the false impression of a severely cut version.

Settings   The studio sets occasionally become romantically picturesque. The Capulet garden has a painted landscape as a background, and a pool which appears to be really a mirror. The Capulet tomb is not underground but consists of a group of stone coffins or biers, with bodies lying on top of them (as is usual in any staging of this play), enclosed by a high iron fence.

Costumes   Velvets, brocades, puffed sleeves. Juliet wears a dress so high-waisted that student viewers sometimes leap to the conclusion she is pregnant, despite her young age.

Interpretation of Roles   Ann Hasson's Juliet can take getting used to. She is very young, and good-looking in a healthy, girl-next-door sort of way, not at all like Olivia Hussey's eerie perfection in Zeffirelli's film. But the audience soon comes to believe in her and sympathize with her. Child-like, she roars with laughter at the nurse's long tale about her husband (I.iii). But when she lies weeping on the floor and the nurse advises her to forget Romeo and marry Paris (III.5), her face suddenly changes. It is as if she has suddenly become a grownup.

Christopher Neame plays Romeo as somewhat fragile and poetic. He seems to lack Juliet's vitality. His love for her is convincing, however. Perhaps he is drawn to the qualities he lacks.

Mercutio is played as a vigorous, good-natured young man. In fighting Tybalt, he goes into acrobatic twirls, offers Tybalt a cup of wine and then blows it in Tybalt's face. The fight becomes more intense, but it has not turned deadly when Romeo so unfortunately interferes.

Lady Capulet (Mary Kenton) seems genuinely fond of her daughter and wants her to be happily married. Old Capulet cannot imagine why Juliet should balk at the the prospect of marrying Paris, but his anger is more annoyance than fury. At the end, his and his wife's sorrow is profound. The uncut text allows him to balance Montague's peacemaking offer and promise a golden statue of Romeo.

Production History; Reviews and Studies   This film was shown on British television and does not seem to have attracted much critical attention.

Purchase/Rental Inquiries   HBO Video; The Writing Company. See Appendix B for addresses.

28 ❧ THE TAMING
OF THE SHREW*_____

❧ **28.1.** *The Taming of the Shrew.* 1929. United Artists. Black-and-white, 68 min.

Directed by Sam Taylor, starring Mary Pickford as Katherine and Douglas Fairbanks as Petruchio. Originally silent, this film then had dialogue dubbed in. In 1966 a new soundtrack added music. Text considerably cut.

The film has recently become available.

_____

❧ **28.2.** *The Taming of the Shrew.* 1966. Royal Films International. Color, 122 min. Producer: Richard McWhorter. Director: Franco Zeffirelli.

KATHERINE	Elizabeth Taylor
PETRUCHIO	Richard Burton
LUCENTIO	Michael York
BAPTISTA MINOLA	Michael Hordern
GRUMIO	Cyril Cusack
BIANCA	Natasha Pyne
TRANIO	Alfred Lynch
GREMIO	Alan Webb
HORTENSIO	Victor Spinetti
VINCENTIO	Mark Dignam
PEDANT	Vernon Dobtcheff
BIONDELLO	Roy Holder
WIDOW	Bice Valori

Pluses Memorable performances. Romping pace, energy, inventiveness; panoramic landscapes and big-budget sets.

Minuses Some viewers object to the frenetic action. Students, however, generally prefer this to all other filmed *Shrews*.

* Note: For films related to Shakespeare's *The Taming of the Shrew*, see Appendix A, "Analogues and Variations."

Textual Cuts and Rearrangements   The "Christopher Sly" frame story (Induction I and II) has been omitted, director Zeffirelli substituting his own beginning. We follow Lucentio through the rolling northern Italian landscape and into Padua, where the beginning of the university term seems to correspond with carnival.

Throughout the play, lines are cut, transposed, and sometimes paraphrased, while the characters rush madly through the streets of Verona. Textual boundaries between scenes disappear in the turbulence. Petruchio, for example, does not have Katherine called into his presence to begin his wooing; he goes in search of her, then follows her as she runs through the house (II.i), their dialogue spoken on the run, while in passing we glimpse through windows or doorways other scenes in progress—Bianca's conversation with her tutors (III.i), or Baptista's virtual auctioning-off of Bianca to the highest-bidding suitor (II.i.332ff.).

Another example of the camera's mobility, in contrast to the one-place-at-a-time fixity of the stage, occurs when Petruchio turns up for his wedding, ludicrously horsed and garbed. Since we see it, there is no need for Biondello's descripton (III.ii.42–63). Similarly, the audience sees the "mad marriage," rather than hearing of it from Gremio (III.ii.150–83).

Settings   The beauty and also the nitty-gritty reality of the external world are important in this *Shrew*. Baptista's house is a Renaissance cornucopia of rich objects (much noticed by Petruchio, who on his courtship visit picks up silver goblets with an appraising look), but it also contains kitchens full of cheese-making gear and a loft filled with wool waiting to be spun. Petruchio's country house, a dusky hulk, would seem far from the environment to which Katherine is accustomed, but the bride takes hold, wins over the serving men, grabs a feather duster, and brings order out of chaos.

The crowds who throng the streets of Padua to celebrate carnival, watch the arrival of Petruchio for his wedding, or observe (from an upper gallery) the feast in the final scene, are a triumph of choreography, a fusion of the beautiful with the grotesque, constantly on the move.

Exterior scenes also include landscapes of lyrical beauty. Lucentio's view of Padua, at the film's opening, is a dream of medieval romance (I.i). The winding, hilly road to Petruchio's house sees Katherine, mounted on a tiny donkey, follow her husband's and Grumio's horses as rain falls from the sky and tears of rage run down her cheeks. Later, having learned to laugh as well as to rage, and having been promoted to a horse, she and Petruchio ride through the same landscape to Bianca's wedding (IV.v).

Costumes   Renaissance opulence is everywhere. Katherine's shrewishness does not prevent her from donning a majestic white wedding dress, although, as it turns out, Petruchio's costume makes an ill match (III.ii). As their relationship comes into harmony, so does their wardrobe, and at Bianca's wedding feast they are symmetrically presentable.

Interpretation of Roles   Elizabeth Taylor gives a virtuoso performance as Katherine. Ferocity, cunning, amazement, and finally love and playfulness all get their turn. She throws herself into the role, literally, as if she had set out to demonstrate the physicality of farce. But at the same time, Taylor's Katherine has a psychological dimension. Her father's preference for her younger sister has clearly hurt her; she longs for the status and the security of marriage. When she realizes that Petruchio's demands—"love, fair looks, and true obedience" (V.ii.153)—are after all reasonable, once put into the context of trust and fair play, she becomes, as her father puts it, "another daughter" (V.ii.114). Her speech to the recalcitrant wives, urging wifely obedience, is neither ironic nor hypocritical, but is spoken as simple truth.

Richard Burton's Petruchio not only changes Kate but undergoes a change of his own, becoming a more generous and more civilized person. The audience realizes that he has been starved for love himself. When he undertakes to marry Kate, sight unseen, strictly for the money (I.ii.75), he is a two-dimensional boorish lout, reeling drunkenly to bed and terrifying the servants of his timid host, Hortensio. On meeting Kate, his ingenuity is awakened; in each of them, antisocial behaviour or no, there is an honesty that the other unconsciously recognizes. Burton's laughter echoes through the film, but when Katherine is able to laugh with him there is a change of tone, from mockery to true merriment.

Michael Hordern plays the overwhelmed father, Baptista, as convincingly frazzled. Students sympathize with him, even though they feel he should not have made Bianca so obviously a favorite.

Michael York is a dreamily romantic Lucentio, a foil to Burton's Petruchio, bedazzled by his love for Bianca. In the final scene the situation reverses. Bianca drops her demure sweetness—"maid's mild behaviour," as Lucentio once called it (I.i.71)—and reveals an uncooperative mind of her own. Played by dimpled blonde Natasha Pyne, Bianca's two moods are equally convincing.

Production History   This film was a box-office hit on its release in 1966, playing for months in first-run movie houses, and has been popular ever since.

Reviews and Studies   Harrison, Carey. "The Taming of the Shrew." In Charles Eckert, ed., *Focus on Shakespearean Films.* 1972. Pp. 158–60.

Jorgens, Jack J. *Shakespeare on Film.* 1977. Pp. 66–78, 258–61, 317–18.

Manvell, Roger. *Shakespeare and the Film.* 1971. Pp. 99–100.

Rothwell, Kenneth S., and Melzer, Annabelle H. *Shakespeare on Screen.* 1990. Item 598, pp. 275–76.

Simon, John. *Movies into Film.* 1972. Pp. 28–30.

Purchase/Rental Inquiries   Filmic Archives. See Appendix B for address.

❧ **28.3.** *The Taming of the Shrew.* 1981. British Broadcasting Company/Time-Life Television: The Shakespeare Plays. Color, 125 min. Producer: Jonathan Miller. Director: Jonathan Miller.

PETRUCHIO	John Cleese
KATHERINE	Sarah Badel
LUCENTIO	Simon Chandler
TRANIO	Anthony Pedley
BAPTISTA	John Franklyn-Robbins
GREMIO	Frank Thornton
HORTENSIO	Jonathan Cecil
BIANCA	Susan Penhaligon
WIDOW	Joan Hickson
BIONDELLO	Harry Waters
GRUMIO	David Kincaid
VINCENTIO	John Barron
PEDANT	John Bird

Pluses   Some interesting characterizations.

Minuses   Slow pace and lugubrious air.

Textual Cuts and Rearrangements   Disappointingly, since the BBC "Shakespeare Plays" series typically uses a full text, the "Christopher Sly" frame story is eliminated. Little else has been cut. Lucentio's confusing line to Biondello about disguising himself because he has killed a man (I.i.232) is retained, for example, though the play contains no other reference to this assertion.

Settings   Padua is represented as a city square rather obviously built of plywood, with a row of arches and a fountain. A few extras occasionally wander about; toward the end we seem to have a helmeted policeman standing out-of-focus to one side, but his function is unclear.

The interior of Baptista's house consists of a sequence of rooms, sometimes viewed as a row of receding doorways, with tiled floors and light coming through side windows. The effect, as is often the case in Jonathan Miller's Shakespeare films for the BBC, is of seventeenth-century Dutch paintings.

Costumes   Renaissance costumes, on the decorous rather than the flamboyant side.

Interpretation of Roles   John Cleese, a comedian whose movie and TV roles show considerable versatility, here plays a solemn and un-funny Petruchio. Some critics were pleased by this refreshing variation. Student audiences are more likely to be baffled. Cleese also rubs his nose, pulls his beard, and generally pokes and pulls at himself in a distracting manner.

Katherine (Sarah Badel) has a good deal of brisk energy and seems to hold up under Petruchio's taming more sturdily than he does. Petruchio, explaining how his tantrums have kept Katherine from sleeping (IV.i), cannot stop yawning, but Katherine's alertness seems undiminished. In the last scene, she does not bring the two unwilling wives before their husbands by force; instead they follow meekly behind her. It is as if this production were doing all it could to avoid the least suspicion of slapstick. Katherine's exhortation toward wifely subservience is done in a crisp, no-nonsense way, typical of the character as here interpreted.

Disguised characters come off well in this film. Hortensio, pretending to be a music teacher, is comically ineffective. Tranio, taking the place of his master, Lucentio, does his best to wrench his accent to a higher station in life. Lucentio becomes a credible teacher of literature. And the "Pedant," the traveler who is persuaded to impersonate Lucentio's father, comes to enjoy his new power and has a charming moment when he can't quite recall his new name (V.i).

The film's ending is inventive, literally productive of social harmony. At the end of the feast, Gremio, Bianca's elderly former suitor, distributes sheets of music, and the wedding company sings Psalm 128, "How blest is he that fears the Lord, and walketh in his way . . ."

Production History   *The Taming of the Shrew* was shown on British television in October of 1980 and on American television in January of 1981. It was part of the British Broadcasting Company's project (1978–85) of filming the entire canon of Shakespeare's plays.

Reviews and Studies   Bulman, J. C., and Coursen, H. R., eds. *Shakespeare on Television*. 1988. Extracts from reviews of this film, pp. 266–68.

Rothwell, Kenneth S., and Melzer, Annabelle H. *Shakespeare on Screen*. 1990. Item 603, pp. 278–79.

Purchase/Rental Inquiries   Ambrose Video; Filmic Archives; Insight Media; The Writing Company. See Appendix B for addresses.

⅜ 28.4. *The Taming of the Shrew*. 1982. Bard Productions. Color, 117 min. Producer: Jack Nakano. Director: John Allison.

KATHERINE	Karen Austin
PETRUCHIO	Franklyn Seales
BIANCA	Kathryn Johnson
BAPTISTA	Larry Drake
LUCENTIO	David Chemel
TRANIO	Bruce Davison
BIONDELLO	Nathan Adler
HORTENSIO	Charles Berendt
GRUMIO	Jeremy Lawrence
GREMIO	Kay E. Kuter
VINCENTIO	Bill Erwin
PEDANT	Jay Robinson

Pluses   Energetic and colorful.

Minuses   Acting quality is uneven.

Textual Cuts and Rearrangements   The "Christopher Sly" frame story is omitted once again. Speeches are thinned of complicated metaphors and classical allusions. In the final scene, much of the widow's and Bianca's repartee has been cut. An addition to the text is, however, Shakespearean; Lucentio, on first sight of Bianca, starts to quote Sonnet 18 ("Shall I compare thee to a summer's day?"); Tranio, gently teasing, finishes the line.

Setting   The single studio set is designed in imitation of an Elizabethan stage and incorporates several acting areas, an upper gallery, and stairways. Most frequently the stage represents the marketplace of Padua and includes a fountain, into which various characters manage to fall. Baptista's garden is indicated with shrubbery and trees.

During the meeting of Petruchio and Katherine, and in fact during most of the Padua scenes, extras crowd the stage and supply a choral reaction, "oohing" and "aahing" to both the dialogue and the slapstick physicality.

Costumes   Bright colors are the rule. Men's costumes are perhaps even more flamboyant than women's, featuring jerkins, tights, and codpieces in contrasting colors. Women wear billowing skirts, multicolored petticoats, low necklines and laced bodices.

Petruchio's swarthy good looks are enhanced by a shirt that opens to the belt. For his wedding, he wears a costly but ridiculous outfit of satin and plumes, with a wreath of vegetables about his neck.

Lucentio and Tranio exchange identities by exchanging cloaks and hats, Tranio thus gaining larger plumes as well as higher social status.

Interpretation of Roles   Karen Austen's Katherine seems to have channeled her rage at the world into an aggressive sexuality, a challenge to which Petruchio (Franklyn Seales) responds in kind. Their relationship lacks subtlety but not vigor, and the audience feels they are well matched. Their first encounter becomes a wrestling match. Katherine gets the upper hand several times, at one point pushing Petruchio into the fountain, but Petruchio eventually triumphs (II.i).

During Petruchio's "taming school" episode, Katherine does manage to snatch some food, but in order to conceal the fact that she is secretly munching apples she has to remain silent, to her great frustration (IV.iii). The turning point for her sense of humor comes on the return to Padua, when she joins her husband in playing a joke on Vincentio, Lucentio's aged father. As she kneels to ask Vincentio's pardon for having mistakenly called him a "young budding virgin," she begins to laugh—as does Vincentio (IV.v.45).

The more complex subplot involving Bianca's suitors is only slightly more decorous. At one point the rivals give each other ferocious blows with the bunches of flowers they have brought to give Bianca (III.i).

In the final scene, Katherine brings in the recalcitrant wives by twisting their arms behind them, then throws them on the floor (V.ii). Her lecture on wifely duty is smiling and self-assured. When at the end she starts to kneel to Petruchio, he stands up and prevents her, presumably symbolizing their equality. Then the slapstick impulse takes over; somehow they both end up in the fountain.

Production History   The Bard series of Shakespeare films typically uses a set designed as an Elizabethan-style playhouse. See the general introduction, p. 5, for other films in the series.

Reviews and Studies   This film seems to have attracted little critical attention.

Purchase/Rental Inquiries   Crest Video; Filmic Archives; The Writing Company. See Appendix B for addresses.

&⋅ **28.5.** *The Taming of the Shrew.* 1986. Stratford Shakespeare Festival, Canada. Color. Running time not specified.

Directed by Peter Dews, with Sharry Flett as Katherine and Len Cariou as Petruchio. Filmed stage production; lively and funny, with the "Christopher Sly" frame retained. A shortened version, with Sharry Flett doing bridge narration, is part of the "From Page to Stage" series. (See Appendix A, 28.E.)

At present the full-length version is not available.

29 ❧ THE TEMPEST*

❧ **29.1.** *The Tempest.* 1960. Hallmark Hall of Fame. Originally black-and-white; available in color. 76 min. Producer: George Schaefer. Director: George Schaefer.

PROSPERO	Maurice Evans
MIRANDA	Lee Remick
ARIEL	Roddy McDowall
CALIBAN	Richard Burton
TRINCULO	Tom Poston
GONZALO	Liam Redmond
FERDINAND	William H. Bassett
ALONSO	Geoffrey Lamb
ANTONIO	William Le Massena
SEBASTIAN	Paul Ballantyne
BOATSWAIN	Chris Gampel

Pluses   Charming and upbeat.

Minuses   For some viewers, frustratingly slight.

Textual Cuts and Rearrangements   Since the play has been reduced to an hour and a quarter, cuts are considerable. The opening scene has lost its dialogue; we simply see the ship in the storm while a non-Shakespearean narrator introduces the characters. Sebastian's and Antonio's villainous scheming is shortened (II.i). The castaways' magical banquet does not appear, nor does the conversation about it (III.iii), and the masque-like show that Prospero puts on for the newly engaged couple is curtailed (IV.i).

Some of the long descriptive and narrative passages are not only shortened but illustrated. Prospero, while telling Miranda of their history on the island (I.ii), displays these past events in a crystal ball.

Prospero's "Our revels now are ended" speech is moved from its usual place (IV.i.148ff.) to the end of the film, where it replaces the epilogue.

* Note: For films related to Shakespeare's *Tempest*, see Appendix A, "Analogues and Variations." *Prospero's Books* (1991) will be found there (29.E).

210

Settings   Locations are greatly stylized, with no sense of an actual island or an outdoor geography. Prospero's cave has an ice palace effect; Caliban lives in a wicker cage. Ferdinand wanders through a forest of what seem to be bare poles.

Costumes   Miranda wears a Grecian-looking gown, long and pleated. Ferdinand also has a classical look, in an armoured breastplate and a fluttering cape. Caliban is more human than not, but he does have froggy feet and a beaky nose. Alonzo and his courtiers wear Renaissance costume, with occasional ruffs, but their dress is not so elaborate as to prevent their getting about.

Ariel's distinctly non-human costume includes what seem to be petrified flames, with an all-over silvery effect. Trick photography makes him various sizes, so that he is able, for example, to stand on Prospero's shoulder (IV.i).

The "strange shapes" who startle the visitors (III.iii) appear here to be lightweight boulders, perhaps papier-mache, equipped with dancing human legs.

Interpretation of Roles   Maurice Evans's Prospero is not feeble but very much in charge of things. Lee Remick's Miranda is all youthful charm. Caliban (Richard Burton) is here a thoughtful sort of monster, and viewers are pleased that he is fond of music (III.ii.135ff.) and that he escapes punishment in the end.

Production History   This film was made by NBC and telecast on the Hallmark Hall of Fame in February of 1960.

Reviews and Studies   Bulman, J. C., and Coursen, H. R., eds. *Shakespeare on Television*. 1988. Extracts from reviews of this production, p. 241.

Rothwell, Kenneth S., and Melzer, Annabelle H. *Shakespeare on Screen*. 1990. Item 613, pp. 284–85.

Purchase/Rental Inquiries   Films for the Humanities and Sciences. See Appendix B for address.

❧ **29.2.** *The Tempest.* 1979. British Broadcasting Company/ Time-Life Television: The Shakespeare Plays. Color, 125 min. Producer: Cedric Messina. Director: John Gorrie.

PROSPERO	Michael Hordern
ARIEL	David Dixon
MIRANDA	Pippa Guard
FERDINAND	Christopher Guard
ANTONIO	Derek Godfrey

ALONSO	David Waller
CALIBAN	Warren Clarke
STEPHANO	Nigel Hawthorne
TRINCULO	Andrew Sachs
GONZALO	John Nettleton
SEBASTIAN	Alan Rowe
FRANCISCO	Paul Greenhalgh
ADRIAN	Christopher Bramwell
BOATSWAIN	Kenneth Gilbert
JUNO	Gwynneth Lloyd
CERES	Elizabeth Gardner
IRIS	Judith Rees

Pluses   A thorough production with interesting moments.

Minuses   Pace sometimes drags.

Settings   The island is fairly realistic and consists of sand, cliffs, and groves of trees. It is also rather bleak visually, a collection of flat, basic shapes. Except during the storm, the sea is neither seen nor heard.

A sort of jetty near Prospero's cave serves as a take-off and landing strip for Ariel. He makes a running jump from it and then, thanks to trick photography, dissolves into air. This transformation occurs several times.

Costumes   The castaways are richly dressed, as the text requires, since Gonzalo is surprised to find that their garments are magically unharmed by the sea water (II.i.62). Alonso wears his crown through all his troubles. The three goddesses in Prospero's masque wear flowing garments. Prospero's Milanese garments, which he puts on when he plans to reveal himself to his former enemies, are a splendid gold-and-white.

Ariel is dressed in very little, a sort of G-string, and stands about in off-balance postures, as if he had been permanently warped by his imprisonment in the cloven pine. He is occasionally joined by a band of male dancers, also nearly nude, who bring in the castaways' banquet (III.iii) and fill in as the hounds who chase Trinculo, Stephano, and Caliban (IV.i).

Interpretation of Roles   Michael Hordern plays a Prospero who loves his daughter and puts himself to a great deal of magical trouble to ensure her future happiness. At the same time, there are hints that he enjoys his power. He is not exactly sadistic, but with a flick of his mental magic he has Ariel writhing on the ground and promising to do his spriting gently (I.ii.297). And while Prospero does eventually forgive his brother and his brother's allies, he does not mind gloating about the fact that all his enemies are at his mercy (IV.i.263). Questions about imperialism, colonialism, and authority generally may be implied here.

As a pretty and fragile Miranda, Pippa Guard succeeds in appearing natural rather than goody-goody. Student audiences approve of her falling in love with Ferdinand and standing up to her father's opposition, even though that opposition is fake and Prospero is really in favor of the marriage all along.

Caliban (Warren Clarke) is brutish but more naive than wicked, and his scenes with Trinculo (Andrew Sachs) and Stephano (Nigel Hawthorne) are distinguished by good comic timing and a sense of the ironic parallels between the government they drunkenly invent and that of Milan and Naples, where usurpation and betrayal also are not unknown.

Production History   *The Tempest* was shown on British and American television in the spring of 1980, during the second year of the British Broadcasting Company's successful attempt to film the entire Shakespeare canon.

Reviews and Comments   Bulman, J. C., and Coursen, H. R., eds. *Shakespeare on Television*. 1988. Extracts from reviews of this film, p. 263.

Rothwell, Kenneth S., and Melzer, Annabelle H. *Shakespeare on Screen*. 1990. Item 620, pp. 287–88.

Purchase/Rental Inquiries

Ambrose Video; Filmic Archives; Insight Media; The Writing Company. See Appendix B for addresses.

➻ **29.3.** *The Tempest.* 1985. Bard Productions. Color, 126 min. Producer: Ken Campbell. Director: William Woodman.

PROSPERO	Efrem Zimbalist
MIRANDA	J. E. Taylor
FERDINAND	Nicholas Hammond
CALIBAN	William Hootkins
ALONSO	William H. Bassett
ANTONIO	Ted Sorel
GONZALO	Kay E. Kuter
SEBASTIAN	Edward Edwards
ARIEL	Duane Black
TRINCULO	Ron Palillo
STEPHANO	David Graf

BOATSWAIN	Hector Elias
ADRIAN	Mark Pinter
IRIS	Callan White
CERES	Gina Friedlander
JUNO	Roberta Farkas

Pluses   Colorful and for the most part briskly paced.

Minuses   Uneven acting quality.

Textual Cuts and Rearrangements   Cuts are few. The roles of Adrian and Francisco, Alonso's courtiers, seem to have been combined. The pageant of the three goddesses omits mention of Venus (IV.i.86ff.) Prospero speaks his epilogue to an empty stage, and as there is no live audience, the line "Please you draw near" (V.i.319) has been cut.

Settings   The play is filmed on an Elizabethan-style stage built of warm-toned and polished wood. Stairways, an upper gallery, and several levels on the main stage create numerous acting areas. Camera angles are varied, showing different parts of the stage. Close-ups are interspersed with longer shots.

Costumes   Costumes are colorful. Trinculo wears a jester's outfit with one red and one blue leg, topped by a yellow shirt. Men wear tights, shirts with full sleeves, and cloaks of richly textured fabrics. Miranda wears a ballgown, with a full skirt, low neckline, and puffed sleeves.

Caliban, who is on the paunchy side, looks like the stereotype of a motorcyclist, girded with various leather straps and wrist guards. Ariel is nearly nude and seems to have been dusted with flour. To become a harpy at the castaway's banquet, he adds many-colored wings and red tights (III.iii). The spirits of the isle on this occasion wear animal masks.

Interpretation of Roles   Efrem Zimbalist plays Prospero with authority. Viewers who remember him in television's *The FBI*, 1960s and 1970s, find the connection appropriate, as Prospero is, of course, greatly concerned with the discovery of facts.

Zimbalist's words and gestures seem spontaneous, and he is clearly changed when, on Ariel's description of the woes of the repentant castaways (V.i), he decides to have mercy on them. As is frequently done on stage and screen, he speaks to Ariel without looking at him, implying perhaps that Ariel chiefly exists within Prospero's mind.

Caliban (William Hootkins) has a threatening manner which might justify Prospero's keeping him under tight control. He looks older than the twenty four years the play's chronology allows him (assuming Caliban to have been an infant when Sycorax died, whereupon twelve years pass before the arrival of Prospero and twelve years after that arrival). Caliban's rage is considerable when he discovers that Trinculo and Stephano are false gods, and he drags Trinculo across the stage.

Ferdinand (Nicholas Hammond) is a pleasant young man, necessarily passive as the plot does not give him much to do.

Among the less effective roles are Trinculo (Ron Palillo), Stephano (David Graf), and Miranda (J. E. Taylor), all of whom seem to have difficulty in speaking Shakespearean verse.

Production History   The Bard series of Shakespeare videos makes use of an Elizabethan-style stage and, usually, of American actors. For other titles in this series, see the general introduction, p. 5.

Reviews and Studies   Vaughan, Virginia Mason. "The Bard *Tempest*." *Shakespeare on Film Newsletter* 15.1 (1990): 11.

Purchase/Rental Inquiries   Crest Video; Filmic Archives; The Writing Company. See Appendix B for addresses.

30 ❧ TIMON OF ATHENS _____

❧ **30.1.** *Timon of Athens.* 1981. British Broadcasting Company/ Time-Life Television: The Shakespeare Plays. Color, 130 min. Producer: Jonathan Miller. Director: Jonathan Miller.

TIMON	Jonathan Pryce
TIMANDRA	Diana Dors
APEMANTUS	Norman Rodway
ALCIBIADES	John Shrapnel
FLAVIUS	John Welsh
LUCILIUS	Max Arthur
FLAMINIUS	Geoffrey Collins
SERVILIUS	Terence McGinity
LUCULLUS	James Cossins
VENTIDIUS	Donald Gee
LUCIUS	Hugh Thomas
SEMPRONIUS	John Bailey
POET	John Fortune
PAINTER	John Bird
JEWELLER	David Kinsey
PHRYNIA	Elaine Sharling

Pluses   Intelligent readings of the lines allow the play's psychological patterns to reveal themselves. The visit of the poet and the painter to Timon (V.i), when they discuss the imaginary artistic works they will pretend to have undertaken as they seek Timon's largesse, is an example. Student audiences find the character of Timon surprisingly understandable. His compulsive generosity, his willingness to do anything if only people will like him, and his insecurity underneath it all, form a pattern that students recognize.

Minuses   This play is in many ways an allegory, or perhaps a parable, and to put it into convincing form for a present-day audience is difficult. Timon's sojourn in the wilderness (beginning IV.iii) is particularly static. The lengthy speeches in which his head fills the screen upside down (he is lying in a cave) can give audiences the fidgets.

Textual Cuts and Rearrangements   These are not extensive. Timon's invitation to the lady masquers to partake in his banquet is cut, and we see them lounging about in their Amazon costumes, pantomiming polite conversation, until the other guests leave the room and they can fall upon the food. Food in this play seems to represent various kinds of nourishment and becomes an important motif, so that this change is functional.

Opening lines of scenes sometimes disappear; the dialogue between Apemantus and Timon's fool (II.ii) is omitted. In act five, scenes two and three are cut, with no loss to the plot, as the soldier who finds Timon's grave (V.iii) brings his copy of the inscription to Alcibiades in the final scene.

Settings   Spacious interiors are used for the first part of the play. Candlesticks, tapestries, and other Renaissance ornaments give a sense of luxury.

For the wilderness scenes, the set closes in. We find ourselves on a shingle beach, with surf murmuring in the distance and pebbles scrunching underfoot. Timon's cave is a shallow burrow beneath a block of stone.

Costumes   Timon is a legendary figure of Greek literature, an emblem of the misanthrope. His story is mentioned by Plutarch (first century A.D.) in his "Life of Antony," and a more detailed version appears in one of the dialogues of Lucian (second century A.D.). In view of this Greek association, it may seem a jolt to find these characters wearing the seventeenth-century garments favored by director Jonathan Miller in other of his BBC Shakespeare films. (The rationale seems to be that Shakespeare's actors dressed according to their own times rather than in period costumes.) Thus Timon and his associates look as if they have walked out of a Rembrandt group portrait, in black with touches of white.

In the wilderness, Timon wears only a loincloth.

Interpretation of Roles   Jonathan Pryce as Timon shows versatility in shifting from insistent generosity to raging disillusion. At Timon's first banquet (I.i), the guests applaud as their host delivers a friend from debtors' prison or underwrites the marriage of one of his servants. At Timon's second banquet (III.vi), the guests lift the lids of the covered dishes set at each place, find only warm water, and laugh nervously. The laughter dies out as Timon dips into his dish of water and starts to sprinkle them with it, increasingly heavily, until at last he throws the dishes about and wrecks the table.

Alcibiades, played by John Shrapnel as a bluff military man, becomes a parallel to Timon in that he too assumed his friends would repay their obligations to him. Instead, he finds himself banished. Unlike Timon, Alcibiades is active rather than passive in misfortune, and he is able to reach a mental state of forgiveness and mercy while Timon is stuck in hatred. The relationship, incidentally, between this fictional Alcibiades and the Athenian general of that name (fifth century B.C.) is somewhat oblique. There are a few links, but the fictional Alcibiades should not be taken as a portrait.

In the small roles of the prostitutes Timandra and Phrynia, Diana Dors and Elaine Sharling let Timon's ferocious moral injunctions roll over them as they hold out their hands for more gold.

As Flavius, Timon's steward, John Welsh shows a human concern when he tries to stop Timon from letting his generosity bankrupt him. In the closing scene, the camera lingers on him as he touches the inscription copied from Timon's tomb: "Here lie I, Timon, who, alive, all living men did hate;/ Pass by and curse thy fill, but pass and stay not here thy gait."

Production History   *Timon of Athens* was filmed by the British Broadcasting Company as part of "The Shakespeare Plays," a series of video productions of the entire Shakespeare canon. It was shown on both British and American television during 1981.

Reviews and Comments   Bulman, J. C., and Coursen, H. R. *Shakespeare on Television*. 1988. Extracts from reviews of this film, pp. 279–81.

Rothwell, Kenneth S., and Melzer, Annabelle H. *Shakespeare on Film*. 1990. Item 632, pp. 294–95.

Willis, Susan. *The BBC Shakespeare Plays*. 1991. Pp. 125–26.

Purchase/Rental Inquiries   Ambrose Video; Filmic Archives; Insight Media; The Writing Company. See Appendix B for address.

31 ❧ TITUS ANDRONICUS _____

❧ **31.1.** *Titus Andronicus.* 1985. British Broadcasting Company/ Time-Life Television: The Shakespeare Plays. Color, 150 min. Producer: Shaun Sutton. Director: Jane Howell.

TAMORA	Eileen Atkins
AARON	Hugh Quarshie
LAVINIA	Anna Calder-Marshall
YOUNG LUCIUS	Paul Davies-Prowles
TITUS	Trevor Peacock
MARCUS	Edward Hardwicke
AEMILIUS	Walter Brown
SATURNINUS	Brian Protheroe
BASSANIUS	Nicholas Gecks
SEMPRONIUS	Derek Fuke
ALARBUS	Peter Searles
DEMETRIUS	Neil McCaul
CHIRON	Michael Crompton
LUCIUS	Gavin Richards
QUINTUS	Crispin Redman
MARTIUS	Tom Hunsinger
PUBLIUS	Paul Kelly

Pluses   A carefully thought-out rendition of this grotesque play. The focus on Young Lucius (see below) adds interest, especially for student audiences.

Minuses   For viewers who think of *Titus* as a parody of the vengeance-ridden Senecan genre, this production may seem unduly restrained. Many of the stabbings take place just outside the camera frame, for example. Other viewers may think the gore over-emphasized. Chiron and Demetrius, for example, are hung upside down in a slaughterhouse complete with butchered animals before Titus slits their throats (V.ii).

Textual Cuts and Rearrangements   For the most part, the text is followed faithfully. The opening scene is rearranged, with the sacrifice of Tamora's eldest son preceding the entrance of Saturninus and Bassianus.

A few elements are added. Young Lucius, Titus' grandson, frequently appears at the edge of the action, solemnly watching the bloodshed through anachronistic round spectacles.

Again, the text implies that in the final scene Aaron's baby is produced alive ("Behold the child," V.iii.119), but in this film Marcus holds up a small black coffin.

Settings   The studio set is suggestive of city squares and streets or, when draped with netting, of a forest, appropriately dismal.

Costumes   Since the story of *Titus* is completely fictional, not anchored to a specific point in history and only nominally attached to ancient Rome, costumes are free of any need for authenticity. Instead they work through associations and suggestions. The Goths wear leather and shaggy furs, while the Romans wear various mixtures of armor, togas, and tunics.

Tamora, queen of the Goths, starts the play in a frizz of orange hair, clinging leather garments, and a necklace of bones. On becoming empress she keeps the hair but wears a blue toga, matching that of her emperor husband, Saturninus.

Aaron, Tamora's black lover, glitters in gold and silver cloaks, with a heavy gold necklace against his bare chest.

Many of the soldiers, senators, and others wear masks, blank and impersonal, with slits for eyes. An effective sense of distance results. When Titus pleads for the lives of his sons Martius and Quintus, for example (III.i), the senators pass by anonymously and imperviously.

Realistic false heads are used for Martius and Quintus and for the chopped-off hand of Titus (III.i). Lavinia's hands were apparently left where they fell and do not make a separate appearance. Both she and her father have bloody stumps which show to grisly advantage as they wave their arms about in hugging each other. The stumps, however, are not very convincing. The length of the actors' forearms convinces viewers that the hands are really in there, beneath the bloody bandages.

Interpretation of Roles   The frequency of young Lucius' appearance has been explained by the director, Jane Howell, as an intimation that the whole play is Lucius' nightmare. Some viewers may welcome this option as making a certain kind of sense out of chaos. Paul Davies-Prowles plays young Lucius as a solemn, self-contained youngster of about twelve. At the beginning and ending of the film, his face shares the screen with a skull. In the final scene he lingers beside the coffin of Aaron's baby, implying sympathy for this innocent victim.

Hugh Quarshie plays Aaron not as a terrifying blackamoor but as a strong, confident loner, with a slyly self-mocking sense of humor. The audience finds itself on his side both for these qualities and for his paternal instincts, which are quite winning. He falls in love at first sight with his and Tamora's infant son and, like any parent, starts planning the baby's future—to "be a warrior and command a camp" (IV.ii.180).

As Tamora, Eileen Atkins is an effective blend of sexuality and savagery. Oozing hypocrisy, she pretends to make peace while plotting vengeance. All her appetites are keen, and it is in character for her to dig hungrily into the meat pie Titus serves her—only to learn too late that it contains two of her sons.

The role of Titus' daughter Lavinia is by contrast somewhat pallid. Since her tongue is cut out early in the action (II.iv), she has little opportunity for memorable lines. Her personality strikes present-day viewers as irritatingly passive. She does her father's bidding, even to carrying his severed hand in her teeth (III.i), and in the last scene (V.iii) allows him to stab her to death without demur or alarm. Anna Calder-Marshall probably does as much with the part as anyone could.

In Trevor Peacock's Titus, one senses an energetic and single-minded loyalty to ideals, even if these ideals seem distorted. When he pretends to be mad, ordering his family to shoot arrows into the heavens with messages for the gods (IV.iii), Peacock displays a crafty inventiveness. By the final scene, when the characters do each other in so briskly that one suspects the elder Lucius remains alive to become emperor only because somebody neglected to kill him, Titus is among a fairly early round of casualties. Difficult as it is to mourn a character in this play—there isn't time, for one thing—the audience does miss Peacock's Titus. His knee-jerk patriotism, his disillusioned fury, his bizarre conviction that whatever he was doing was the right thing to do, have a strangely compelling quality.

Production History   This was the last of "The Shakespeare Plays," the complete Shakespeare canon, undertaken by the British Broadcasting Company between 1978 and 1985. It was shown on British and American television in April of 1985.

Reviews and Studies   Bulman, J. C., and Coursen, H. R., eds. *Shakespeare on Television*. 1988. Extracts from reviews of this film, pp. 313–15.

Maher, Mary Z. "Production Design in the BBC's *Titus Andronicus*." In *Shakespeare on Television*, cited above. Pp. 133–50.

———. "Vision in the BBC's *Titus*." *Shakespeare on Film Newsletter* 10.1 (1985): 5–6.

Rothwell, Kenneth S., and Melzer, Annabelle H. *Shakespeare on Screen*. 1990. Item 633, pp. 296–97.

Willis, Susan. *The BBC Shakespeare Plays*. 1991. Pp. 292–318.

Purchase/Rental Inquiries   Ambrose Video; Filmic Archives; Insight Media; The Writing Company. See Appendix B for addresses.

32 ❧ TROILUS
AND CRESSIDA_____

❧ 32.1. *Troilus and Cressida.* 1982. British Broadcasting Company/ Time-Life Television: The Shakespeare Plays. Color, 180 min. Producer: Jonathan Miller. Director: Jonathan Miller.

TROILUS	Anton Lesser
CRESSIDA	Suzanne Burden
PANDARUS	Charles Gray
THERSITES	The Incredible Orlando, aka Jack Birkett
HELEN	Ann Pennington
ANDROMACHE	Merelina Kendall
CASANDRA	Elayne Sharling
PARIS	David Firth
PRIAM	Esmond Knight
HECTOR	John Shrapnel
AENEAS	Tony Steedman
CALCHAS	Peter Whitbread
AGAMEMNON	Vernon Dobtcheff
MENELAUS	Bernard Brown
ACHILLES	Kenneth Haigh
AJAX	Anthony Pedley
ULYSSES	Benjamin Whitrow
NESTOR	Geoffrey Chater
DIOMEDES	Paul Moriarty
PATROCLES	Simon Cutter

Pluses   A capable treatment of this complex play.

Minuses   Flaws are few, bearing in mind that *Troilus and Cressida* usually evokes idiosyncratic treatments in production and that the viewer should expect some here.

Textual Cuts and Rearrangements   Cuts are few, and some might well be accidental. An actor may have dropped a line or two, for example, when studio time was running out and the scene could not be retaped. Diomedes' entrance into Troy, to get custody of Cressida and take her to her father in the Greek camp (IV.iii), is omitted, but this is a short scene anyhow. Dialogue also tends to disappear in the heat of battle.

Settings   The city of Troy is an assemblage of geometric plywood shapes, mostly arches and stairways.

Trojan interiors are slightly more specific. The royal family confers around a large table, with women as well as men in attendance even though the women's presence is not indicated in Shakespeare's text (II.ii). During the argument over whether or not to give Helen back to the Greeks, the participants are able to point to her, leaning against a wall and fuming. Cassandra is present throughout the council as well. (In Shakespeare's text she enters in the middle of it.) When her prophetic ravings become distracting, the others shut her into a cage apparently kept there for the purpose.

The Greek camp, by contrast to the antiseptic streets of Troy, is full of busy detail. Dogs bark, roosters crow, and camp followers splash through the mud puddles. Tents are of khaki, with the sides rolled up and metal cots visible. The Greek commanders sit about drawing plans (including preliminary diagrams of the Trojan horse) and quaffing wine. The viewer remembers that the siege has gone on for ten years. The participants have settled in.

Costumes   Clothing is Renaissance rather than Greek. Elaborate armor is worn in battle. Women, whose dress sometimes looks like a cross between seventeenth- and nineteenth-century modes, occasionally appear in wide-brimmed hats as if bound for a garden party.

When not in battle, Trojan men wear well-kept garments, usually in pastel tints. The Greeks, a scruffier lot, wear olive drab.

Thersites, the "parasite" of Achilles and Ajax, wears a low-necked velvet gown and presumably gives the camp followers some competition.

Interpretation of Roles   Charles Gray plays Pandarus, Cressida's uncle, who brings Troilus and Cressida together and whose name consequently explains itself (III.ii.300). Leering, insinuating, he is the archetypal voyeur. The audience assumes he is impotent and gets his thrills as best he can. Helen and Paris seem to pick up this idea; when Pandarus calls on them with a message from Troilus (III.i), the lovers continue their dalliance in Pandarus' presence, all three seeming to enjoy the situation. Again, as Troilus and Cressida shyly converse (III.ii), Pandarus tries to embrace both of them, and warms up the conversation with lecherous comments before pushing them off to bed.

As Cressida, Suzanne Burden is waifish and weepy, an interpretation that is not very heroic but does fit her situation. She is after all a piece of merchandise.

Pandarus has found a buyer for her in Troy, just as her father, who has abandoned Troy and gone over to the Greeks, is open to negotiations from the soldiers there (III.iii.28). Cressida's attempt to get Troilus to declare his love for her—or to make a commitment, as students phrase it—is unsuccessful (III.ii), and in Suzanne Burden's face we can see her growing despair. When she finally tells him she loves him, hoping no doubt for a reciprocal confession from him, he has the perfect comeback: "Why was my Cressid then so hard to win?" (III.ii.116). When word arrives that Cressida must go to the Greeks, it is she who tries to refuse. Troilus merely wonders why he always has such bad luck (IV.ii.69).

Among the Greeks, Benjamin Whitrow as Ulysses gives his speech on "degree, priority, and place" (I.ii.85–124), often cited as a central statement of Renaissance cosmology, with plain-spoken urgency. He wants his audience to see his point, not as an abstract doctrine but as the essence of the situation at hand. Other of Ulysses' common-sense observations include some cynical remarks about Cressida (IV.v.54), whose fortunes continue to decline.

Menelaus (Bernard Brown), Helen's cuckolded husband, is in this film not a highly respected figure among the Greeks. He hovers at the edge of conversational circles and even runs errands for his brother, Agamemnon (I.iii.213).

Kenneth Haigh plays Achilles in an ironic mode. Clearly he is neither the man of honor nor the mighty warrior that he (and his fellow Greeks) think he is. Usually we see him lounging on his bed; when he does join the battle, it is to plot the death of Hector by unfair means (V.vii).

Production History   *Troilus and Cressida* was shown on British television in November of 1981 and in America in May of 1982. It is part of the British Broadcasting Company's 37-play series of films of Shakespeare's plays (1978–1985).

Reviews and Studies   Bulman, J. C., and Coursen, H. R., eds. *Shakespeare on Television.* 1988. Extracts from reviews of this film, pp. 281–82.

Rothwell, Kenneth S., and Melzer, Annabelle H. *Shakespeare on Screen.* 1990. Item 638, pp. 299–300.

Willis, Susan. *The BBC Shakespeare Plays.* 1991. Pp. 229–59.

Purchase/Rental Inquiries   Ambrose Video; Filmic Archives; Insight Media; The Writing Company. See Appendix B for addresses.

33 ❧ TWELFTH NIGHT*

❧ **33.1. *Twelfth Night.*** 1980. British Broadcasting Company/ Time-Life Television: The Shakespeare Plays. Color, 130 min. Producer: Cedric Messina. Director: John Gorrie.

MALVOLIO	Alec McCowan
VIOLA	Felicity Kendal
OLIVIA	Sinead Cusack
FESTE	Trevor Peacock
ORSINO	Clive Arrindell
SIR TOBY BELCH	Robert Hardy
MARIA	Annette Crosbie
SIR ANDREW AGUECHEEK	Ronnie Stevens
FABIAN	Robert Lindsay
ANTONIO	Maurice Roeves
SEBASTIAN	Michael Thomas
VALENTINE	Malcolm Reynolds
CURIO	Ryan Michael
SEA CAPTAIN	Ric Morgan

Pluses   Excellent acting; creates a world of mixed humor and poignancy.

Minuses   Hard to fault, unless one insist that a *Twelfth Night* production bring out all the play's potential dark shadows. This one is basically sunny.

Textual Cuts and Rearrangements   Cuts are few. Occasional passages of dialogue are slightly thinned. In the second act, the first and second scenes are transposed, so that Malvolio intercepts Viola, to return the ring he thinks she gave Olivia, immediately after she leaves Olivia's house at the end of act one.

Settings   The film has studio-built sets which manage to look like solid, realistic Tudor houses with surrounding gardens and courtyards. Orsino's house is grander and contains, among other things, a small consort of Elizabethan musicians. We spend more time at Olivia's house and so get to know not only the main hall and adjacent courtyard but the kitchen, with its large fireplace, and a linen cupboard where Olivia and Maria fold what appear to be pillowcases.

---

* Note: For films related to Shakespeare's *Twelfth Night*, see Appendix A, "Analogues and Variations."

The rooms have a lived-in, cared-for appearance, with polished wooden furniture, many-paned windows sparkling in the sunlight, and tapestries on the walls. The season is spring or summer.

Costumes   Characters wear Renaissance costumes that reveal both personalities and social status. Malvolio is in stewardly black, with his chain of office on display. Olivia at first wears mourning, but on falling in love changes to lavenders and grays. Orsino first appears as a correctly disheveled Renaissance lover but spruces up as the action continues, closing his shirt at the collar and eventually putting on a doublet.

Maria is dressed as a housekeeper in a dark gown and apron, not, as in some productions of this play, as a lady-companion wearing her mistress's cast-off finery.

On her first appearance as a castaway, Viola wears ruffled feminine garments and is not wet at all. Apparently she came ashore in a boat. As the disguised Caesario, she wears a black page's suit with touches of white.

Interpretation of Roles   Felicity Kendal is a pretty Viola, big-eyed and fluffy-haired. She is slightly passive, as the text directs, willing to wait for time to untangle the plot (II.ii.40). It is quite believable that this Viola would be unable to reveal her love for Orsino. She also looks like her twin brother, Sebastian (Michael Thomas), though the resemblance is partly a matter of similar hair styles and costumes.

Sinead Cusack creates an Olivia who is impulsive, vowing to mourn her brother for seven years and then falling instantly in love with Orsino's page, but at the same time methodical and, one feels, well brought up. Her house is in excellent order, as Sebastian notes when he wonders briefly if she is crazy (IV.iii.17).

Robert Hardy's Sir Toby is a dedicated roisterer but is secretly getting a bit tired. He sits down whenever he gets a chance. His decision that the joke on Malvolio has gone far enough (IV.ii.67) is consequently convincing.

Annette Crosbie's Maria is middle aged and rather plain, loyal to her mistress, with a warm sense of humor. Sir Toby's description of her—"A beagle, true bred, and one that adores me" (II.iii.179)—would seem apt.

As Malvolio, Alec McCowen shows just the right amount of pomposity and self-delusion to fall into the trap set for him. He does not question Maria's forged letter, and he believes his mistress is in love with him. His appearance in yellow stockings, cross-gartered, and worn with a facial expression of smug superiority, is one of the high points of the film. At the end, he is more indignant than heartbroken. The viewer assumes that he will return to his place in the household—where, as depicted in this film at least, people are mischievous but not cruel.

Trevor Peacock plays Feste as a plain, simple sort of jester, neither sophisticated nor neurotic. He clumps about, at home wherever he might be, singing his songs and unaffected by the turbulence about him. His closing song, "For the rain it raineth every day," seems merely to state a fact of life, and Feste is not particularly upset by it.

Production History   *Twelfth Night* was shown on British and American television in January and February, respectively, of 1980, during the second season of the British Broadcasting Company's project of filming Shakespeare's entire canon (1978–85).

Reviews and Studies   Bulman, J. C., and Coursen, H. R., eds. *Shakespeare on Television*. 1988. Extracts from reviews of this film, pp. 256–57.

Carr, Virginia. "The Second Season: *Twelfth Night.*" *Shakespeare on Film Newsletter* 4.2 (1980): 5.

Rothwell, Kenneth S., and Melzer, Annabelle H. *Shakespeare on Film*. 1990. Item 659.1, pp. 307–08.

Willis, Susan. *The BBC Shakespeare Plays*. 1991. Pp. 191–92.

Purchase/Rental Inquiries   Ambrose Video; Filmic Archives; Insight Media; The Writing Company. See Appendix B for addresses.

❧ **33.2.** *Twelfth Night.* 1988. Renaissance Theatre Company. Color. Running time not specified. Producer: David Parfitt. Director: Kenneth Branagh.

VIOLA	Frances Barber
FESTE	Anton Lesser
OLIVIA	Caroline Langrishe
MARIA	Abigail McKern
MALVOLIO	Richard Briers
ORSINO	Christopher Ravenscroft
SIR TOBY BELCH	James Saxon
SIR ANDREW AGUECHEEK	James Simmons
FABIAN	Shaun Prendergast
SEBASTIAN	Christopher Hollis
SEA CAPTAIN	Tim Barker
ANTONIO	Tim Barker

CURIO   Christopher Hollis
VALENTINE   Julian Gartside

Pluses   An imaginative, lively production, taking some chances.

Minuses   Some viewers may feel the results are overly zany, or, perhaps, overly gloomy.

Textual Cuts and Rearrangements   No really substantive cuts. Some of the dialogue is thinned—Sir Toby's puzzling reference to "Mistress Mall's picture," for example (I.iii.127). The film's first two scenes are swapped round, so that we first come in on Viola's arrival in Ilyria and afterwards learn of Orsino's lovelorn state. Sir Toby's song, "On the Twelfth Day of December" (II.iii.84), is changed to "The Twelve Days of Christmas," in keeping with the film's wintry ambience.

Settings   Orsino and Olivia are neighbors in a cemetery, or so the set would seem to indicate. We have tombstones, statues, marble benches, a pair of iron gates, all touched with snow that sometimes falls on the actors. A Chagall touch is added by a grandfather clock among the monuments, its hands stopped at 3:35. Occasionally the characters pause to decorate a Christmas tree. Most of the action takes place in this exterior set, despite the apparent cold.

Scenes in Orsino's part of the cemetery are shot in black-and-white, or blue-and-white rather, perhaps indicating Orsino's gloomy obsession with his unrequited love. When the action switches to Olivia's household, color returns.

Costumes   Dress is late Victorian. Olivia's statuesque blonde beauty is set off by a fur-trimmed black cape. Sir Toby wears a derby hat and a coat with fur lapels. Viola is in tatters as a castaway but as a page appears in a double-breasted suit that resembles a school uniform. Sir Andrew's attempt to impress Olivia includes putting on red and gold military gear.

Interpretation of Roles   As Viola, Frances Barber is diminutive and fragile, expressing emotions with her face but hesitant to take action. On hearing herself called "Sebastian" (III.iv.366), she is so dazed by joy and suspense—is it possible her brother is alive?—that she can do nothing else. This interpretation satisfies student audiences, who wonder, on reading the text, why Viola doesn't immediately begin an investigation.

Contrastingly self-assured but equally bedazzled by love, Caroline Langrishe's Olivia sweeps Sebastian off to the altar without noticing he has grown a foot or so taller (IV.iii).

Sir Toby (James Saxon) remains ebullient throughout the action, his cigar at a jaunty angle, often reaching behind the nearest tombstone for a hidden bottle. Maria (Abigail McKern) is young, pretty, and flirtatious.

Malvolio, played by Richard Briers, has in this film a large capacity for bitterness. His precise, perfectionist ways are mocked by his associates; his loyalty and high standards seem to count for nothing. His escape into self-delusion might well be the result of pressure. Imprisoned as a madman in a mausoleum-like cell, he emerges stooped over, as if he has not had room to stand up. His "I'll be revenged on the whole pack of you!" (V.i.378), heard after his final exit, is a cry from a severely wounded heart.

Anton Lesser gives the jester/musician Feste a mysterious rendition. Student audiences label him a "burnout," and he seems a man with a past. His eyes and voice are pained; tears stand in his eyes as he sings "Mistress Mine" (II.iii). With lanky hair and hollow cheeks, constantly swigging from his pocket flask, he follows Maria with his eyes, and her marriage to Sir Toby is apparently a last straw. After singing his last song about the inevitable fall of rain, Feste collects some bundles from under the Christmas tree—his luggage? somebody else's gifts?—and goes out the iron gates in an apparently final departure.

Viewers might be warned about a potentially confusing bit of casting. Tim Barker doubles as the sea captain who rescues Viola and as Antonio, Sebastian's friend. He has a beard for one role and none for the other, but he looks like himself nevertheless. Students unfamiliar with the play are likely to assume that a single person has escorted Viola to shore and then smuggled Sebastian in by another route, concealing one from the other for some reason to be revealed later in the plot.

Production History This film was shown on British television in December of 1988. It is based on a successful stage version by Kenneth Branagh's Renaissance Stage Company.

Reviews and Studies Coursen, H. R. "The Renaissance Theatre's Television *Twelfth Night.*" *Shakespeare on Film Newsletter* 13.2 (1989): 3.

Rothwell, Kenneth S., and Melzer, Annabelle H. *Shakespeare on Screen.* 1990. Item 663.2, p. 310.

Purchase/Rental Inquiries Films for the Humanities and Sciences. See Appendix B for address.

34. ❧ THE TWO GENTLEMEN OF VERONA_____

❧ 34.1. *The Two Gentlemen of Verona.* 1983. British Broadcasting Company/ Time-Life Television: The Shakespeare Plays. Color, 135 min. Producer: Shaun Sutton. Director: Don Taylor.

VALENTINE	John Hudson
PROTEUS	Tyler Butterworth
JULIA	Tessa Peake-Jones
SILVIA	Joanne Pearce
LAUNCE	Tony Haygarth
CRAB, THE DOG	Bella
LUCETTA	Hetta Charnley
ANTONIO	Michael Byrne
THURIO	David Collings
SIR EGLAMOUR	Frank Barrie
SPEED	Nicholas Kaby
DUKE OF MILAN	Paul Daneman
PANTHINO	John Woodnutt

Pluses   Visually graceful, with much Renaissance music.

Minuses   Nothing will quite counterbalance the fact that *The Two Gentlemen of Verona* is a very slight play.

Textual Cuts and Rearrangements   Cuts are almost nonexistent. The few that occur, such as the first three lines of V.iv, are not noticeable.

Settings   Verona, Milan, and the forest are all portrayed as a palace courtyard. We see various permutations of stairways, terraces, gazebos, balconies, and figured pavements, with statuary scattered about.

When the courtyard represents the duke's palace in Milan, it becomes a symbolic garden of love, with young gilded cupids flinging confetti (II.i). In a later scene we see the cupids, gold paint washed off, sweeping up the confetti (V.ii). It would appear that even fantasy entertainments need their clean-up committee.

To suggest the forest, garlands of greenery are looped about the courtyard's columns, augmented by numerous metal poles brought in for the nonce.

230

Costumes   Pleasant Renaissance garb. Velvets, brocades, ruffled skirts.

Julia, in her disguise as a page, pins up her long hair beneath her cap; her face is the same, but Proteus, her changeable lover, does not recognize her. (For once, this film convention of not recognizing the lightly disguised, so annoying to student audiences as it seems deliberately to offend their common sense, has a function in the play. It makes Proteus that much more superficial.) When Julia wants to return to her earlier self, she simply lets her hair down (V.iv).

Interpretation of Roles   Proteus (Tyler Butterworth) and Valentine (John Hudson) are played by energetic young actors who do their best to make these two friends, fond of each other but caught up in the emotional maelstroms of adolescence, convincing enough for the audience to feel some identification with their problems.

In the final scene, Valentine's offer to give Sylvia to Proteus, just to show how sincerely he accepts Proteus's apology (V.ii.83), is spoken straight, not turned into a facetious joke as sometimes happens. We do not find out whether or not Valentine means what he says. Proteus has no chance to take Valentine up on his offer, since Julia immediately begins the dialogue that ends with the revelation of her identity.

Master-servant relationships form a cheerful pattern, reflecting the orderly society toward which this comedy bends. Julia and her maidservant Lucetta (Hetta Charnley) giggle together, understanding perfectly well that Julia is attracted to Proteus even though she pretends not to be (I.ii). Speed, Valentine's young page, is most competently played by Nicholas Kaby. He speaks his complex, artificially witty lines with delight, clearly reveling in the game. Proteus's servant Launce (Tony Haygarth) is upstaged, as Launce is doomed to be in any production that uses a live dog, by his faithful Crab, here an affectionate black creature something like a poodle.

Production History   *Two Gentlemen of Verona* was shown on American television in April of 1984 as part of the British Broadcasting Company's project of filming Shakespeare's entire canon.

Reviews and Studies   Bulman, J. C., and Coursen, H. R., eds. *Shakespeare on Television*. 1988. Extracts from reviews of this film, p. 307.

Keyishian, Harry. *"Two Gentlemen of Verona." Shakespeare on Film Newsletter* 9.1 (1984): 6.

Rothwell, Kenneth S., and Melzer, Annabelle H. *Shakespeare on Screen*. 1990. Item 667, p. 312.

Purchase/Rental Inquiries   Ambrose Video; Filmic Archives; Insight Media; The Writing Company. See Appendix B for addresses.

35 &❧ THE WINTER'S TALE _____

&❧ **35.1.** *The Winter's Tale.* 1968. Cressida-Hurst Park Productions. Color, 151 min.

Directed by Frank Dunlop, with Laurence Harvey (Leontes), Jane Asher (Perdita), Moira Redmond (Hermione). Based on a stage production at the 1966 Edinburgh Festival.

This film is currently not available.

&❧ **35.2.** *The Winter's Tale.* 1980. British Broadcasting Company/ Time-Life Television: The Shakespeare Plays. Color, 185 min. Producer: Jonathan Miller. Director: Jane Howell.

LEONTES	Jeremy Kemp
HERMIONE	Anna Calder-Marshall
PERDITA	Debbie Farrington
FLORIZELL	Robin Kermode
AUTOLYCUS	Rikki Fulton
POLIXENES	Robert Stevens
PAULINA	Margaret Tyzack
CAMILLO	David Burke
ARCHIDAMUS	John Welsh
ANTIGONUS	Cyril Luckham
MAMILLIUS	Jeremy Dimmick
EMILIA	Marelina Kendall
SHEPHERD	Arthur Hewlett
CLOWN	Paul Jesson
MOPSA	Maggie Wells
DORCAS	Janette Legge

Pluses   A thought-provoking production.

Minuses   Pace can be slow.

Textual Cuts and Rearrangements   In general, Shakespeare's text is followed closely. The dance of the satyrs at the sheep-shearing festival has been cut (IV.iv).

Setting   Most of the action takes place on the same set, a stylized geometrical construction of cones and pyramids, with a tree that is painted white in Sicilia but puts forth some green leaves when the action transfers itself to Bohemia. Sicilia also has an interior throne room, used infrequently, and a green space with a trellis for Paulina's garden house, where the statue of Hermione comes to life (V.iii).

Costumes   Since Sicilia is depicted as a very cold kingdom, its inhabitants wear furs. Leontes in fact gets furrier and furrier, progressing from fur hats to fur cloaks, and thus links himself visually with the bear that devours Antigonus (III.iii).

The allegorical figure Time, who tells the audience that sixteen years have passed (IV.i), wears a white cloak and carries an hourglass.

In pastoral Bohemia, shepherds and shepherdesses wear bucolic attire, and there is a flurry of false beards as Polixenes, Camillo, and Autolycus switch their identities about.

Interpretation of Roles   Glowering, narrow-eyed Leontes (Jeremy Kemp), in the grip of jealousy and unable to open his mind enough to question his own conclusions, dominates the first part of the film. When the action later returns to Sicilia (V.i), he is exhausted and repentant. He has by this time known for sixteen years that he falsely accused his wife. Whether he really deserves this much punishment is a question students like to debate, but it may be worth remembering that the "romance" genre to which *The Winter's Tale* belongs is not a realistic one, and that Leontes' story might be more easily seen as a narrative abstraction than as a case history.

Anna Calder-Marshall becomes a fragile, vulnerable Hermione, defending herself against a charge of adultery that bewilders and horrifies her. Her friend Paulina, forcefully played by Margaret Tyzack, expresses moral indignation on Hermione's behalf (II.iii).

Polixenes (Robert Stevens), with whom Leontes claims Hermione had an affair, is in the first act an easygoing, rather pudgy gentleman. Student audiences claim to find him an unlikely temptation to adultery. In the later part of the play he is required by the plot to become a heavy father and to forbid Florizell's marriage with Perdita (IV.iv). Stevens does not make this switch entirely convincing — but then, this is not a realistic play.

Perdita is played by Debbie Farrington as a pretty, sensible shepherd girl. The film ends before she has time to get used to the fact that she is actually a misplaced princess. Florizell (Robin Kermode) has little to do except stare in amazement, but he does that.

Mamillius, Leontes' young son, is believably played by Jeremy Dimmick as a playful, observant child who enjoys telling ghost stories: "There was a man dwelt by a churchyard . . . " (II.i.30).

Autolycus (Rikki Fulton), rogue and peddler, gains audience sympathy by revealing his tricks to us and thus becoming, at least for the audience, harmless and amusing. He receives his come-uppance when two of his victims, the old shepherd and his son (the "clown," or rustic), are transformed into gentlemen at the court of Leontes and so can treat Autolycus with the condescension that he once bestowed on them (V.ii.126ff.).

Production History   *The Winter's Tale* was the sixteenth of the British Broadcasting Company's project of filming all 37 of Shakespeare's plays. It was shown on British and American television in 1981.

Reviews and Studies   Bulman, J. C., and Coursen, H. R., eds. *Shakespeare on Television*. 1988. Extracts from reviews of this film, pp. 276–77.

Rothwell, Kenneth S., and Melzer, Annabelle H. *Shakespeare on Film*. 1990. Item 673, pp. 314–15.

Willis, Susan. *The BBC Shakespeare Plays*. 1991. Pp. 165–70.

Purchase/Rental Inquiries   Ambrose Video; Filmic Archives; Insight Media; The Writing Company. See Appendix B for addresses.

⽆ Appendix A
Analogues and Variations_____

The following list contains films that are related to Shakespeare's plays in one way or another. Some have similar themes (e.g., *West Side Story* as a retelling of *Romeo and Juliet*). There are a few ballet and opera versions, and even some animated cartoons.

Several films which are in fact renditions of Shakespeare's plays but which for various reasons are not suited for general classroom use are included here. Examples are Peter Greenaway's *Prospero's Books* (29.E), a version of *The Tempest* which enthralls some viewers while horrifying others, and two of the Westinghouse Studio One modern-dress films of the 1950s (*Coriolanus* and *The Taming of the Shrew*), each with a running time of one hour and thus severely cut.

Background films on Shakespearean criticism, films about acting techniques, etc., are included here only if they focus on one specific play rather than surveying a large number of them. I have listed some films that include discussions of, and/or scenes taken from, up to four different plays, on the assumption that an instructor can cue the tape or disk to the part that deals with the play the class has been reading. (Literature students generally tune out if subjected to an analysis of a work with which they are completely unfamiliar. Acting students, on the other hand, will watch with interest an acting demonstration of virtually anything.)

Films about Shakespeare's life, scenic explorations of Stratford-upon-Avon, "talking head" video lectures without a performance component, and similar resource materials are omitted. The catalogs of Filmic Archives, Films for the Humanities and Sciences, Insight Media, and The Writing Company typically include a large range of these.

Films in this list are grouped under the titles of the Shakespeare plays to which they are related. Thus their arabic numbers will correspond with the chapters in the main body of this book. (If there are no analogous films for, say, *Cymbeline*, number 6 in the main list, then that number is skipped, and we will go from number 5, *Coriolanus*, to number 7, *Hamlet*.) Beneath the umbrella of each play, films are then listed chronologically, distinguished by a letter of the alphabet rather than by a second number. I hope that this method will prevent confusion in cross-listings.

Distributors are mentioned here if the film has been included in a fairly recent catalog. The absence of a distributor's name does not necessarily mean the film is hard to find.

2. *Antony and Cleopatra*

A. *Shakespeare Wallah*. 1965. Merchant-Ivory Productions. Black-and-white, 115 min. Directed by James Ivory, with Felicity Kendal, Shashi Kapoor, Geoffrey Kendal, Laura Liddell. An English acting troupe tours post-independence India. Excerpts are shown from their performances of *Antony and Cleopatra*, *Othello*, *Hamlet*, and *Twelfth Night*. Passages from *Antony and Cleopatra* include Enobarbus' descripton of Cleopatra (II.ii) and Cleopatra's farewell to the dying Antony (IV.xv).

B. *Preparing to Perform Shakespeare*. 1984(?). Color, 50 min. One of the "Playing Shakespeare" series with director John Barton. Patrick Stewart discusses Enobarbus' speech from *Antony and Cleopatra*, "The barge she sat in . . ." (II.ii.191ff.). The video also includes a scene from *Troilus and Cressida*. Intended for acting students but useful for literature classes. Purchase/ rental inquiries: Films for the Humanities and Sciences. See Appendix B for address.

C. *The Roman Tragedies*. 1985(?). Color, 60 min. One of the series "Shakespeare Workshops with the New Shakespeare Company," directed by David Whitworth. An examination of Shakespeare's Roman tragedies, using examples from *Antony and Cleopatra* (and also from *Julius Caesar* and *Coriolanus*). Purchase/ rental inquiries: Films for the Humanities and Sciences. See Appendix B for adddress.

3. *As You Like It*

A. *As You Like It*. 1985. "From Page to Stage." Stratford Shakespeare Festival, Canada. Color, 30 min. Filmed excerpts from a live production with Roberta Maxwell (Rosalind), Andrew Gillies (Orlando). Rosemary Dunsmore, who plays Celia, does bridge narration between scenes.

B. *As You Like It: Rosalind and Celia*. 1991. Color, 20 min. Actresses Juliet Stevenson and Fiona Shaw discuss the interpretation of these two roles. Part of the series "Shakespearean Explorations with Patrick Stewart." Purchase/ rental inquiries: Insight Media. See Appendix B for address.

C. *Acting in Shakespearean Comedy with Janet Suzman*. 1992. Color, 60 min. Workshop in Shakespearean comedy; scenes from *As You Like It*. (Also *Much Ado about Nothing* and *Twelfth Night*.) Purchase/ rental inquiries: Insight Media. See Appendix B for address.

5. Coriolanus

A. *Coriolanus*. 1951. Westinghouse Studio One. Black-and- white, 60 min. Directed by Paul Nickel, with Richard Greene and Judith Evelyn. Twentieth-century wartime setting, with trenches and barbed wire. Civilians in 1950s dress. Much cutting, including most of the Coriolanus/ Aufidius relationship. Purchase/ rental inquiries: Video Yesteryear. See Appendix B for address.

B. *The Roman Tragedies*. 1985(?). Color, 60 min. One of the series "Shakespeare Workshops with the New Shakespeare Company," David Whitworth, director. Examines Shakespeare's Roman tragedies, using examples from *Coriolanus*. (Also discusses *Julius Caesar* and *Antony and Cleopatra*.) See above (2.C).

7. Hamlet

A. *To Be or Not To Be*. 1942. United Artists. Black-and- white, 99 min. Produced and directed by Ernest Lubitsch, starring Jack Benny and Carole Lombard. World War II setting. Scenes from *Hamlet* are mixed with the comedy.

B. *The Bad Sleep Well*. 1963. Black-and-white, 135 min. A variation of the *Hamlet* story set in Japan. Directed by Akira Kurosawa.

C. *Shakespeare Wallah*. 1965. See above (2.A). Scenes from *Hamlet* include parts of Gertrude's and Hamlet's closet scene (III.iv) and Ophelia's mad scene (IV.v).

D. *To Be or Not To Be*. 1983. Color, 108 min. A remake of Lubitsch's film (7.A) by the irrepressible Mel Brooks. With Anne Bancroft.

E. *Understanding Hamlet*. 1984. Color, 120 min. Workshop given for members of the National Youth Theatre of Great Britain. Purchase/ rental inquiries: Insight Media. See Appendix B for address.

F. *The Tortured Mind*. 1985(?). Color, 60 min. One of the series "Shakespeare Workshops with the New Shakespeare Company," directed by David Whitworth. Examines the mind of Ophelia in *Hamlet*. (Also discusses the characters Othello, Lady Macbeth, and King Lear.) Purchase/ rental inquiries: Films for the Humanities and Sciences. See Appendix B for address.

G. *Rosencrantz and Guildenstern Are Dead*. 1990. Color, 117 min. With Richard Dreyfuss as the Chief Player. Film version of Tom Stoppard's play of the same name. The *Hamlet* story from the perspective of these minor characters. Purchase/ rental inquiries: The Writing Company. See Appendix B for address.

H. *Discovering Hamlet*. 1990. Unicorn Projects. Color, 60 min. Documentary. We watch Derek Jacobi directing Kenneth Branagh as Hamlet, in a stage production at the Birmingham Theatre Company. Patrick Stewart narrates. Rehearsals; discussions; a few glimpses of the finished product. Purchase/ rental inquiries: PBS Video. See Appendix B for address.

I. *Performing Shakespeare*. 1990. Color, 120 min. Follows the development of a scene from *Hamlet*; Kathleen Conlin, director of the Ohio University School of Theatre, works with two student actors. Purchase/ rental inquiries: Insight Media. See Appendix B for address.

J. *Hamlet: Claudius*. 1991. Color, 25 min. Patrick Stewart discusses his interpretation of Claudius. Part of the series "Shakespeare Explorations with Patrick Stewart." Purchase/ rental inquiries: Insight Media. See Appendix B for address.

K. *Hamlet: Polonius*. 1991. Color, 37 min. See above (7.J). Here Stewart discusses Polonius.

L. *Laurence Olivier: A Life*. 1992. Color, 159 min. Interviews with Olivier and many of his colleagues. Excerpts include scenes from Olivier's film of *Hamlet*. (Also from *Henry V*.) Purchase/ rental inquiries: Insight Media. See Appendix B for address.

M. *Hamlet*. 1992. Shakespeare: The Animated Tales. Color, 30 min. An abridged cartoon version for children, made by the Soyuzmultfilm Studios of Moscow. Shakespeare's text is used, or snippets of it, with voice-over narration for the story line. This international venture was funded by sources in Britain, Japan, Russia, and the United States. Scripts were prepared by Leon Garfield in consultation with other Shakespearean scholars. Other cartoons in the series are *Macbeth* (17.D), *A Midsummer Night's Dream* (21.D), *Romeo and Juliet* (27.E), *The Tempest* (29.F), and *Twelfth Night* (33.E). *Hamlet* is animated by a painting-on-glass technique. Purchase/ rental inquiries: Random House; The Writing Company. See Appendix B for addresses.

8. *Henry IV, Part One and Two*

A. *My Own Private Idaho*. 1991. Produced by Laurie Parker, directed by Gus Van Sant. With Keanu Reaves, River Phoenix. A Prince Hal figure must choose between his respectable family and his street friends, drifting male prostitutes, and other outcasts.

10. *Henry V*

A. *Laurence Olivier: A Life*. See above (7.L).

13. *Julius Caesar*

A. *The Roman Tragedies*. 1985(?). Color, 60 min. One of the series "Shakespeare Workshops with the New Shakespeare Company," directed by David Whitworth. Examines Shakespeare's Roman tragedies, using examples from *Julius Caesar*. (Also discusses *Antony and Cleopatra* and *Coriolanus*.) See above (2.C).

15. *King Lear*

A. *Harry and Tonto.* 1974. Twentieth-Century Fox. Color, 115 min. Directed by Paul Mazursky, with Art Carney and Ellen Burstyn. An old man, evicted from his apartment in New York, travels with his cat, Tonto, across the country to live with his children.

B. *The Dresser.* 1985. Columbia Pictures. Color, 110 min. Produced and directed by Peter Yates, with Albert Finney and Tom Courtenay. Set during World War II. A dying Shakespearean actor and his "dresser" tour in a production of *King Lear.* (A dresser is a British theatrical phenomenon, employed by a leading actor or actress as a personal valet or maid, and yet more than that.)

C. *Ran.* 1985. Orion Classics. Color, 160 min. Directed by Akira Kurosawa. A medieval Japanese warlord tries to give his lands and power to his sons. Purchase/ rental inquiries: The Writing Company. See Appendix B for address.

D. *The Tortured Mind.* 1985 ?). Color, 60 min. One of the series "Shakespeare Workshops with the New Shakespeare Company," directed by David Whitworth. Examines the mind of King Lear. (Also discusses Othello, Lady Macbeth, and Ophelia in Hamlet). See above (7.F).

17. *Macbeth*

A. *Throne of Blood; The Castle of the Spider's Web; Kumonos-Djo.* 1957. Black-and-white, 105 min. Directed by Akira Kurosawa. Macbeth and Banquo are translated into medieval Japanese warriors.

B. *Macbeth.* 1977. Color, 60 min. BBC presentation with Corin Redgrave. Excerpts from stage play; commentary.

C. *The Tortured Mind.* 1985(?) Color, 60 min. One of the series "Shakespeare Workshops with the New Shakespeare Company," directed by David Whitworth. Examines the mind of Lady Macbeth. Also discusses the characters Ophelia (*Hamlet*), King Lear, and Othello. See above (7.F).

D. *Macbeth.* 1992. Shakespeare: The Animated Tales. Color, 30 min. An animated version for children. See above (7.M). *Macbeth* was produced in cel animation.

19. *The Merchant of Venice*

A. *Exploring a Character.* 1984. London Weekend Television. Color, 51 min. One of the "Playing Shakespeare" series with director John Barton. Focuses entirely on *Merchant*, with Patrick Stewart and David Suchet demonstrating different approaches to Shylock. Intended for drama students but useful for literature classes. Purchase/ rental inquiries: Films for the Humanities and Sciences. See Appendix B for address.

B. *The Merchant of Venice: Shylock.* 1991. Color, 27 min. Patrick Stewart discusses his interpretation of this role. Part of the "Shakespeare Explorations with Patrick Stewart" series. Purchase/ rental inquiries: Insight Media. See Appendix B for address.

20. *The Merry Wives of Windsor*

A. *Falstaff.* 1983. Color, 141 min. Guiseppe Verdi's opera, conducted by Carlo Maria Guilini. Royal Opera House, Covent Garden. Renato Bruson sings Falstaff. English subtitles.

21. *A Midsummer Night's Dream*

A. *A Midsummer Night's Sex Comedy.* 1982. Color, 88 min. Directed by Woody Allen, starring Allen, Mia Farrow, Jose Ferrer, Julie Hagerty. Thematic connections to Shakespeare's play via lovers switching partners, magical doings, and Mendelssohn's music.

B. *The Comic Spirit.* 1985(?). Color, 60 min. One of the series "Shakespeare Workshops with the New Shakespeare Company," directed by David Whitworth. Examines theories of comedy, using examples from *A Midsummer Night's Dream.* (Also discusses *Twelfth Night* and *Two Gentlemen of Verona.*) Purchase/ rental inquiries: Films for the Humanities and Sciences. See Appendix B for address.

C. *Dead Poet's Society.* 1989. Color, 128 min. Directed by Peter Weir, with Robin Williams, Robert Leonard. An English teacher at a boys' school directs a performance of *A Midsummer Night's Dream.*

D. *A Midsummer Night's Dream.* 1992. Shakespeare: The Animated Tales. Color, 30 min. An animated cartoon version for children. See above (7.M). *A Midsummer Night's Dream* was produced in cel animation.

22. *Much Ado about Nothing*

A. *Acting in Shakespearean Comedy with Janet Suzman.* 1992. Color, 60 min. A workshop in Shakespearean comedy, including scenes from *Much Ado.* (Also *As You Like It* and *Twelfth Night.*) See above (3.C).

23. *Othello*

A. *Othello.* 1922. Warner Film. Silent. Black-and-white, 93 min. Directed by Dimitri Buchowetzki, with Emil Jannings (Othello) and Werner Krauss (Iago).

Many startling and haunting moments. Iago does not hide his evil nature, at least from the camera, but displays it in facial grimaces and bodily contortions.

B. *A Double Life*. 1947. Black-and-white, 103 min. Produced by Michael Kanin, directed by George Cukor. With Ronald Colman, Shelley Winters. An actor playing Othello confuses the events of his life with those of the play.

C. *Jubal*. 1956. Columbia Pictures. Color, 101 min. Produced by William Fadiman, directed by Delmer Daves. With Glenn Ford, Ernest Borgnine, Rod Steiger. Set in the American West. Othello is a ranch owner; Iago, a ranch hand passed over for promotion; Desdemona, the rancher's wife; Cassio, the interloper who got the job.

D. *Shakespeare Wallah*. 1965. See above (2.A). The film includes passages from Othello's murder of Desdemona (V.ii).

E. *The Tortured Mind*. 1985(?). Color, 60 min. One of the series "Shakespeare Workshops with the New Shakespeare Company," directed by David Whitworth. Examines the mind of Othello. Also discusses the characters Ophelia (in *Hamlet*), King Lear, and Lady Macbeth. See above (7.F).

F. *Otello*. 1986. Color, 123 min. Verdi's opera, directed by Franco Zeffirelli and starring Placido Domingo and Katia Ricciarelli. English subtitles.

26. *Richard III*

A. *The Goodbye Girl*. 1977. Color, 110 min. Richard Dreyfuss plays an actor playing Richard III; scenes from this play-within-a-play.

27. *Romeo and Juliet*

A. *West Side Story*. 1961. United Artists. Color, 155 min. Produced by Robert Wise, directed by Jerome Robbins. With Natalie Wood, Rita Moreno. A musical in which the Capulets and Montagues become rival New York gangs. Purchase/rental inquiries: Filmic Archives. See Appendix B for address.

B. *Shakespeare Wallah*. 1965. See above (2.A). The film includes passages from the marriage of Romeo and Juliet (II.vi).

C. *Romeo and Juliet*. 1966. Color, 124 min. Ballet with Margot Fontayne and Rudolph Nureyev. Prokofiev's music conducted by John Lanchbery of the Orchestra of the Royal Opera House, Covent Garden.

D. *Romeo and Juliet*. 1985. "From Page to Stage." Stratford Shakespeare Festival, Canada. Color, 30 min. Filmed excerpts from a live production with Colm Feore (Romeo) and Seana McKenna (Juliet). Richard Monette, who plays Mercutio, does bridge narration.

E. *Romeo and Juliet*. 1992. Shakespeare: The Animated Tales. Color, 30 min.

A cartoon version for children. See above (7.M). *Romeo and Juliet* is produced in cel animation.

F. *Zebrahead*. 1992. Color, 102 min. Produced by Oliver Stone, written and directed by Anthony Drazen. The star-crossed lovers here inhabit present-day Detriot.

28. The Taming of the Shrew

A. *The Taming of the Shrew*. 1950. Westinghouse Studio One. Black-and-white, 60 min. A condensed version in modern (1950s) dress, with Charlton Heston and Lisa Kirk. Purchase/ rental inquiries: Filmic Archives. See Appendix B for address.

B. *Kiss Me, Kate*. 1953. Metro-Goldwyn-Mayer. Color, 190 min. Produced by Jack Cummings, directed by George Sidney. With Howard Keel, Kathryn Grayson, Ann Miller. Musical; a group of actors perform *The Taming of the Shrew*, with backstage parallels to Shakespeare's plot. Purchase/ rental inquiries: The Writing Company. See Appendix B for address.

C. *McClintock!* 1963. Color, 130 min. With John Wayne and Maureen O'Hara. The untamable Kate has here been transplanted to the American West.

D. *Kiss Me, Petruchio*. 1981. New York City Shakespeare Company. Color, 58 min. A documentary about a production of *The Taming of the Shrew*, with Meryl Streep and Raul Julia, staged in Central Park in 1978. Interviews with the actors.

E. *The Taming of the Shrew*. 1985. "From Page to Stage." Stratford Shakespeare Festival, Canada. Color, 30 min. Excerpts from a live productionn. With Sharry Flett (Katherine) and Len Cariou (Petruchio). Sharry Flett does bridge narration between excerpts.

29. The Tempest

A. *Forbidden Planet*. 1956. Metro-Goldwyn-Mayer. Color, 96 min. Directed by Fred McLeod Wilcox, with Walter Pigeon, Anne Francis. Prospero's island becomes an isolated planet; Ferdinand and the other castaways arrive on a space ship. Purchase/ rental inquiries: The Writing Company. See Appendix B for address.

B. *The Tempest*. 1980. Color, 96 min. Directed by Derek Jarman. Surreal visions based on Shakespeare's text.

C. *The Tempest*. 1982. Columbia Pictures. Color, 140 min. Directed by Paul Mazursky, with Susan Sarandon, Molly Ringwald, Raul Julia. Set in the twentieth century. A New York architect exchanges the complexities of civilization for a Greek island, taking his teenage daughter with him.

D. *The Tempest*. 1985. "From Page to Stage." Stratford Shakespeare Festival,

Canada. Color, 30 min. Filmed excerpts of a live stage production. With Sharry Flett (Miranda), Len Cariou (Prospero). Nicholas Pennell, who plays Stephano, does bridge narration between excerpts.

E. *Prospero's Books*. 1991. Miramax Films. Color; running time not specified. Produced by Kees Kasander, directed by Peter Greenaway. John Gielgud plays Prospero and speaks all the lines, everyone else's as well as his own. The idea is that Prospero/ Shakespeare is writing the play. We see on the screen what is going through his mind. The words of Shakespeare's text are not altered, though passages are sometimes cut or rearranged. Dreamlike to the point of hallucination; hundreds of extras, much nudity, much blood. Four Ariels of graduated sizes. Director Greenaway explains his intentions, with many pictures and a screenplay, in *Prospero's Books: A Film of Shakespeare's The Tempest* (New York: Four Walls Eight Windows, in association with Chatto and Windus, 1991).

F. *The Tempest*. 1992. Shakespeare: The Animated Tales. Color, 30 min. A cartoon version for children. See above (7.M). *The Tempest* is animated by puppets.

32. *Troilus and Cressida*

A. *Preparing to Perform Shakespeare*. 1984(?). Color, 50 min. One of the "Playing Shakespeare" series with director John Barton. Discussion of a scene from *Troilus and Cressida* (also from *Antony and Cleopatra*). See above (2.B).

33. *Twelfth Night*

A. *Shakespeare Wallah*. 1965. See above (2.A). The film includes part of the "yellow stockings" scene from *Twelfth Night* (III.iv).

B. *Rehearsing the Text*. 1984. London Weekend Television. Color, 51 min. One of the "Playing Shakespeare" series with director John Barton. Focuses entirely on *Twelfth Night*. Richard Pasco and Judi Dench demonstrate rehearsal techniques. Intended for drama students but useful for literature classes. Purchase/ rental inquiries: Films for the Humanities and Sciences. See Appendix B for address.

C. *The Comic Spirit*. 1985(?). Color, 60 min. One of the series "Shakespeare Workshops with the New Shakespeare Company," directed by David Whitworth. Examines theories of comedy, using examples from *Twelfth Night*. (Also discusses *A Midsummer Night's Dream* and *Two Gentlemen of Verona*.) See above (21.B).

D. *Acting in Shakespearean Comedy with Janet Suzman*. 1992. Color, 60 min. A workshop in Shakespearean comedy, using scenes from *Twelfth Night*. (Also *As You Like It* and *Much Ado about Nothing*.) See above (3.C).

E. *Twelfth Night*. 1992. Shakespeare: The Animated Tales. Color, 30 minutes.

A cartoon version for children. See under *Hamlet* (7.M) for more information on this series. *Twelfth Night* is animated by puppets.

34. *Two Gentlemen from Verona*

A. *The Comic Spirit*. 1985(?). Color, 60 min. One of the series "Shakespeare Workshops with the New Shakespeare Company," directed by David Whitworth. Examines theories of comedy, using examples from *Two Gentlemen*. (Also discusses *A Midsummer Night's Dream* and *Twelfth Night*.) See above (21.B).

❧ Appendix B
Video Distributors

Ambrose Video Publishing, Inc.
Dept. 92SP
1290 Avenue of the Americas, Suite 2245
New York, NY 10102-1010
(800) 526-4663

Corinth Films
34 Gansevoort St.
New York, NY 10014
(800) 221-4720

Crest Video Marketing
415 North Figueroa St.
Wilmington, CA 90744

Critic's Choice Video
P.O. Box 809
Itasca, IL 60143-0809
(800) 367-7765

Drama Classics Video
P.O. Box 2128
Manorhaven, NY 11050

Embassy Home Entertainment
1901 Avenue of the Stars
Los Angeles, CA 90067

Filmic Archives
The Cinema Center
Botsford, CT 06404-0386
(800) 366-1920

Films for the Humanities and Sciences
P.O. Box 2053
Princeton, N.J. 08543-2053
(800) 257-5126

HBO Video
1100 Avenue of the Americas
New York, NY 10036

Insight Media
121 West 85th St.
New York, NY 10024
(212) 721-6316

NTA Home Entertainment
P.O. Box 66930
Los Angeles, CA 90066-0930

Pacific Arts
11858 La Grange Ave.
Los Angeles, CA 90025
(800) 538-5856

PBS Video
Public Broadcasting Service
1320 Braddock Place
Alexandria, VA 22314-1698

Random House, Inc.
400 Hahn Rd.
Westminster, MD 21157-4698
(800) 773-3000

RMI Media Productions
2807 West 47th St.
Shawnee Mission, KS 66205
(800) 745-5480

Rockbottom Productions
18653 Ventura Blvd., #131B
Tarzana, CA 91356

Thorn EMI Video
1370 Avenue of the Americas
New York, NY 10019

The Video Catalog
P.O. Box 64428
St. Paul, MN 55164-0428
(800) 733-2232

Video Yesteryear
Box C-137
Sandy Hook, CT 06482
(800) 243-0987

Viewfinders, Inc.
P.O. Box 1665
Evanston, IL 60204-1665
(800) 342-3342

The Writing Company
10200 Jefferson Blvd.
P.O. Box 802
Culver City, CA 90232-0802
(800) 421-4246

⁊ Bibliography ————————————————

Introductory Note

Readers whose backgrounds are more literary than cinemagraphic (who, in other words, are not film buffs, or not yet) will be well served by most of the books listed here. Technical vocabulary is explained, or becomes intelligible in context.

This bibliography includes all the books listed under "Reviews and Studies" of individual plays, with fuller information about them (place of publication and name of publisher); these data were omitted in "Reviews and Studies" to save space.

Journal listings from "Reviews and Studies" are not repeated here for reasons of space. However, the reader will want to keep a number of periodicals in mind for browsing and staying up to date. The *Shakespeare on Film Newsletter*, edited from 1976 by Bernice W. Kliman and Kenneth S. Rothwell, ceased publication in 1992, but the *Shakespeare Bulletin* has taken on its function of relaying film news, reviews, and critical articles.

The *Shakespeare Quarterly* is alert to film as well as stage performances. Its annual bibliography includes a section on "Film, Cinema, Radio, Television" under the more general heading of "Productions, Stage History."

Shakespeare and the Classroom, a newsletter for teachers of Shakespeare, began publication in 1993 and includes material on the use of film in teaching. Inquiries about this newsletter may be sent to Eva McManus, Ohio Northern University, Ada, OH 45810.

Literature/ Film Quarterly occasionally devotes an entire issue to Shakespeare films. See volumes and issues 1.4 (1973), 4.2 (1976), 5.4 (1977), 8.4 (1980), 11.3 (1983), 14.4 (1986), 20.4 (1992).

Periodicals intended for film scholars and critics pay frequent attention to Shakespeare, often in the forms of reviews of new productions, interviews with directors, etc. Especially useful for browsing are *Film Quarterly*, *Films in Review*, *Film Criticism*, *Quarterly Review of Film and Video*, and *Sight and Sound*.

Mass-circulation newspapers and magazines carry material on Shakespeare films when there is a news hook such as the opening of a big-budget production with well-known stars. Reviews, interviews, etc., can be found in the *New York Times* and other newspapers, magazines such as the *New Yorker* or *Vanity Fair*, etc.

For reviews of television offerings, one needs to keep an eye on the above categories, not forgetting *TV Guide*.

Ball, Robert Hamilton. *Shakespeare on Silent Film: A Strange Eventful History*. London: George Allen & Unwin, 1968. A pioneer work in Shakespearean film scholarship.

Branagh, Kenneth. *Henry V: A Screen Adaptation*. London: Chatto and Windus, 1989.

———. *Much Ado about Nothing: Screenplay, Introduction, and Notes on the Making of the Movie*. New York and London: W. W. Norton, 1993.

Buchman, Lorne M. *Still in Movement: Shakespeare on Screen*. New York and Oxford: Oxford University Press, 1991.

Bulman, J. C., and Coursen, H. R., eds. *Shakespeare on Television: An Anthology of Essays and Reviews*. Hanover and London: University Press of New England, 1988. A wide-ranging collection. Essays on numerous aspects, including some detailed discussions of individual films. Also a useful section of extracts from contemporary reviews of televised productions from 1949 through 1985. Covers all the BBC's series "The Shakespeare Plays."

Collick, John. *Shakespeare, Cinema and Society*. Manchester and New York: Manchester University Press, 1989. Part of Manchester University's "Cultural Politics" series.

Crowl, Samuel. *Shakespeare Observed: Studies in Performance on Stage and Screen*. Athens: Ohio University Press, 1992.

Davies, Anthony. *Filming Shakespeare's Plays: The Adaptations of Laurence Olivier, Orson Welles, Peter Brook and Akira Kurosawa*. Cambridge and New York: Cambridge University Press, 1988.

Davison, Peter. *Text in Performance: Hamlet*. London: The Macmillan Press, 1982.

Dessen, Alan. *Titus Andronicus*. Shakespeare in Performance Series. Manchester and New York: Manchester University Press, 1992.

Dick, Bernard F. *Joseph L. Mankiewicz*. Boston: Twayne Publishers, 1983.

Donaldson, Peter S. *Shakespearean Film/ Shakespearean Directors*. Boston: Unwin Hyman, 1990.

Eckert, Charles W., ed. *Focus on Shakespearean Films*. Englewood Cliffs, N.J.: Prentice-Hall, 1972. Collection of essays by various hands.

Grant, Cathy, ed. *As You Like It: Audio Visual Shakespeare*. London: The British Universities Film and Video Council, 1992. Lists resources available on film and on audio- and videocassette in Great Britain.

Greenaway, Peter. *Prospero's Books: A Film of Shakespeare's The Tempest*. New York: Four Walls Eight Windows, in association with Chatto and Windus, 1991. Many illustrations. A helpful key to this unusual film.

Jorgens, Jack J. *Shakespeare on Film*. Bloomington and London: Indiana University Press, 1977. Deals with 18 films, often with close attention to individual scenes. Interesting comparisons.

Kliman, Bernice W. *Hamlet: Film, Television, and Audio Performance*. London and Toronto: Associated University Presses, 1988. Thorough, detailed, and readable. Technical vocabulary is explained.

————. *Macbeth*. Shakespeare in Performance Series. Manchester and New York: Manchester University Press, 1993.

Leaming, Barbara. *Polanski: A Biography: The Filmmaker as Voyeur*. New York: Simon and Schuster, 1981.

Levenson, Jill. *Romeo and Juliet*. Shakespeare in Performance Series. Manchester and London: Manchester University Press, 1987.

Loney, Glenn. *Staging Shakespeare: Seminars on Production Problems*. New York and London: Garland Publishers, 1990.

Lyons, Bridget Gellert, ed. *Chimes and Midnight: Orson Welles, Director*. New Brunswick and London: Rutgers University Press, 1988. Includes the shooting script and reminiscent essays by the actors.

MacLiammoir, Michael. *Put Money in Thy Purse: The Filming of Orson Welles' Othello*. 2d revised edition. London: Methuen, 1976. MacLiammoir's well-written recollections of this milestone in the history of Shakespearean film.

Manvell, Roger. *Shakespeare and the Film*. New York and Washington: Praeger Publishers, 1971. Essays on 25 major productions.

Polanski, Roman. *Roman by Polanski*. New York: William Morrow, 1984.

Rothwell, Kenneth S., and Melzer, Annabelle H. *Shakespeare on Screen: An International Filmography and Videography*. New York and London: Neal-Schuman Publishers, 1990. An essential reference book for anyone interested in Shakespeare films from a historical perspective. Includes virtually everything — silents, talkies, surviving fragments, lost fragments, background films, derivatives, dating from the 1880s through the 1980s. Gives casts, designers, composers. Evaluations of individual films. Well indexed. Useful bibliography.

Spoto, Donald. *Laurence Olivier: A Biography*. New York: HarperCollins Publishers, 1992.

Warren, Roger. *Text and Performance: A Midsummer Night's Dream*. London: The Macmillan Press, 1983.

Willis, Susan. *The BBC Shakespeare Plays: Making the Televised Canon*. Chapel Hill and London: The University of North Carolina Press, 1991. Gives an overview of this enormous project, and also close-up descriptions of filmmaking which the author watched in progress. Much attention to comparative styles of directors.

DATE DUE

SEP 0 1 2000 MAR 3 1 2007	

GAYLORD   PRINTED IN U.S.A.